DATA VISUALIZATION WITH PYTHON FOR BEGINNERS

Visualize Your Data Using Pandas, Matplotlib and Seaborn

AI PUBLISHING

First Printing, 2020

Edited by AI Publishing
Ebook Converted and Cover by Gazler Studio
Published by AI Publishing LLC

ISBN-13: 978-1-7330426-8-0

How to Contact Us

If you have any feedback, please let us know by sending an email to contact@aispublishing.net.

This feedback is highly valued, and we look forward to hearing from you. It will be very helpful for us to improve the quality of our books.

To get the Python codes and materials used in this book, please click the link below:

https://www.aispublishing.net/book-data-visualization

About the Publisher

At AI Publishing Company, we have established an international learning platform specifically for young students, beginners, small enterprises, startups, and managers who are new to data sciences and artificial intelligence.

Through our interactive, coherent, and practical books and courses, we help beginners learn skills that are crucial to developing AI and data science projects.

Our courses and books range from basic intro courses to language programming and data sciences to advanced courses for machine learning, deep learning, computer vision, big data, and much more, using programming languages like Python, R, and some data science and AI software.

AI Publishing's core focus is to enable our learners to create and try proactive solutions for digital problems by leveraging the power of AI and data sciences to the maximum extent.

Moreover, we offer specialized assistance in the form of our free online content and eBooks, providing up-to-date and useful insight into AI practices and data-science subjects, along with eliminating the doubts and misconceptions about AI and programming.

Our experts have cautiously developed our online courses and kept them concise, short, and comprehensive so that you can understand everything clearly and effectively and start practicing the applications right away.

We also offer consultancy and corporate training in AI and data sciences for enterprises so that their staff can navigate through the workflow efficiently.

With AI Publishing, you can always stay closer to the innovative world of AI and data sciences.

If you are also eager to learn the A to Z of AI and data sciences but have no clue where to start, AI Publishing is the finest place to go.

Please contact us by email at: contact@aispublishing.net.

AI Publishing is Searching for Authors Like You

Table of Contents

Preface

§ Book Approach

The book follows a very simple approach. It is divided into 10 chapters. Chapter 1 contains an introduction while the 2nd and 3rd chapters cover the Matplotlib library. Python's Seaborn library is covered in 4th and 5th chapters while the 6th and 7th chapters explore the Pandas library. The 8th chapter covers 3-D plotting, while the 9th chapter explains how to draw maps via the Basemap library. Finally, the 10th chapter covers interactive data visualization via the Plotly library.

In each chapter, different types of plots have been explained theoretically, followed by practical examples. Each chapter also contains an exercise that students can use to evaluate their understanding of the concepts explained in the chapter. The Python notebook for each chapter is provided in the resources. It is advised that instead of copying the code, you write the code yourself, and in case of error, you match your code with the corresponding Python notebook, find, and then correct the error.

§ Data Science and Data Visualization

Data science and data visualization are two different but interrelated concepts. Data science refers to the science of extracting and exploring data in order to find patterns that can be used for decision making at different levels. Data visualization can be considered as a subdomain of data science where you visualize data with the help of graphs and tables in order to find out which data is most significant and can help in the identification of important patterns. Data visualization can also be considered as a standalone discipline where you just want to visually analyze data and base your decision on the visual representation of data.

This book is dedicated to data visualization and explains how to perform data visualization on a variety of datasets using various data visualization libraries written in the Python programming language. It is suggested that you use this book for data visualization purposes only and not for decision making. For decision making and pattern identification, read this book in conjunction with a dedicated book on machine learning and data science.

§ Who Is This Book For?

This book explains the process of data visualization using various libraries from scratch. Hence, the book is aimed ideally at absolute beginners to data visualization. Though a background in the Python programming language and data visualization can help speed up learning, the book contains a crash course on Python programming language in the first chapter. Therefore, the only prerequisite to efficiently using this book is access to a computer with the internet. All the codes and datasets have been provided. However, to download data visualization libraries, you will need the internet.

In addition to beginners in data visualization, this book can also be used as a reference manual by intermediate and experienced programmers as it contains data visualization code samples using multiple data visualization libraries.

§ How to Use this Book?

As I said earlier, the data visualization libraries taught in this book have been divided into multiple chapters. To get the best out of this book, I would suggest that you first get your feet wet with the Python programming language, especially the object-oriented programming concepts. To do so, you can take a crash course on Python in chapter 1 of this book. Also, try to read the other chapters of this book in order since concepts taught in the subsequent chapters are based on previous chapters. In each chapter, try to first understand the theoretical concepts behind different types of plots and then try to execute the example code. I would again stress that rather than copy and pasting code, try to write the code yourself, and in case of any error, you can match your code with the source code provided in the book as well as in the Python notebooks in the resources. Finally, try to answer the questions asked in the exercises at the end of each chapter. The solutions to the exercises have been given at the end of the book.

About the Author

This book is written by Muhammad Usman Malik

Usman has a Ph.D. in Computer Science from Normandy University, France, with Artificial Intelligence and Machine Learning being the main areas of research. Usman has over 5 years of industry experience in Data Science and has worked with both private and public sector organizations. In his free time, he likes to listen to music and play snooker.

An Important Note to Our Valued Readers:

Download the Color Images

Our print edition books are available only in black & white at present. However, the digital edition of our books is available in color PDF.

We request you to download the PDF file containing the color images of the screenshots/diagrams used in this book here:

https://www.aispublishing.net/book-data-visualization

The typesetting and publishing costs for a color edition are prohibitive. These costs would push the final price of each book to $50, which would make the book less accessible for most beginners.

We are a small company, and we are negotiating with major publishers for a reduction in the publishing price. We are hopeful of a positive outcome sometime soon. In the meantime, we request you to help us with your wholehearted support, feedback, and review.

For the present, we have decided to print all of our books in black & white and provide access to the color version in PDF. This is a decision that would benefit the majority of our readers, as most of them are students. This would also allow beginners to afford our books.

Get in Touch with Us

Feedback from our readers is always welcome.

For general feedback, please send us an Email at contact@aipublishing.net and mention the book title in the subject of your message.

Although we have taken great care to ensure 100 percent accuracy of our content, mistakes do occur. If you come across a mistake in this book, we would be grateful if you report this to us as soon as you can.

If you are interested in becoming an AI Publishing author: If there is any topic that you have expertise in and you are keen on either writing or contributing to a book, please send us an email at authors@aipublishing.net

1

Introduction

1.1. What is Data Visualization

Data visualization is the process of visualizing data in order to identify important patterns in the data that can be used for organizational decision making. Visualizing data graphically can reveal trends that otherwise may remain hidden from the naked eye.

Data visualization is a precursor to many important processes such as Data Science, Machine Learning, Business Intelligence, and Data Analytics. Data visualization is, without any doubt, one of the most important skillsets of the 21st century for a variety of jobs.

In the first chapter of this book, you will see how to set up the Python environment needed to run various data visualization libraries. The chapter also contains a crash Python course for absolute beginners in Python. Finally, the different data visualization libraries that we are going to study in this book have been discussed. The chapter ends with a simple exercise.

1.2. Environment Setup

1.2.1. Windows Setup

The time has come to install Python on Windows using an IDE. In fact, we will use Anaconda throughout this book right from installing Python to writing multithreaded codes in the coming lectures. Now, let us get going with the installation.

This section explains how you can download and install Anaconda on Windows.

To download and install Anaconda, follow these steps.

1. Open the following URL in your browser.

   https://www.anaconda.com/distribution/

2. The browser will take you to the following webpage. Select the latest version of Python (3.7 at the time of writing this book). Now, click the *Download* button to download the executable file. Depending upon the speed of your internet, the file will download within 2-3 minutes.

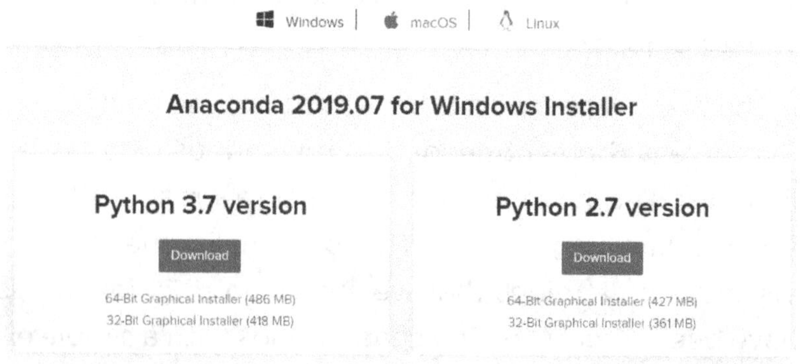

3. Run the executable file after the download is complete. You will most likely find the download file in your

download folder. The name of the file should be similar to "Anaconda3-5.1.0-Windows-x86_64." The installation wizard will open when you run the file, as shown in the following figure. Click the *Next* button.

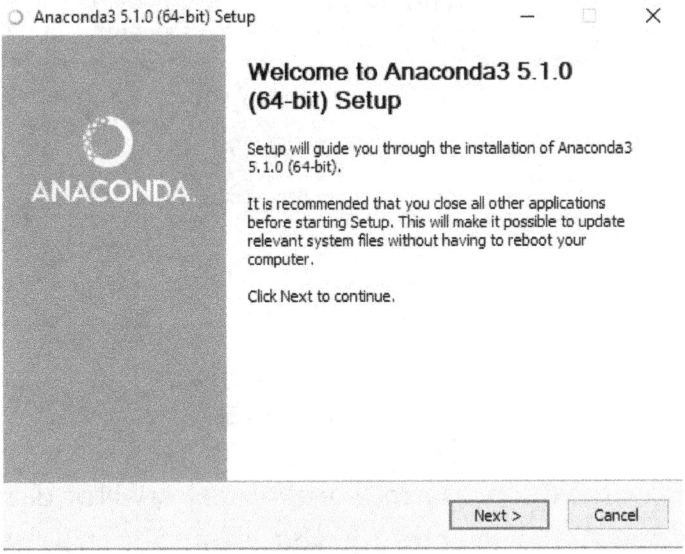

4. Now click *I Agree* on the *License Agreement* dialog, as shown in the following screenshot.

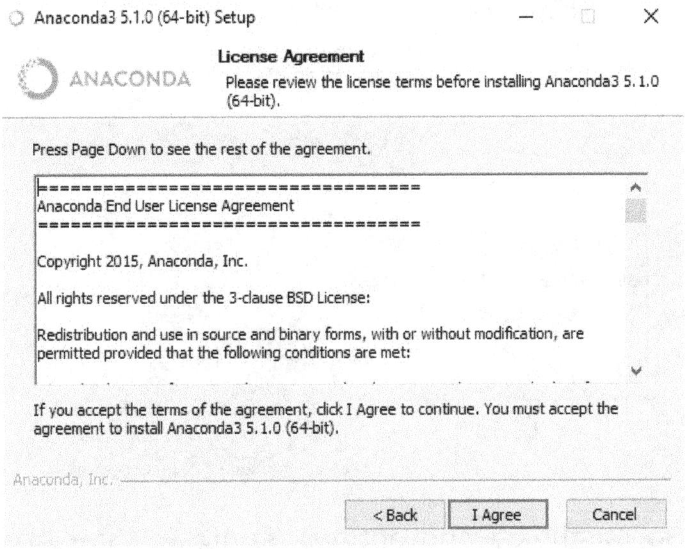

5. Check the *Just Me* radio button from the *Select Installation Type* dialogue box. Click the *Next* button to continue.

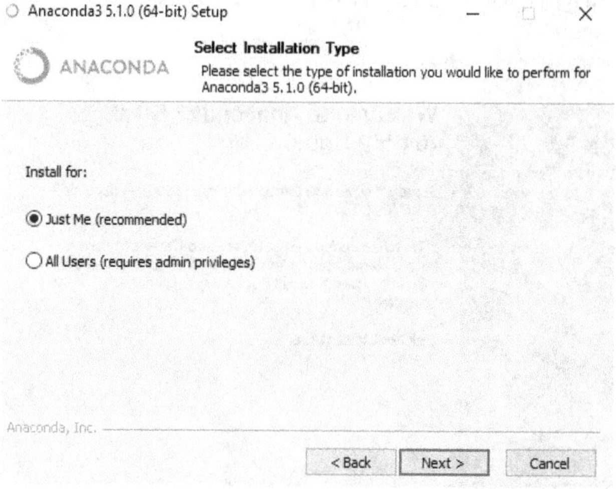

6. Now, the *Choose Install Location* dialog will be displayed. Change the directory if you want, but the default is preferred. The installation folder should at least have 3 GB of free space for Anaconda. Click the *Next* button.

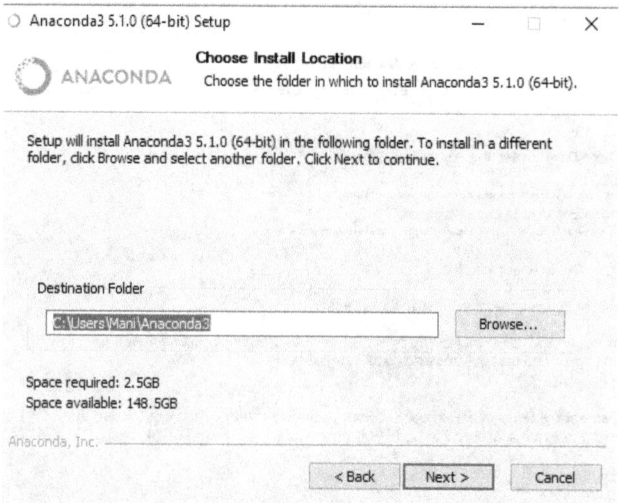

7. Go for the second option, *as my Register Anaconda*

default Python 3.7 in the *Advanced Installation Options* dialogue box. Click the *Install* button to start the installation, which can take some time to complete.

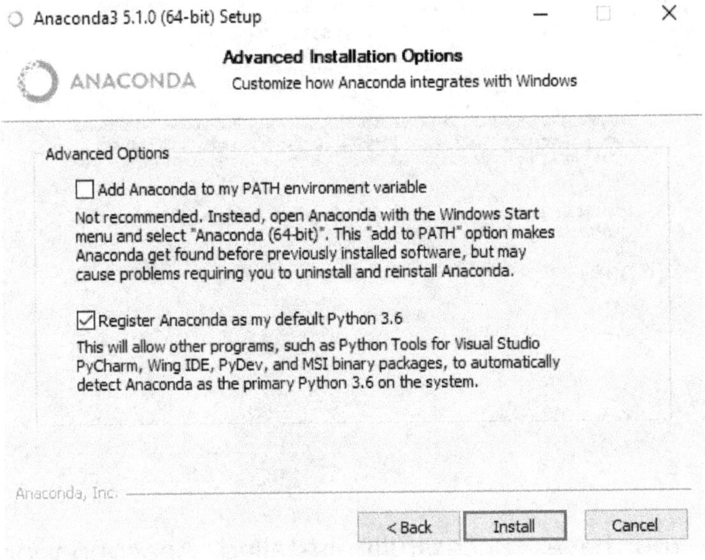

8. Click *Next* once the installation is complete.

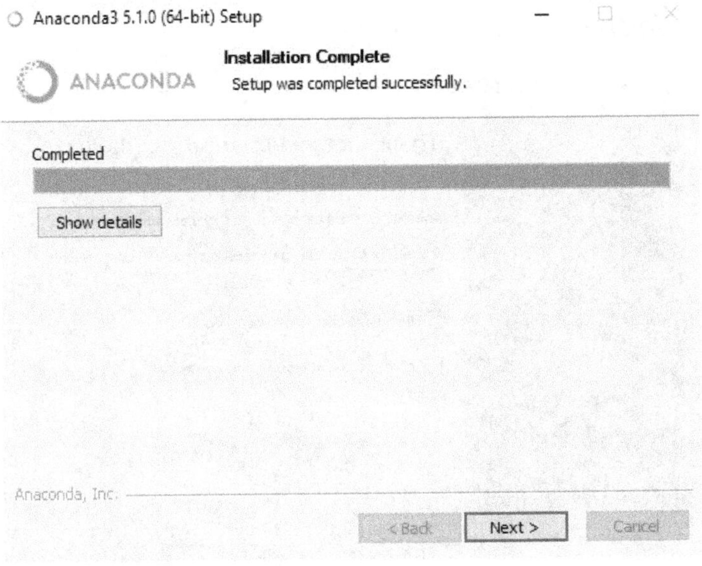

9. Click *Skip* on the *Microsoft Visual Studio Code Installation* dialog box.

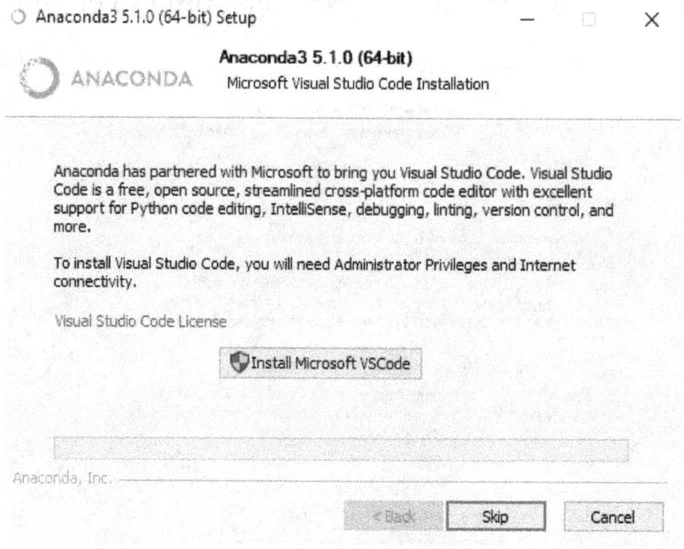

10. You have successfully installed Anaconda on your Windows. Excellent job. The next step is to uncheck both checkboxes on the dialog box. Now, click on the *Finish* button.

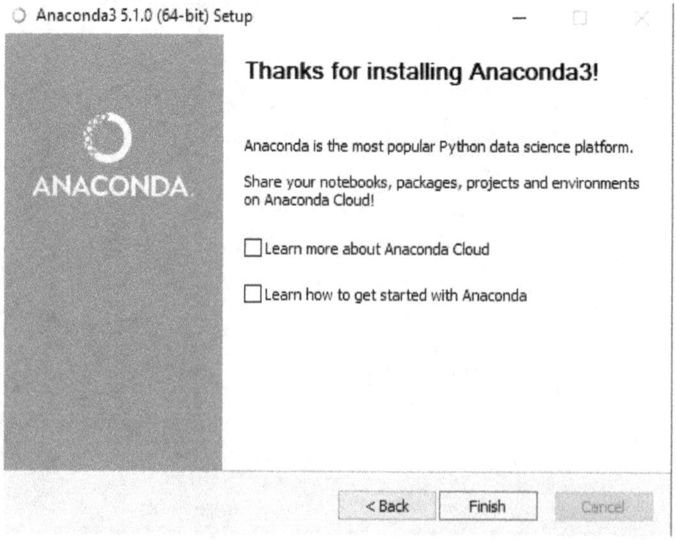

1.2.2. Mac Setup

Anaconda's installation process is almost the same for Mac. It may differ graphically, but you will follow the same steps you followed for Windows. The only difference is that you have to download the executable file, which is compatible with the Mac operating system.

This section explains how you can download and install Anaconda on Mac.

To download and install Anaconda, follow these steps.

1. Open the following URL in your browser.

   https://www.anaconda.com/distribution/

2. The browser will take you to the following webpage. Select the latest version of Python for Mac (3.7 at the time of writing this book). Now, click the *Download* button to download the executable file. Depending upon the speed of your internet, the file will download within 2-3 minutes.

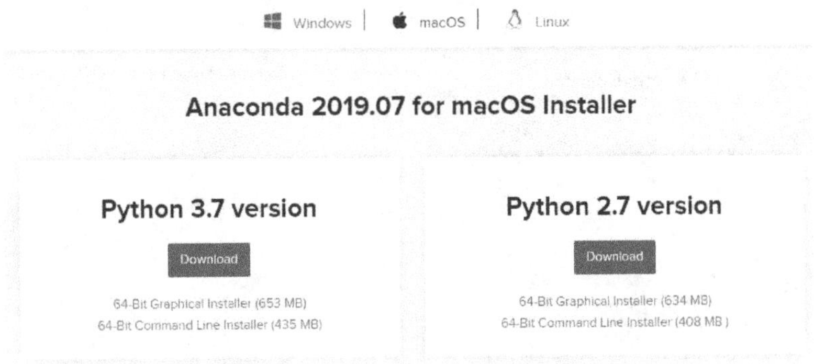

3. Run the executable file after the download is complete. You will most likely find the downloaded file in your download folder. The name of the file should be much

the same as "Anaconda3-5.1.0-Windows-x86_64." The installation wizard will open when you run the file, as shown in the following figure. Click the *Continue* button.

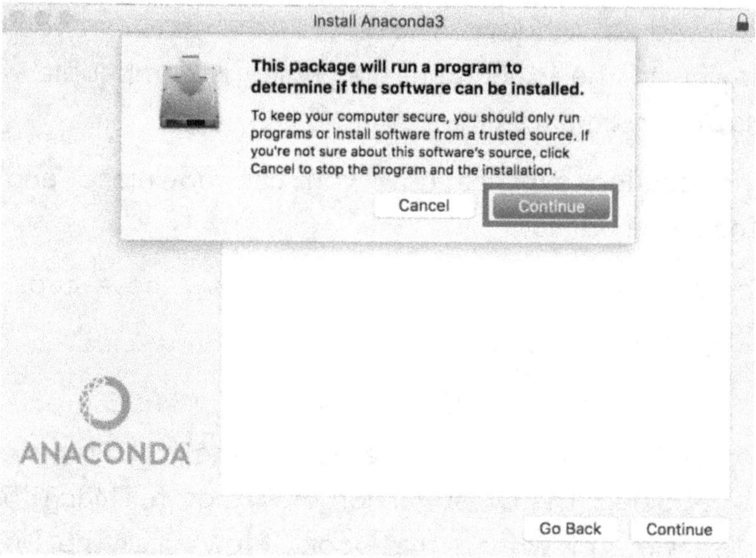

4. Now click *Continue* on the *Welcome to Anaconda 3 Installer* window, as shown in the following screenshot.

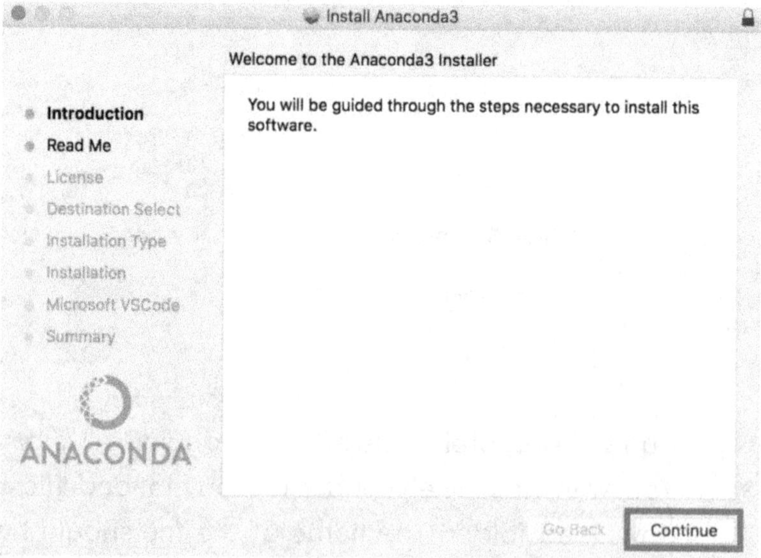

5. The *Important Information* dialog will pop up. Simply, click *Continue* to go with the default version, that is, Anaconda 3.

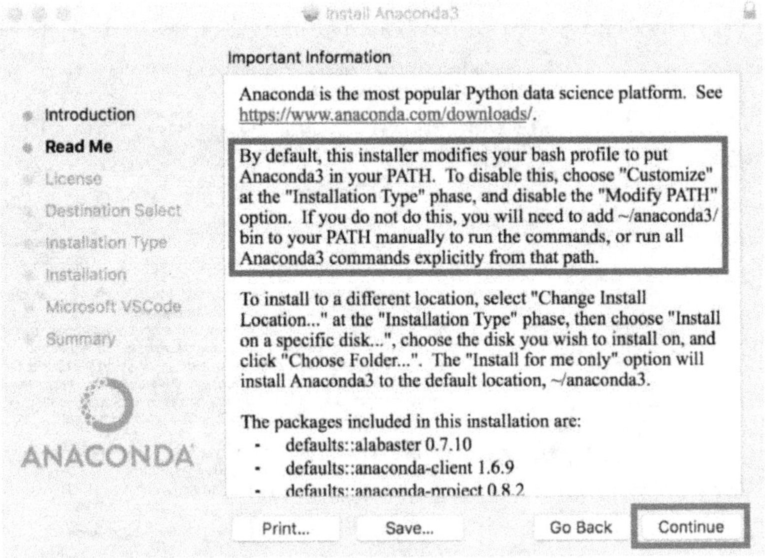

6. Click *Continue* on the *Software License Agreement* Dialog.

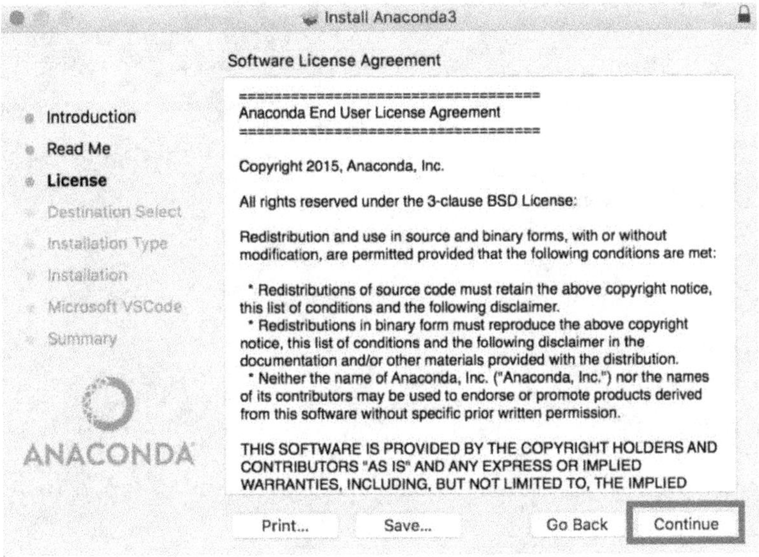

7. It is mandatory to read the license agreement and click the *Agree* button before you can click the *Continue* button again.

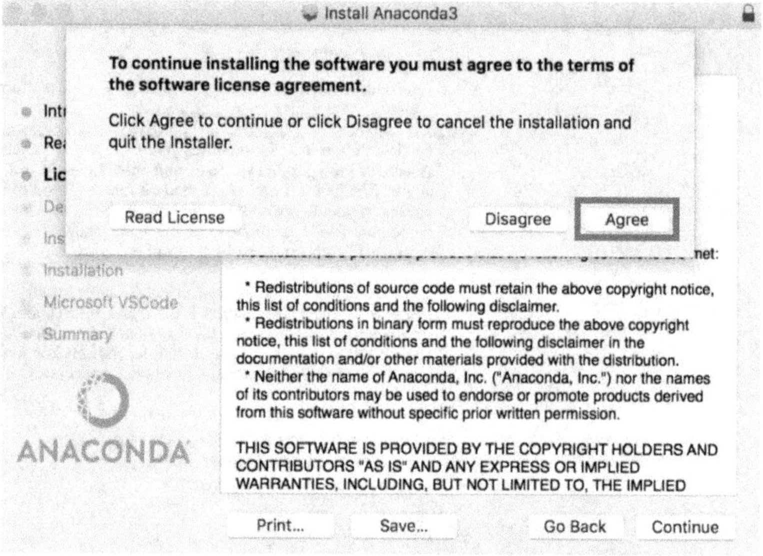

8. On the next window that appears, just click *Install.*

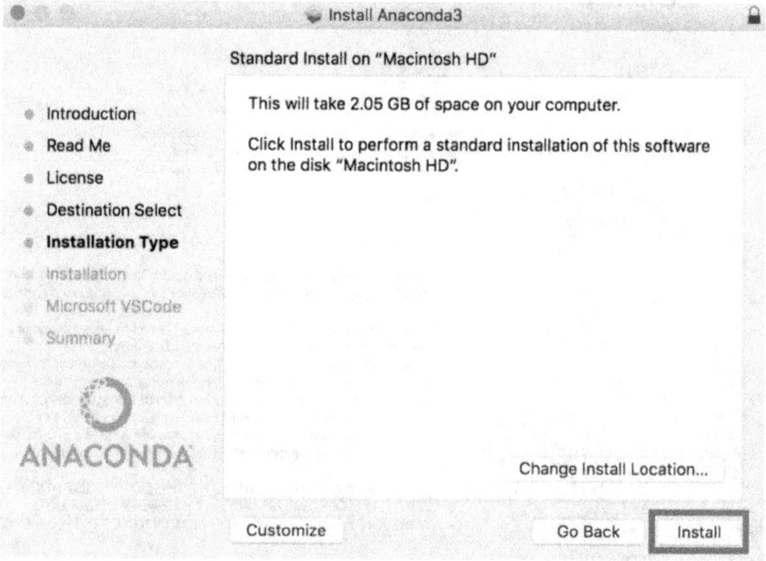

The system will prompt you to give your password. Use the same password you use to login to your Mac computer. Now, click on *Install Software*.

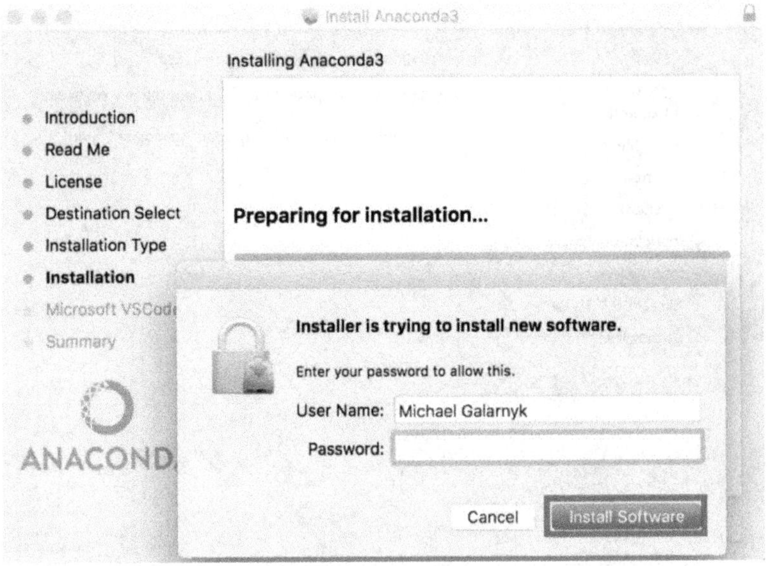

9. Click *Continue* on the next window. You also have the option to install Microsoft VSCode at this point.

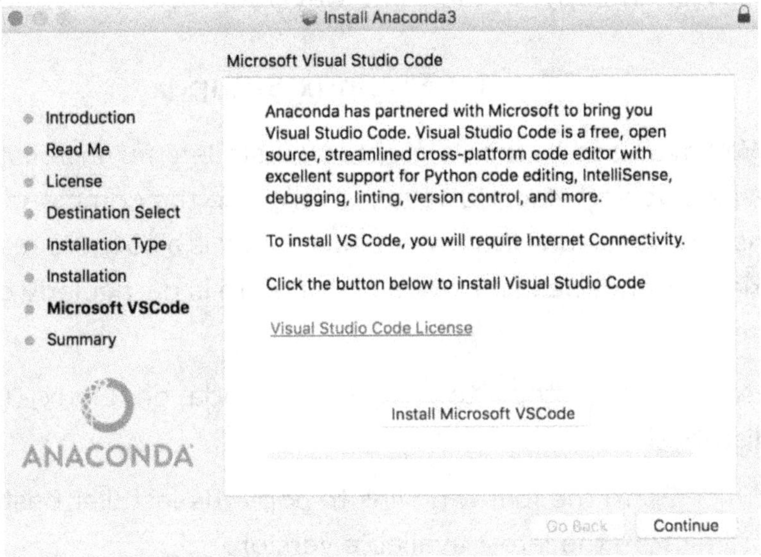

The next screen will display the message that the installation has completed successfully. Click on the *Close* button to close the installer.

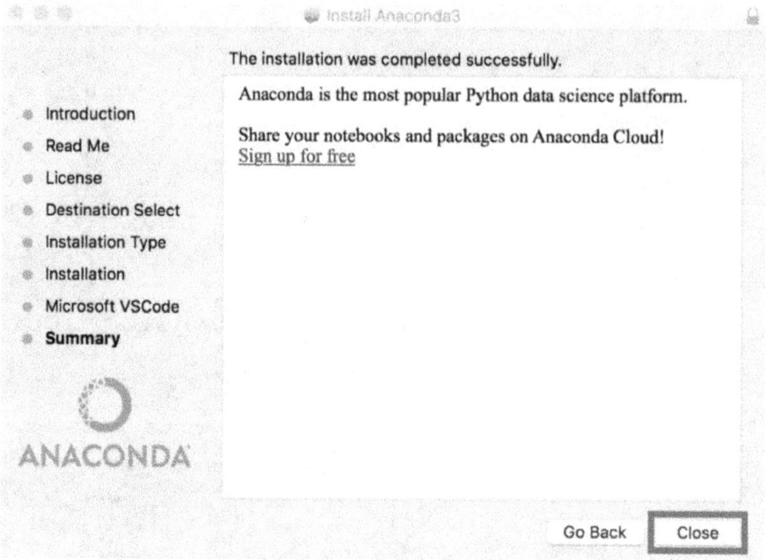

There you have it. You have successfully installed Anaconda on your Mac computer. Now, you can write Python code in Jupyter and Spyder the same way you wrote it in Windows.

1.2.3. Linux Setup

We have used Python's graphical installers for installation on Windows and Mac. However, we will use the command line to install Python on Ubuntu or Linux. Linux is also more resource-friendly, and the installation of software is particularly easy, as well.

Follow these steps to install Anaconda on Linux (Ubuntu distribution).

1. Go to the following link to copy the installer bash script from the latest available version.

https://www.anaconda.com/distribution/

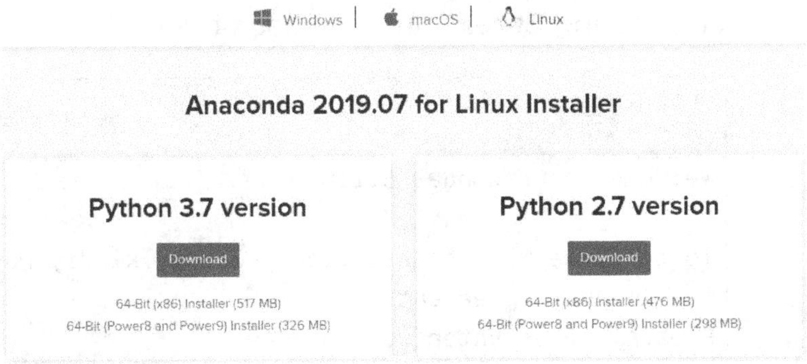

2. The second step is to download the installer bash script. Log into your Linux computer and open your terminal. Now, go to /temp directory and download the bash you downloaded from Anaconda's home page using curl.

```
$ cd / tmp

$ curl -o https://repo.anaconda.com.archive/
Anaconda3-5.2.0-Linux-x86_64.sh
```

3. You should also use the cryptographic hash verification through SHA-256 checksum to verify the integrity of the installer.

```
$ sha256sum Anaconda3-5.2.0-Linux-x86_64.sh
```

You will get the following output.

```
09f53738b0cd3bb96f5b1bac488e5528df9906be2480fe61df-
40e0e0d19e3d48
Anaconda3-5.2.0-Linux-x86_64.sh
```

4. The fourth step is to run the Anaconda Script, as shown in the following figure.

```
$ bash Anaconda3-5.2.0-Linux-x86_64.sh
```

The command line will produce the following output. You will be asked to review the license agreement. Keep on pressing **Enter** until you reach the end.

```
Output

Welcome to Anaconda3 5.2.0

To continue the installation process, kindly review
the license agreement.
Please, press Enter to continue
>>>
...
Do you approve the license terms? [yes|No]
```

Type *Yes* when you get to the bottom of the License Agreement.

5. The installer will ask you to choose the installation location after you agree to the license agreement. Simply press **Enter** to choose the default location. You can also specify a different location if you want.

```
Output

Anaconda3 will now be installed on this location:
/home/tola/anaconda3

- Press ENTER to confirm the location
- Press CTRL-C to abort the installation
- Or specify a different location below

[/home/tola/anaconda3] >>>
```

The installation will proceed once you press **Enter**. Once again, you have to be patient as the installation process takes some time to complete.

6. You will receive the following result when the installation is complete. If you wish to use conda command, type *Yes*.

```
Output
...
Installation finished.
Do you wish the installer to prepend Anaconda3
install location to path in your /home/tola/.bashrc?
[yes|no]
[no]>>>
```

At this point, you will also have the option to download the Visual Studio Code. Type *yes* or *no* to install or decline, respectively.

7. Use the following command to activate your brand-new installation of Anaconda3.

```
$ source `/.bashrc
```

8. You can also test the installation using the conda command.

```
$ conda list
```

Congratulations! You have successfully installed Anaconda on your Linux system.

1.3. Python Crash Course

If you are familiar with the elementary concepts of the Python programming language, you can skip this section. For those who are absolute beginners to Python, this section provides a very brief overview of some of the most basic concepts of Python. Python is a very vast programming language, and this section is by no means a substitute for a complete Python book. However, if you want to see how various operations and commands are executed in Python, you are welcome to follow along the rest of this section.

1.3.4. Writing Your First Program

You have already installed Python on your computer and established a unique environment in the form of Anaconda. Now, it is time to write your first program, that is the Hello World!

In order to write a program in Anaconda, you have to launch Anaconda Navigator. Search *Anaconda Navigator* in your Windows Search Box. Now, click on the Anaconda Navigator application icon, as shown in the following figure.

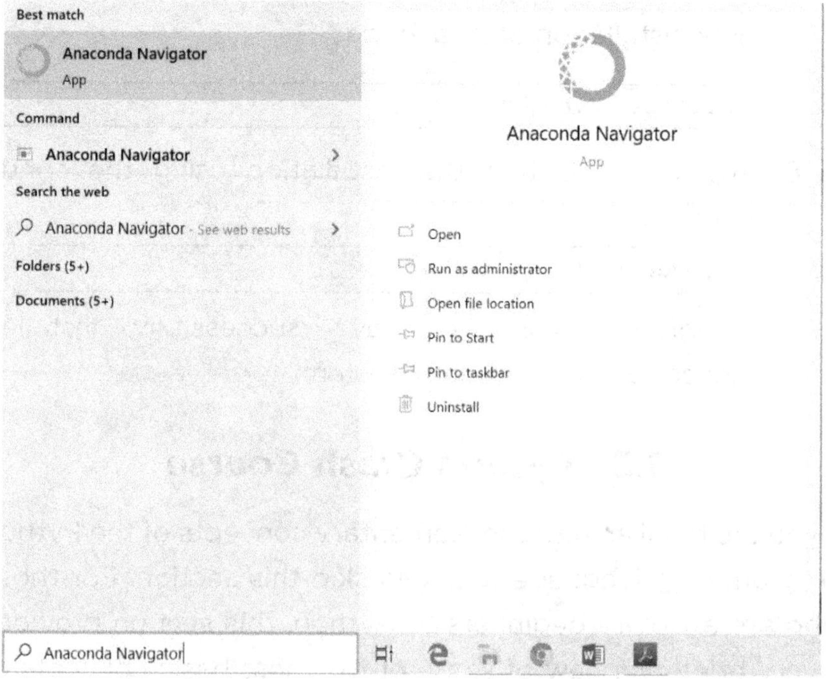

Once you click on the application, the Anaconda's dashboard will open. The dashboard offers you a myriad of tools to write your code. We will use the *Jupyter Notebook*, the most popular of these tools, to write and explain the code throughout this book.

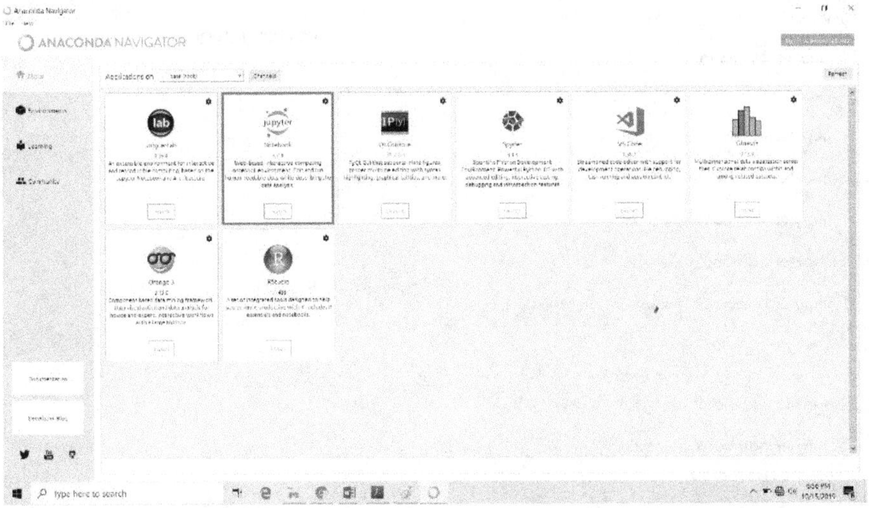

The Jupyter Notebook is available at second from the top of the dashboard. You can use Jupyter Notebook even if you don't have access to the internet as it runs right in your default browser. Another method to open Jupyter Notebook is to type Jupyter Notebook in the Window's search bar. Subsequently, click on the Jupyter Notebook application. The application will open in a new tab on your browser.

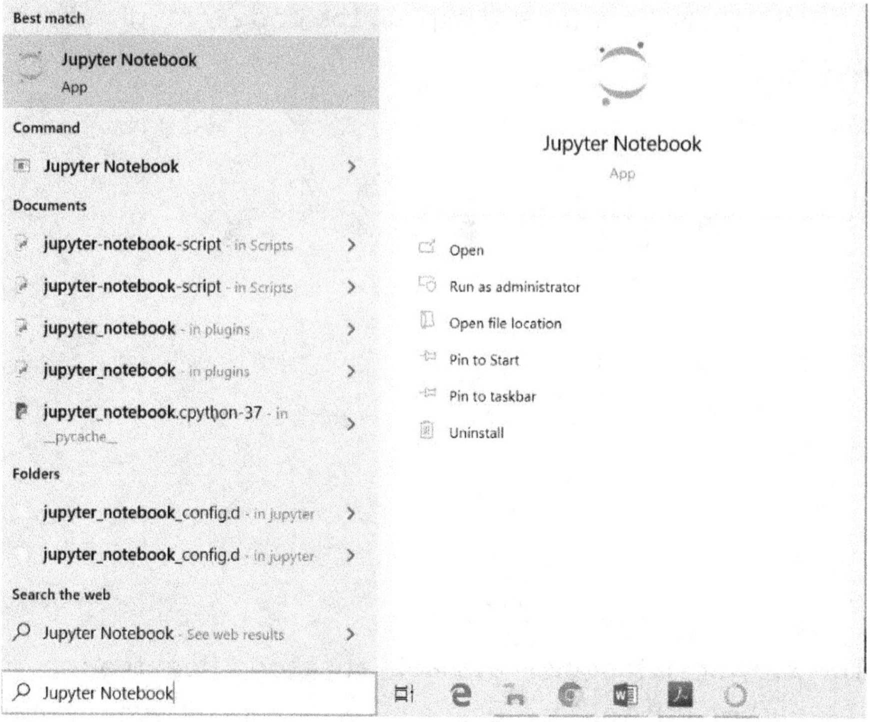

The top right corner of Jupyter Notebook's own dashboard houses a *New* button, which you have to click to open a new document. A dropdown containing several options will appear. Click on *Python 3*.

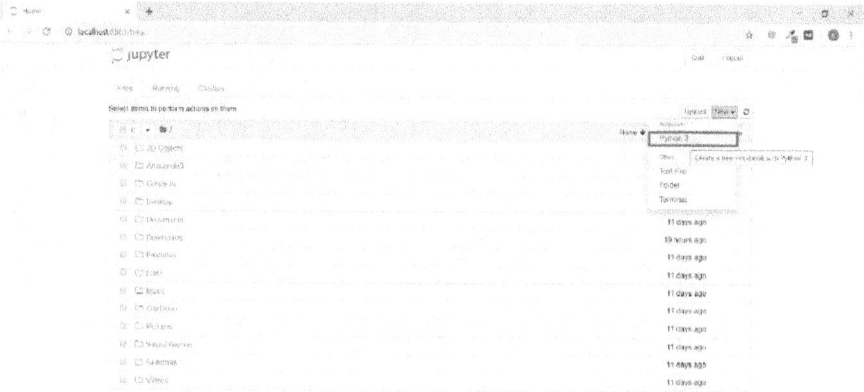

A new Python notebook will appear for you to write your programs. It looks as follows.

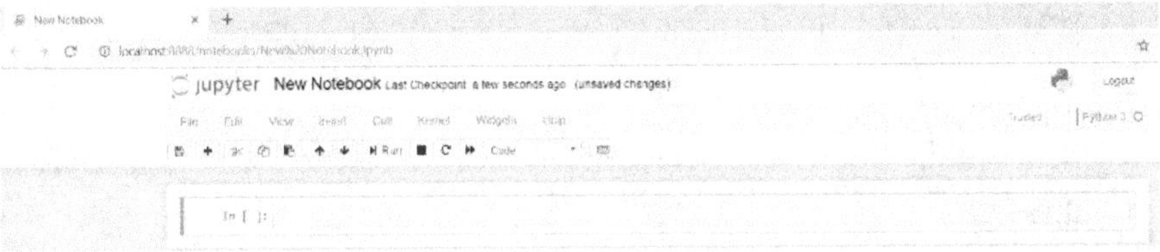

Jupyter Notebook consists of cells, as evident from the above image, making its layout very simple and straightforward. You will write your code inside these cells. Let us write our first ever Python program in Jupyter Notebook.

1.3.1. Writing Your First Program

```
In [1]: print("Welcome to Data Visualization with Python")

        Welcome to Data Visualization with Python
```

The above script basically prints a string value in the output using the **print()** method. The **print()** method is used to print on the console any string passed to it. If you see the following output, you have successfully run your first Python program.

Output:

```
Welcome to Data Visualization with Python
```

Let's now explore some of the other important Python concepts starting with Variables and Data Types.

Requirements - Anaconda, Jupyter, and Matplotlib

- All the scripts in this book have been executed via the Jupyter notebook. Therefore, you should have the Jupyter notebook installed.
- It goes without saying that we will be using the Matplotlib library.
- The Numpy and Pandas libraries should also be installed before this chapter.

Hands-on Time - Source Codes

All IPython notebook for the source code of all the scripts in this chapter can be found in Resources/Chapter 1.ipynb. I would suggest that you write all the code in this chapter yourself and see if you can get the same output as mentioned in this chapter.

1.3.5. Python Variables and Data Types

Data types in a programming language refers to the type of data that the language is capable of processing. The following are the major data types supported by Python.

a. Strings
b. Integers
c. Floating Point Numbers
d. Booleans
e. Lists
f. Tuples
g. Dictionaries

A variable is an alias for the memory address where actual data is stored. The data or the values stored at a memory address can be accessed and updated via the variable name. Unlike other programming languages like C++, Java, and C#, Python is loosely typed, which means that you don't have to state the data type while creating a variable. Rather, the type of data is evaluated at runtime.

The following example demonstrates how to create different data types and how to store them in their corresponding variables. The script also prints the type of the variables via the **type()** function.

Script 2:

```
# A string Variable
first_name = "Joseph"
print(type(first_name))

# An Integer Variable
age = 20
print(type(age))

# A floating point variable
weight = 70.35
print(type(weight))

# A floating point variable
married = False
print(type(married))

#List
cars = ["Honda", "Toyota", "Suzuki"]
print(type(cars))
                                                    ......
```

```
#Tuples
days = ("Sunday", "Monday", "Tuesday", "Wednesday",
"Thursday", "Friday", "Saturday")
print(type(days))

#Dictionaries
days2 = {1:"Sunday", 2:"Monday", 3:"Tuesday",
4:"Wednesday", 5:"Thursday", 6:"Friday", 7:"Saturday"}
print(type(days2))
```

Output:

```
<class 'str'>
<class 'int'>
<class 'float'>
<class 'bool'>
<class 'list'>
<class 'tuple'>
<class 'dict'>
```

1.3.6. Python Operators

Python programming language contains the following types of operators:

a. Arithmetic Operators
b. Logical Operators
c. Comparison Operators
d. Assignment Operators
e. Membership Operators

Let's briefly review each of these types of operators.

Arithmetic Operators

Arithmetic operators are used to perform arithmetic operations in Python. The following table sums up the arithmetic operators supported by Python. Suppose X = 20 and Y = 10.

Operator Name	Symbol	Functionality	Example
Addition	+	Adds the operands on either side	X+ Y= 30
Subtraction	–	Subtracts the operands on either side	X -Y= 10
Multiplication	*	Multiplies the operands on either side	X * Y= 200
Division	/	Divides the operand on the left by the one on right	X / Y= 2.0
Modulus	%	Divides the operand on the left by the one on right and returns remainder	X % Y= 0
Exponent	**	Takes exponent of the operand on the left to the power of right	X ** Y = 1024 x e^{10}

Here is an example of arithmetic operators with output:

Script 3:

```
X = 20
Y = 10
print(X + Y)
print(X - Y)
print(X * Y)
print(X / Y)
print(X ** Y)
```

Output:

```
30
10
200
2.0
10240000000000
```

Logical Operators

Logical operators are used to perform logical **AND, OR**, and **NOT** operations in Python. The following table summarizes the logical operators. Here, **X** is **True,** and **Y** is **False**.

Operator	Symbol	Functionality	Example
Logical AND	and	The condition becomes true if both the operands are true.	(X and Y) = False
Logical OR	or	The condition becomes true if any of the two operands are true.	(X or Y) = True
Logical NOT	not	Used to reverse the logical state of its operand.	not(X and Y) = True

Here is an example that explains the usage of the Python logical operators.

Script 4:

```
X = True
Y = False
print(X and Y)
print(X or Y)
print(not(X and Y))
```

Output:

```
False
True
True
```

Comparison Operators

Comparison operators, as the name suggests, are used to compare two or more than two operands. Depending upon the relation between the operands, comparison operators return

Boolean values. The following table summarizes comparison operators in Python. Here, X is 20, and Y is 35.

Operator	Symbol	Description	Example
Equality	==	If the values of both the operands are equal, then the condition returns true.	(X == Y) = false
Inequality	!=	If the values of both the operands are not equal, then the condition returns true.	(X = Y) = true
Greater than	>	If the value of the left operand is greater than the right one, then the condition returns true.	(X> Y) = False
Smaller than	<	Returns true if value of the left operand is smaller than the right one	(X< Y) = True
Greater than or equal to	>=	If value of the left operand is greater than or equal to the right one, then the condition returns true.	(X > =Y) = False
Smaller than or equal to	<=	Returns true if value of the left operand is smaller than or equal to the right one	(X<= Y) = True

The comparison operators have been demonstrated in action in the following example:

Script 5:

```
X = 20
Y = 35

print(X == Y)
print(X != Y)
print(X > Y)
print(X < Y)
print(X >= Y)
print(X <= Y)
```

Output:

```
False
True
False
True
False
True
```

Assignment Operators

Assignment operators are used to assign values to variables. The following table summarizes the assignment operators. Here, X is 20, and Y is equal to 10.

Operator	Symbol	Description	Example
Assignment	=	Used to assign value of the right operand to the right.	R = X+ Y assigns 30 to R
Add and assign	+=	Adds the operands on either side and assigns the result to the left operand	X += Y assigns 30 to X
Subtract and assign	–	Subtracts the operands on either side and assigns the result to the left operand	X – Y assigns 10 to X
Multiply and Assign	*=	Multiplies the operands on either side and assigns the result to the left operand	X *= Y assigns 200 to X
Divide and Assign	/=	Divides the operands on the left by the right and assigns the result to the left operand	X/= Y assigns 2 to X
Take modulus and assign	%=	Divides the operands on the left by the right and assigns the remainder to the left operand	X %= Y assigns 0 to X
Take exponent and assign	**=	Takes exponent of the operand on the left to the power of right and assign the remainder to the left operand	X **= Y assigns 1024 x e^{10} to X

Take a look at script 6 to see Python assignment operators in action.

Script 6:

```
X = 20; Y = 10
R = X + Y
print(R)

X = 20;
Y = 10
X += Y
print(X)

X = 20;
Y = 10
X -= Y
print(X)

X = 20;
Y = 10
X *= Y
print(X)

X = 20;
Y = 10
X /= Y
print(X)

X = 20;
Y = 10
X %= Y
print(X)

X = 20;
Y = 10
X **= Y
print(X)
```

Output:

```
30
30
10
200
2.0
0
10240000000000
```

Membership Operators

Membership operators are used to find if an item is a member of a collection of items or not. There are two types of membership operators. They are the **in** operator and the **not in** operator. The following script shows the **in** operator in action.

Script 7:

```
days = ("Sunday", "Monday", "Tuesday", "Wednesday",
"Thursday", "Friday", "Saturday")
print('Sunday' in days)
```

Output:

```
True
```

And here is an example of the **not in** operator.

Script 8:

```
days = ("Sunday", "Monday", "Tuesday", "Wednesday",
"Thursday", "Friday", "Saturday")
print('Xunday' not in days)
```

Output:

```
True
```

1.3.7. Conditional Statements

Conditional statements are used to implement conditional logic in Python. Conditional statements help you decide whether to execute a certain code block or not. There are three chief types of conditional statements in Python:

a. If statement

b. If-else statement

c. If-elif statement

IF Statement

If you have to check for a single condition and you do not concern about the alternate condition, you can use the **if** statement. For instance, if you want to check if 10 is greater than 5, and based on that you want to print a statement, you can use the if statement. The condition evaluated by the **if** statement returns a Boolean value. If the condition evaluated by the **if** statement is true, the code block that follows the **if** statement executes. It is important to mention that in Python, a new code block starts at a new line with on tab indented from the left when compared with the outer block.

Here, in the following example, the condition 10 > 5 is evaluated, which returns true. Hence, the code block that follows the **if** statement executes, and a message is printed on the console.

Script 8:

```
# The if statment

if 10 > 5:
    print(«Ten is greater than 10»)
```

Output:

```
Ten is greater than 10
```

IF-Else Statement

The **`If-else`** statement comes handy when you want to execute an alternate piece of code in case the condition for the if statement returns false. For instance, in the following example, the condition 5 < 10 will return false. Hence, the code block that follows the **`else`** statement will execute.

Script 9:

```
# if-else statement

if  5 > 10:
    print("5 is greater than 10")
else:
    print(«10 is greater than 5»)
```

Output:

```
10 is greater than 5
```

IF-Elif Statement

The **`if-elif`** statement comes handy when you have to evaluate multiple conditions. For instance, in the following example, we first check if 5 > 10 which evaluates to false. Next, an **`elif`** statement evaluates the condition 8 < 4, which also returns false. Hence, the code block that follows the last **`else`** statement executes.

Script 10:

```
#if-elif and else

if  5 > 10:
    print(«5 is greater than 10»)
elif 8 < 4:
    print(«8 is smaller than 4»)
else:
    print(«5 is not greater than 10 and 8 is not smaller
than 4»)
```

Output:

```
5 is not greater than 10 and 8 is not smaller than 4
```

1.3.8. Iteration Statements

Iteration statements, also known as loops, are used to iteratively execute a certain piece of code. There are two main types of iteration statements in Python.

a. For loop

b. While Loop

For Loop

The **for loop** is used to iteratively execute a piece of code for a certain number of times. You should use **for loop** when you know exactly the number of iterations or repetitions for which you want to run your code. A **for loop** iterates over a collection of items. In the following example, we create a collection of five integers using **range()** method. Next, a **for loop** iterates five times and prints each integer in the collection.

Script 11:

```
items = range(5)
for item in items:
    print(item)
```

Output:

```
0
1
2
3
4
```

While Loop

The **while loop** keeps executing a certain piece of code unless the evaluation condition becomes false. For instance, the **while loop** in the following script keeps executing unless variable c becomes greater than 10.

Script 12:

```
c = 0
while c < 10:
    print(c)
    c = c +1
```

Output:

```
0
1
2
3
4
5
6
7
8
9
```

1.3.9. Functions

Functions, in any programming language, are used to implement that piece of code that is required to be executed numerous times at different locations in the code. In such cases, instead of writing long pieces of codes, again and again, you can simply define a function that contains the piece of code, and then you can call the function wherever you want in the code.

To create a function in Python, the def keyword is used, followed by the name of the function and opening and closing parenthesis.

Once a function is defined, you have to call it in order to execute the code inside a function body. To call a function, you simply have to specify the name of the function, followed by opening and closing parenthesis. In the following script, we create a function named **myfunc,** which prints a simple statement on the console using the **print()** method.

Script 13:

```
def myfunc():
    print("This is a simple function")

### function call
myfunc()
```

Output:

```
This is a simple function
```

You can also pass values to a function. The values are passed inside the parenthesis of the function call. However, you must specify the parameter name in the function definition, too. In the following script, we define a function named

myfuncparam(). The function accepts one parameter, i.e., **num**. The value passed in the parenthesis of the function call will be stored in this **num** variable and will be printed by the **print()** method inside the **myfuncparam()** method.

Script 14:

```
def myfuncparam(num):
    print("This is a function with parameter value: "+num)

### function call
myfuncparam(«Parameter 1»)
```

Output:

```
This is a function with parameter value:Parameter 1
```

Finally, a function can also return values to the function call. To do so, you simply have to use the return keyword, followed by the value that you want to return. In the following script, the **myreturnfunc()** function returns a string value to the calling function.

Script 15:

```
def myreturnfunc():
    return "This function returns a value"

val = myreturnfunc()
print(val)
```

Output:

```
This function returns a value
```

1.3.10. Objects and Classes

Python supports object-oriented programming (OOP). In OOP, any entity that can perform some function and have some attributes is implemented in the form of an object.

For instance, a car can be implemented as an object since a car has some attributes such as price, color, model and can perform some functions such as drive car, change gear, stop the car, etc.

Similarly, a fruit can also be implemented as an object since a fruit has a price, name, and you can eat a fruit, grow a fruit, and perform functions with a fruit.

To create an object, you first have to define a class. For instance, in the following example, a class **`Fruit`** has been defined. The class has two attributes **`name`** and **`price`,** and one method **`eat_fruit()`**. Next, we create an object **`f`** of class Fruit and then call the **`eat_fruit()`** method from the **`f`** object. We also access the **`name`** and **`price`** attributes of the **`f`** object and print them on the console.

Script 16:

```
class Fruit:

    name = "apple"
    price = 10

    def eat_fruit(self):
        print("Fruit has been eaten")

f = Fruit()
f.eat_fruit()
print(f.name)
print(f.price)
```

Output:

```
Fruit has been eaten
apple
10
```

A class in Python can have a special method called a *constructor*. The name of the constructor method in Python is **__init__().** The constructor is called whenever an object of a class is created. Look at the following example to see the constructor in action.

Script 17:

```
class Fruit:

    name = “apple”
    price = 10

    def __init__(self, fruit_name, fruit_price):
        Fruit.name = fruit_name
        Fruit.price = fruit_price

    def eat_fruit(self):
        print(“Fruit has been eaten”)


f = Fruit(«Orange», 15)
f.eat_fruit()
print(f.name)
print(f.price)
```

Output:

```
Fruit has been eaten
Orange
15
```

Further Readings - Python [1]

To study more about Python, please check Python 3 Official Documentation. Get used to searching and reading this documentation. It is a great resource of knowledge.

1.4. Data Visualization Libraries

Owing to the growing importance of data visualization, several Python libraries have been developed. Some of these libraries have been briefly reviewed in this section.

1.4.1. Matplotlib

Matplotlib is the de facto standard for static data visualization in Python. Being the oldest data visualization library in Python, Matplotlib is the most widely used data visualization library. Matplotlib was developed to resemble MATLAB, which is one of the most widely used programming languages in academia. While Matplotlib graphs are easy to plot, the look and feel of the Matplotlib plots have a distinct feel of the 1990s. Many wrappers libraries like Pandas and Seaborn have been developed on top of Matplotlib. These libraries allow users to plot much cleaner and sophisticated graphs.

1.4.2. Seaborn

Seaborn library is built on top of the Matplotlib library and contains all the plotting capabilities of Matplotlib. However, with Seaborn, you can plot much more pleasing and aesthetic graphs with the help of Seaborn default styles and color palettes.

1.4.3. Basemap

The Basemap library is a Matplotlib Extension and is used to plot Geographical Maps in Python. The working of the Basemap library has been explained in detail in chapter 4 of this book.

1.4.4. Pandas

Pandas library, like Seaborn, is based on the Matplotlib library and offers utilities that can be used to plot different types of static plots in a single line of codes. With pandas, you can import data in various formats such as CSV (Comma Separated View) and TSV (Tab Separated View), and can plot a variety of data visualizations via these data sources.

1.4.5. Plotly

Plotly is an online data visualization platform that supports interactive data visualization. However, you can also create interactive visualizations within the Python notebook using Plotly. Chapter 10 explains how to use Plotly for interactive data visualization in Python.

Hands-on Time - Exercise
Now, it is your turn. Follow the instruction in **the exercises below** to check your understanding of the advanced data visualization with Matplotlib. The answers to these questions are given at the end of the book.

Exercise 1.1

Question 1

Which iteration should be used when you want to repeatedly execute a code specific number of times?

A- For Loop
B- While Loop
C- Both A & B
D- None of the above

Question 2

What is the maximum number of values that a function can return in Python?

A- Single Value
B- Double Value
C- More than two values
D- None

Question 3

Which of the following membership operators are supported by Python?

A- In
B- Out
C- Not In
D- Both A and C

Answer: D

Exercise 1.2

Print the table of integer 9 using a while loop:

2

Basic Plotting with Matplotlib

2.1. Introduction

In the first chapter of the book, you saw briefly what data visualization is, why it is important, and what its various applications are. You also installed different software that we will be using in order to execute data visualization scripts in this book.

In this chapter, we will start a formal discussion about Matplotlib, which is one of the most commonly and frequently used Python libraries for data visualization. Matplotlib is so popular that various advanced data visualization libraries such as Seaborn use Matplotlib as the underlying data visualization library.

In this chapter, you will see how to draw some of the most commonly used plots with the Matplotlib library.

Requirements - Anaconda, Jupyter, and Matplotlib

- All the scripts in this book have been executed via the Jupyter notebook. Therefore, you should have the Jupyter notebook installed.
- It goes without saying that we will be using the Matplotlib library.
- The Numpy and Pandas libraries should also be installed before this chapter.

Hands-on Time - Source Codes

All IPython notebooks for the source code of all the scripts in this chapter can be found in Resources/Chapter 2.ipynb. I would suggest that you write all the code in this chapter yourself and see if you can get the same output as mentioned in this chapter.

Finally, before you can plot any graphs with Matplotlib library, you will need to import the **pyplot** module from the Matplotlib library. And since all the scripts will be executed inside Jupyter notebook, the statement **%matplotlib inline** has been used to generate plots inside Jupyter notebook. Execute the following script:

```
import matplotlib.pyplot as plt
%matplotlib inline
```

2.2. Line Plots

The first plot that we are going to plot in this chapter is a line plot. A line plot is the simplest of all the Matplotlib plots. A line plot is basically used to plot the relationship between two numerical sets of values. Usually, a line plot is used to plot an increasing or decreasing trend between two dependent variables. For instance, if you want to see how the weather changed over a period of 24 hours, you can use a line plot where the x-axis contains hourly information, and the y-axis contains weather in degrees. Let us plot a line plot that displays the square root of 20 equidistance numbers between 0 and 20. Look at Script 1.

Script 1:

```
import matplotlib.pyplot as plt
import numpy as np
import math

x_vals = np.linspace(0, 20, 20)
y_vals = [math.sqrt(i) for i in x_vals]
plt.plot(x_vals, y_vals)
```

In script 1, we generate 20 equidistance numbers using **np.linspace()** function. The numbers are stored in the **x_vals** variable. Next, we iterate through each value in the **x_vals** list and take the square root of each value. The resultant list is stored in the **y_vals** variable. To plot a line plot via the **pyplot** module, you only need to call the **plot()** method of the **pyplot** module and then pass it the values for the x and y axes. It is important to mention that **plt** is an alias for **pyplot** in script 1. You can name it anything you want. Here is the output for the script 1.

Output:

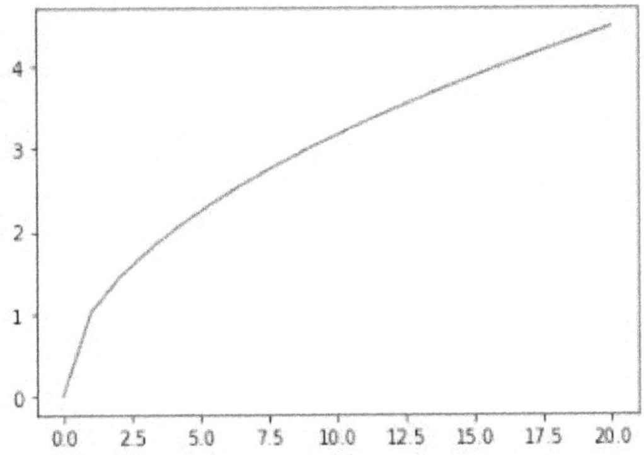

This is one of the ways to plot a graph via Matplotlib. There is another way to do so. You first have to call the **figure()** method via the **plt** module, which draws an empty figure. Next, you can call the **axes()** method, which returns an **axes** object. You can then call the **plot()** method from the **axes** object to create a plot, as shown in the following script.

Script 2:

```
import matplotlib.pyplot as plt
import numpy as np
import math

x_vals = np.linspace(0, 20, 20)
y_vals = [math.sqrt(i) for i in x_vals]

fig = plt.figure()
ax = plt.axes()
ax.plot(x_vals, y_vals)
```

Here is the output of the above script. This method can be used to plot multiple plots, which we will see in the next chapter. In this chapter, we will stick to the first approach, where we call the **plot()** method directly from the **pyplot** module.

Output:

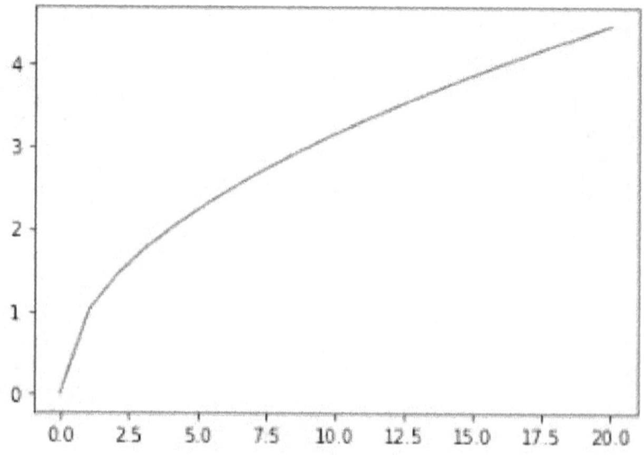

You can also increase the default plot size of a Matplotlib plot. To do so, you can use the **rcParams** list of the **pyplot** module and then set two values for the **figure.figsize** attribute. The following script sets the plot size to 8 inches wide and 6 inches tall.

Script 3:

```
import matplotlib.pyplot as plt
import numpy as np
import math

plt.rcParams["figure.figsize"] = [8,6]

x_vals = np.linspace(0, 20, 20)
y_vals = [math.sqrt(i) for i in x_vals]
plt.plot(x_vals, y_vals)
```

In the output, it is evident that the default plot size has been increased.

Output:

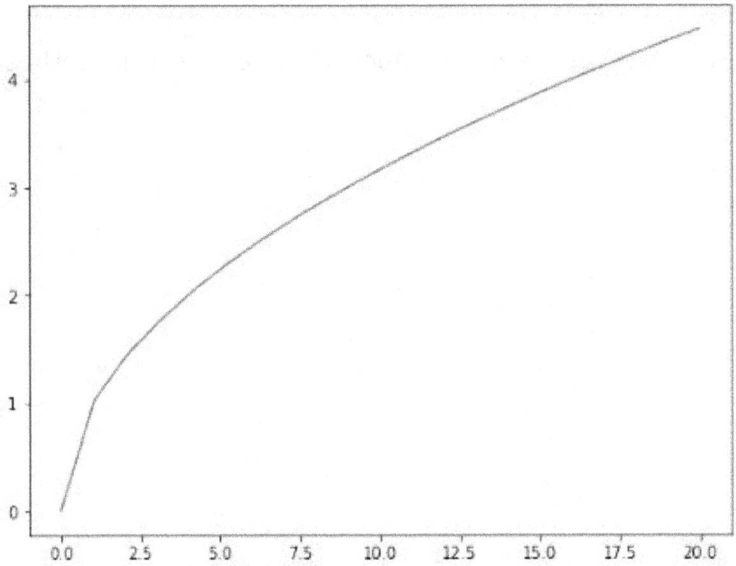

2.3. Titles, Labels, and Legends

You can improve the aesthetics and readability of your graphs by adding titles, labels, and legends to your graph. Let's first see how to add titles and labels to a plot.

To add labels on x and y axes, you need to pass string values respectively to the **xlabel** and **ylabel** methods of the **pyplot** module. Similarly, to set the title, you need to pass a string value to the **title** method, as shown in script 4.

Script 4:

```
import matplotlib.pyplot as plt
import numpy as np
import math

x_vals = np.linspace(0, 20, 20)
y_vals = [math.sqrt(i) for i in x_vals]
plt.xlabel('X Values')
plt.ylabel('Y Values')
plt.title('Square Roots')
plt.plot(x_vals, y_vals)
```

Here in the output, you can see the labels and titles that you specified in the script 4.

Output:

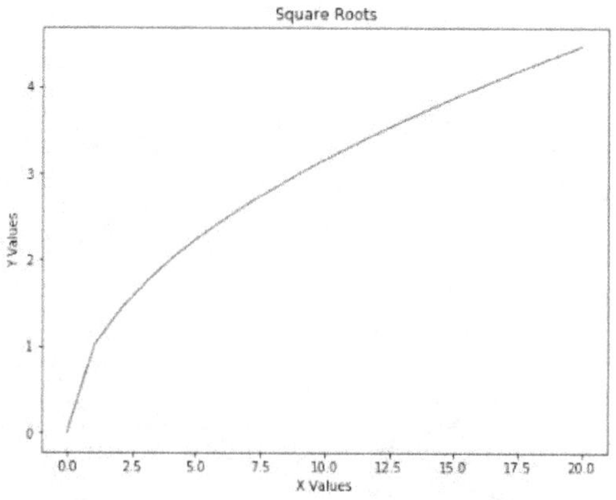

In addition to changing titles and labels, you can also specify the color for the line plot. To do so, you simply have to pass shorthand notation for the color name to the **plot()** function, for example, "r" for red, "b" for blue, and so on. Here is an example:

Script 5:

```
import matplotlib.pyplot as plt
import numpy as np
import math


x_vals = np.linspace(0, 20, 20)
y_vals = [math.sqrt(i) for i in x_vals]
plt.xlabel('X Values')
plt.ylabel('Y Values')
plt.title('Square Roots')
plt.plot(x_vals, y_vals, 'r')
```

Output:

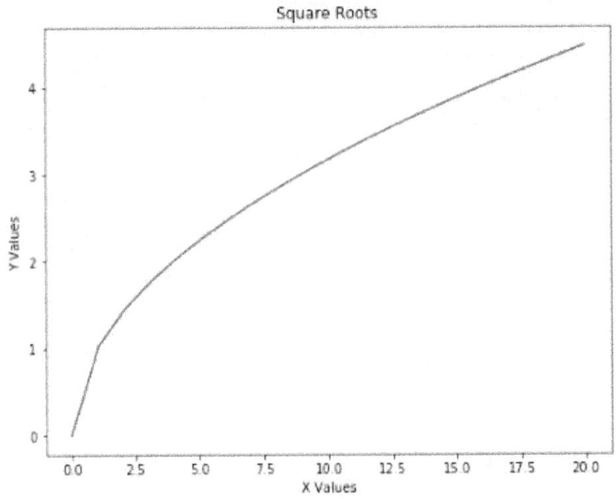

To add a legend, you need to make two changes. First, you have to pass a string value for the **label** attribute of the **plot()** function. Next, you have to pass the value for the **loc**

attribute of the **legend** method of the **pyplot** module. In the **loc** attribute, you have to pass the location of your legend. The following script plots a legend at the upper center corner of the plot.

Script 6:

```
import matplotlib.pyplot as plt
import numpy as np
import math

x_vals = np.linspace(0, 20, 20)
y_vals = [math.sqrt(i) for i in x_vals]
plt.xlabel('X Values')
plt.ylabel('Y Values')
plt.title('Square Roots')
plt.plot(x_vals, y_vals, 'r', label = 'Square Root')
plt.legend(loc='upper center')
```

Output:

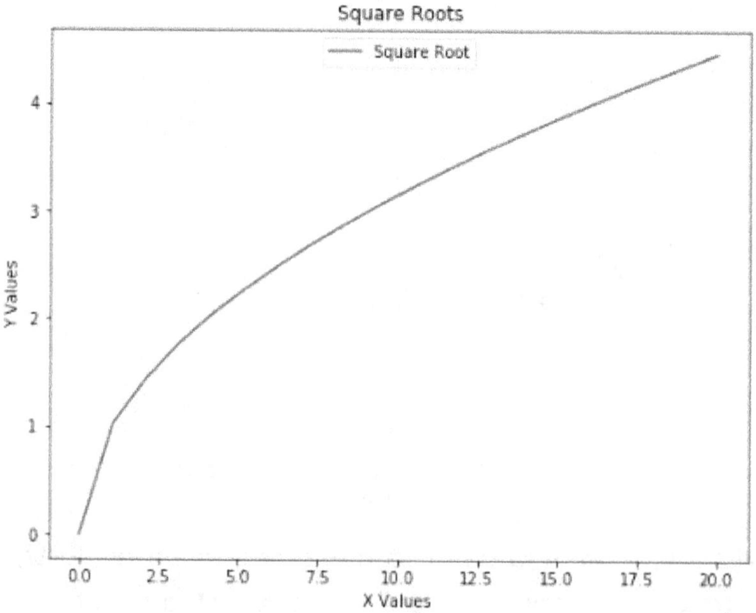

You can also plot multiple line plots inside one graph. All you have to do is call the **plot()** method twice with different values for x and y axes. The following script plots a line plot for square root in red and for a cube function in blue.

Script 7:

```
import matplotlib.pyplot as plt
import numpy as np
import math

x_vals = np.linspace(0, 20, 20)
y_vals = [math.sqrt(i) for i in x_vals]
y2_vals = x_vals ** 3
plt.xlabel('X Values')
plt.ylabel('Y Values')
plt.title('Square Roots')
plt.plot(x_vals, y_vals, 'r', label = 'Square Root')
plt.plot(x_vals, y2_vals, 'b', label = 'Cube')
plt.legend(loc='upper center')
```

Output:

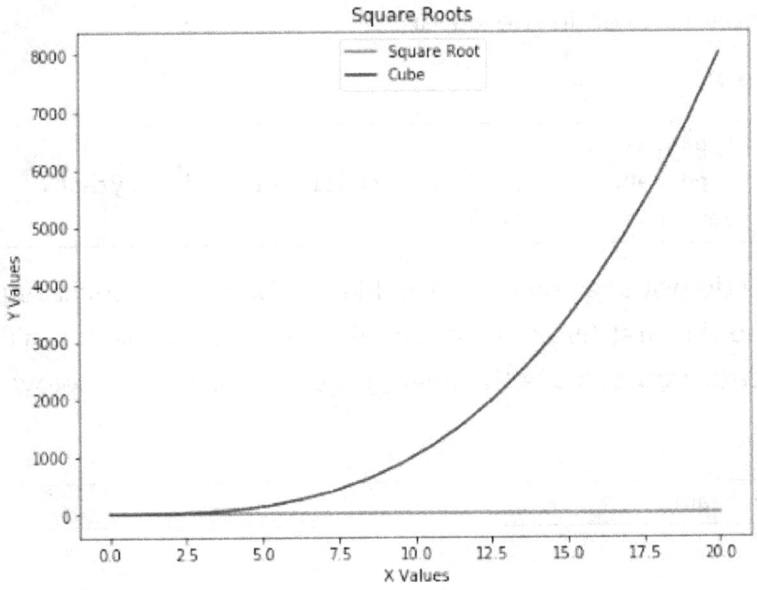

Further Readings - Matplotlib Line Plot [1]

To study more about the Matplotlib line plot, please check Matplotlib's official documentation for line plots. Get used to searching and reading this documentation. It is a great resource of knowledge.

2.4. Plotting Using CSV Data Source

In addition to plotting Matplotlib's graph using in-memory data, you can read data from sources such as CSV (Comma Separated View) and TSV (Tab Separated View) files. The finest way to read data from a CSV file is via the **read_csv()** method of the Pandas library. You will study the Pandas library in detail in another chapter. For now, just remember that the **read_csv()** method from Pandas library can read CSV files and store the file data in a Pandas **dataframe**. Let's read the **iris_data.csv** file. The file is available in the datasets folder of the resources. You can download locally. In the **read_csv()** method, you simply have to pass the path of the CSV file. An example is given in the script 8.

Script 8:

```
import pandas as pd
data = pd.read_csv(«E:\Data Visualization with Python\
Datasets\iris_data.csv»)
```

If you do not see any error, the file has been read successfully. To see the first five rows of the Pandas **dataframe** containing the data, you can use the **head()** method as shown below:

Script 9:

```
data.head()
```

Output:

	sepal_length	sepal_width	petal_length	petal_width	species
0	5.1	3.5	1.4	0.2	setosa
1	4.9	3.0	1.4	0.2	setosa
2	4.7	3.2	1.3	0.2	setosa
3	4.6	3.1	1.5	0.2	setosa
4	5.0	3.6	1.4	0.2	setosa

You can see that the **iris_data.csv** file has five columns. We can use values from any of these two columns to plot a line plot. To do so, for x and y axes, we need to pass the data **dataframe** column names to the **plot()** function of the **pyplot** module. To access a column name from a Pandas **dataframe**, you need to specify the **dataframe** name followed by a pair of square brackets. Inside the brackets, the column name is specified. The following script plots a line plot, where the x-axis contains values from the **sepal_length** column, whereas the y-axis contains values from the **petal_length** column of the **dataframe**.

Script 10:

```
import matplotlib.pyplot as plt
import numpy as np
import math

plt.xlabel('Sepal Length')
plt.ylabel('Petal Length')
plt.title('Sepal vs Petal Length')
plt.plot(data[«sepal_length»], data[«petal_length»],
'b')
```

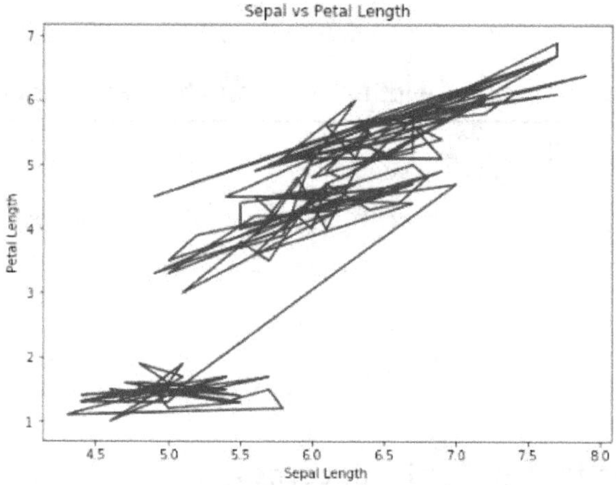

2.5. Plotting Using TSV Data Source

Like CSV, you can also read a TSV file via the **read_csv()** method. You have to pass **'\t'** as the value for the **sep** parameter. The script 11 reads **iris_data.tsv** file and stores it in a Pandas **dataframe.** Next, the first five rows of the dataframe have been printed via the **head()** method.

Script 11:

```
import pandas as pd
data = pd.read_csv(«E:\Data Visualization with
Python\Datasets\iris_data.tsv», sep='\t')
data.head()
```

Output:

	SepalLength	SepalWidth	PetalLength	PetalWidth	TrainingClass
0	5.1	3.5	1.4	0.2	Iris-setosa
1	4.9	3.0	1.4	0.2	Iris-setosa
2	4.7	3.2	1.3	0.2	Iris-setosa
3	4.6	3.1	1.5	0.2	Iris-setosa
4	5.0	3.6	1.4	0.2	Iris-setosa

The remaining process to plot the line plot remains the same as it was for the CSV file. The following script plots a line plot where the x-axis contains sepal length, and the y-axis displays petal length.

Script 12:

```
import matplotlib.pyplot as plt
import numpy as np
import math

plt.xlabel('Sepal Length')
plt.ylabel('Petal Length')
plt.title('Sepal vs Petal Length')
plt.plot(data[«SepalLength»], data[«PetalLength»], «b»)
```

Output:

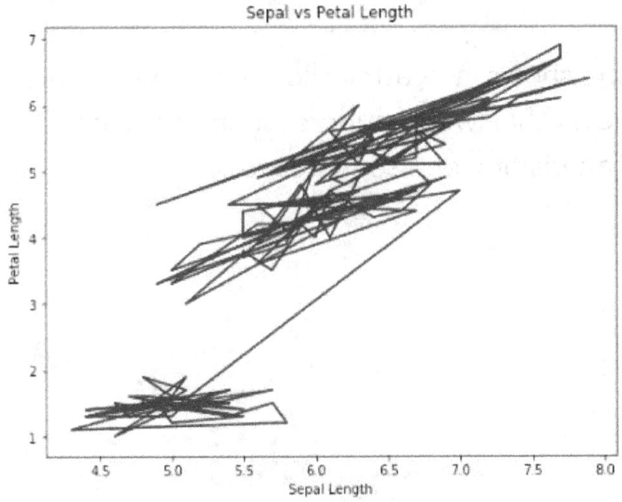

2.6. Scatter Plot

A scatter plot is used to plot the relationship between two numeric columns in the form of scattered points. Normally, a scatter plot is used when for each value in the x-axis, there exist multiple values in the y-axis. To plot a scatter plot, the **scatter()** function of the **pyplot** module is used. You have to pass the values for the x-axis and the y-axis. In addition, you have to pass a shorthand notation of color value to the **c** parameter. The script 13 shows how to plot a scatter plot between sepal length and petal length of iris plants.

Script 13:

```
import matplotlib.pyplot as plt
import numpy as np
import math

plt.xlabel('Sepal Length')
plt.ylabel('Petal Length')
plt.title('Sepal vs Petal Length')
plt.scatter(data[«SepalLength»], data[«PetalLength»], c =
«b»)
```

The output shows a scatter plot with blue points. The plot clearly shows that with an increase in sepal length, the petal length of an iris flower also increases.

Output:

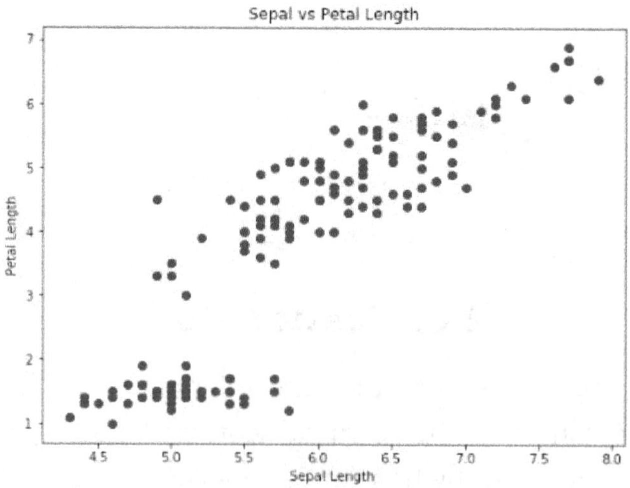

You can change the default markers used to plot points on a scatter plot. To do so, you have to pass the marker value to the **marker** parameter of the **scatter()** method. The following script uses the letter **x** as the marker for the points in the scatter plot.

Script 14:

```
import matplotlib.pyplot as plt
import numpy as np
import math

plt.xlabel('Sepal Length')
plt.ylabel('Petal Length')
plt.title('Sepal vs Petal Length')
plt.scatter(data[«SepalLength»], data[«PetalLength»], c =
«b», marker = «x»)
```

Output:

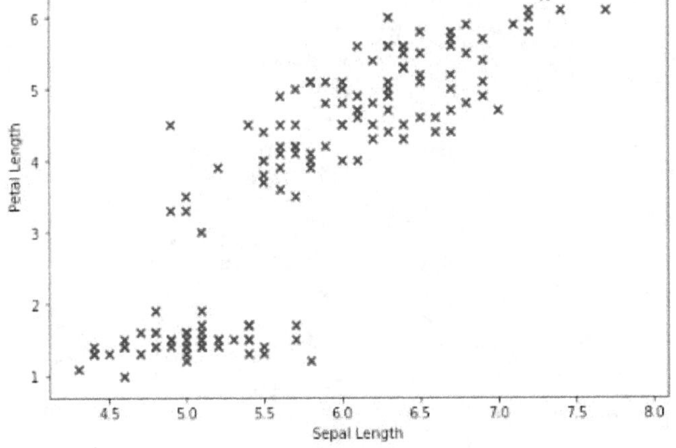

Like line plots, you can plot multiple scatter plots inside one graph. To do so, you have to call the scatter() method twice with the same value for the x-axis while different values for the y-axis. In the following script, you will see two scatter plots. The first scatter plot plots the relation between sepal vs. petal length using blue markers, and the second scatter plot plots the relation between sepal length and sepal width using red markers.

Script 15:

```
import matplotlib.pyplot as plt
import numpy as np
import math

plt.xlabel('Sepal Length')
plt.ylabel('Petal Length')
plt.title('Sepal vs Petal Length')
plt.scatter(data[«SepalLength»], data[«PetalLength»], c =
«b», marker = «x», label=»Petal Length»)
plt.scatter(data[«SepalLength»], data[«SepalWidth»], c =
«r», marker = «o», label=»Sepal Width»)
plt.legend(loc='upper center')
```

Output:

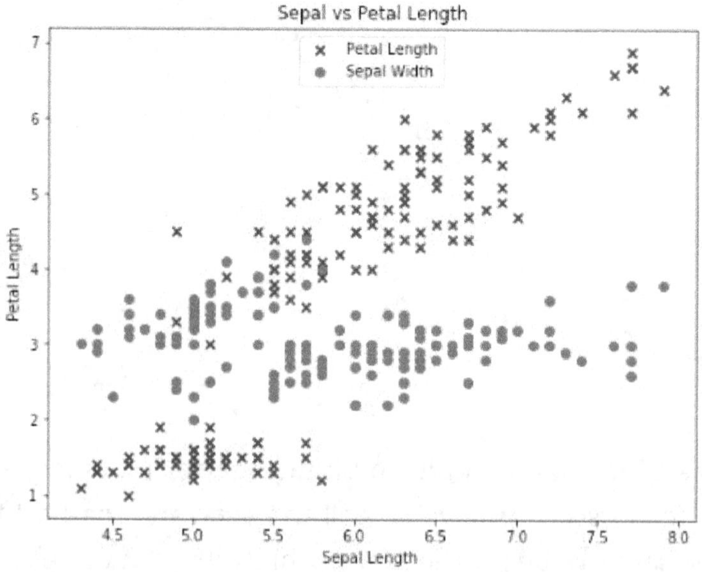

Further Readings - Matplotlib Scatter Plot [2]

To study more about Matplotlib scatter plot, please check Matplotlib's official documentation for scatter plots. Get used to searching and reading this documentation. It is a great resource of knowledge.

2.7. Bar Plots

Bar plot is used to plot the relationship between unique values in a categorical column grouped by an aggregate function such as sum, mean, median, etc. Before we plot a bar plot, let's first import the dataset that we are going to use in this chapter. Execute the following script to read the **`titanic_data.csv`** file. You find the CSV file in the datasets folder in *resources*. The following script also displays the first 5 rows of the dataset.

Script 16:

```
import pandas as pd
data = pd.read_csv(r»E:\Data Visualization with Python\
Datasets\titanic_data.csv»)
data.head()
```

Output:

	PassengerId	Survived	Pclass	Name	Sex	Age	SibSp	Parch	Ticket	Fare	Cabin	Embarked
0	1	0	3	Braund, Mr. Owen Harris	male	22.0	1	0	A/5 21171	7.2500	NaN	S
1	2	1	1	Cumings, Mrs. John Bradley (Florence Briggs Th...	female	38.0	1	0	PC 17599	71.2833	C85	C
2	3	1	3	Heikkinen, Miss. Laina	female	26.0	0	0	STON/O2. 3101282	7.9250	NaN	S
3	4	1	1	Futrelle, Mrs. Jacques Heath (Lily May Peel)	female	35.0	1	0	113803	53.1000	C123	S
4	5	0	3	Allen, Mr. William Henry	male	35.0	0	0	373450	8.0500	NaN	S

To plot a bar plot, you need to call the **`bar()`** method. The categorical values are passed on the x-axis, and corresponding aggregated numerical values are passed on the y-axis. The following script plots a bar plot between genders and ages of the *Titanic* ship.

Script 17:

```
import matplotlib.pyplot as plt
import numpy as np
import math

plt.xlabel('Gender')
plt.ylabel('Ages')
plt.title('Gender vs Age')
plt.bar(data[«Sex»], data[«Age»])
```

Output:

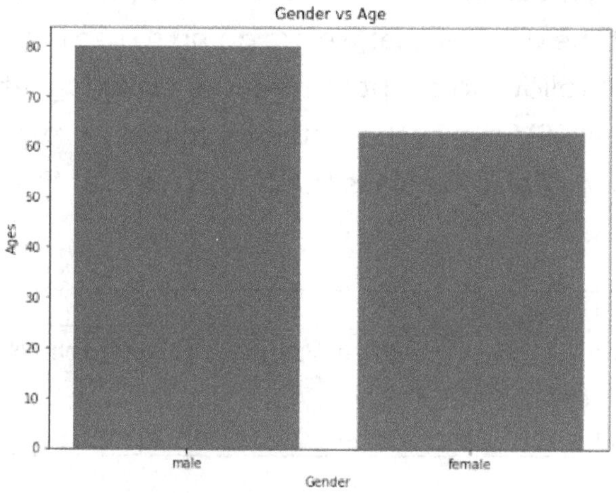

You can also create horizontal bar plots. To do so, you need to call the **barh()** method, as shown below:

Script 18:

```
import matplotlib.pyplot as plt
import numpy as np
import math

plt.xlabel('Ages')
plt.ylabel('Class')
plt.title('Class vs Age')
plt.barh(data[«Pclass»], data[«Age»])
```

Output:

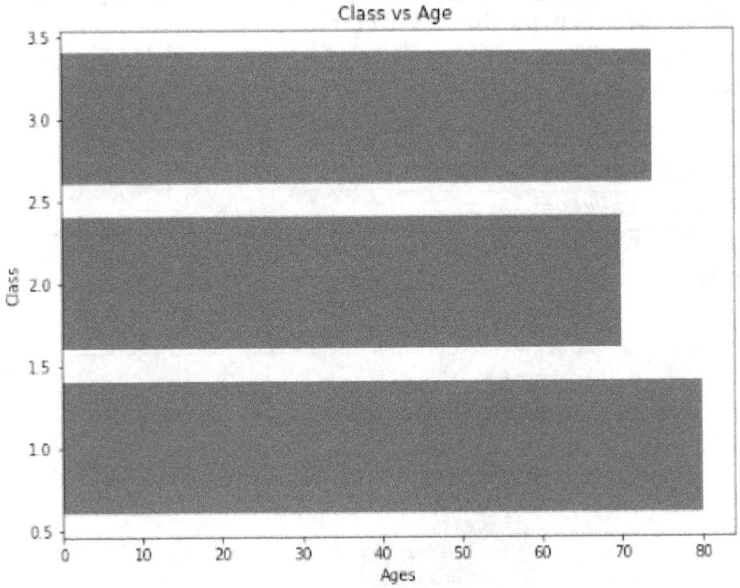

The output shows the relationship between the passenger class and the ages of the passengers in the unfortunate *Titanic* ship.

Further Readings - Matplotlib Bar Plot [3]

To study more about Matplotlib bar plots, please check Matplotlib's official documentation for bar plots. Get used to searching and reading this documentation. It is a great resource of knowledge.

2.8. Histograms

Histograms are used to display the distribution of data for a numeric list of items. To plot a histogram, the **`hist()`** method is used. You simply have to pass a collection of numeric values to the **`hist()`** method. For instance, the following histogram plots the distribution of values in the Age column of the Titanic dataset.

Script 19

```
import matplotlib.pyplot as plt
import numpy as np
import math

plt.title('Age Histogram')
plt.hist(data[«Age»])
```

Output:

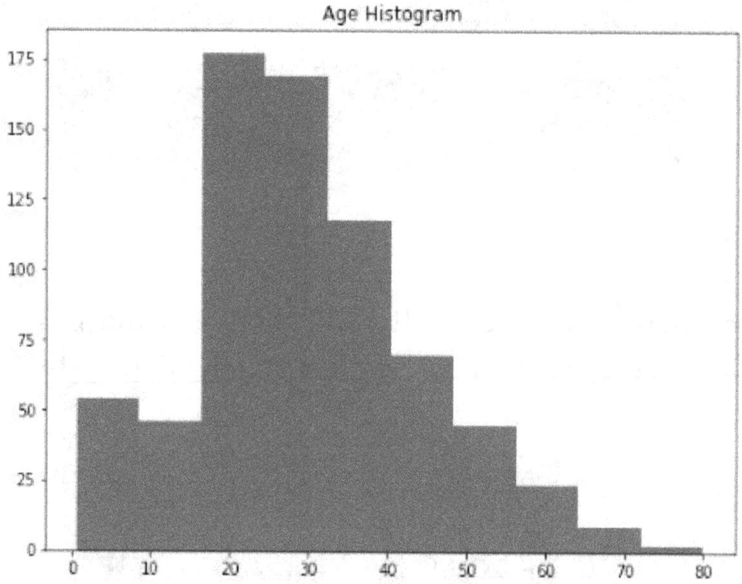

The output shows that the majority of the passengers (175) were aged between 20 and 25. Similarly, the passengers aged between 70 and 80 are least in number. By default, the age is distributed into 10 bins or 10 groups.

Similarly, the following script plots a histogram for the fare column of the titanic dataset.

Script 20

```
import matplotlib.pyplot as plt
import numpy as np
import math

plt.title('Fare Histogram')
plt.hist(data[«Fare»])
```

Output:

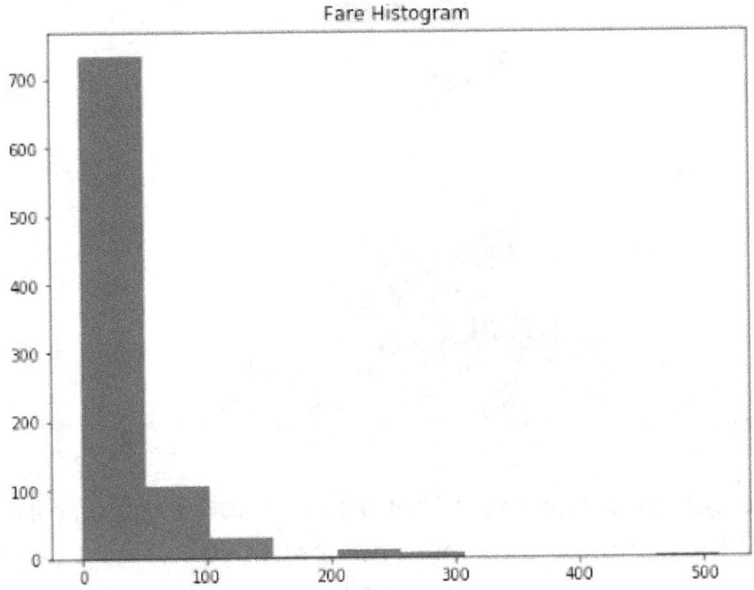

The output shows that the majority of passengers (more than 700) paid amounts between 0 and 50 as fares.

The default bin size for the histograms in Matplotlib can be changed. To do so, you need to pass bin size in an integer as the value for the **bins** parameter of the **hist()** method. Look at the following script where bin size has been set to 5.

Script 21:

```
import matplotlib.pyplot as plt
import numpy as np
import math

plt.title('Age Histogram')
plt.hist(data[«Age»], bins = 5)
```

Output:

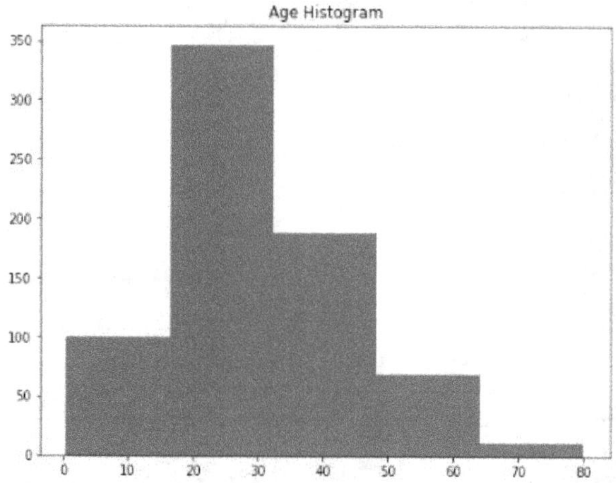

In the output, it is evident that age has now been distributed in five bins, and the maximum number of passengers (around 350) are aged between 20 and 30.

Further Readings – Matplotlib Histogram [4]

To study more about Matplotlib histograms, please check Matplotlib's official documentation for histograms. Get used to searching and reading this documentation. It is a great resource of knowledge.

2.9 Pie Charts

Pie chart, as the name suggests, displays the percentage distribution of values in a categorical column in terms of an aggregated function. For instance, the following script shows the percentage distribution of jobs with respect to job categories, i.e., IT, Marketing, Data Science, and Finance. To plot a pie chart, the **pie()** method of the **pyplot** module is used. The first parameter is the list of numeric values that you want to be converted and displayed into percentages. Next, you have to pass a list of categories to the **labels** parameter. The **explode** parameter defines the magnitude of the split for each category in the pie chart. The **autopct** parameter defines the format in which the percentage will be displayed on the pie chart.

Script 22:

```
labels = 'IT', 'Marketing', 'Data Science', 'Finance'
values = [500, 156, 300, 510]
explode = (0.05, 0.05, 0.05, 0.05)

plt.pie(values, explode=explode, labels=labels,
autopct='%1.1f%%', shadow=True)
plt.show()
```

Output:

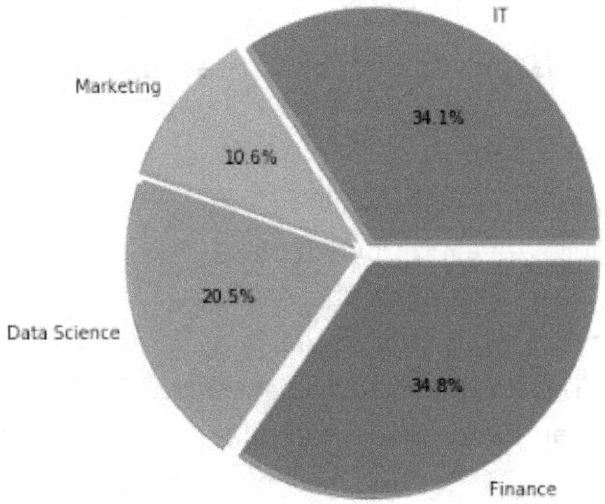

In the previous section, you saw how to plot a pie plot using raw values. Let's see how to plot a pie plot using a Pandas dataframe as the source.

Suppose, we want to plot the percentage distribution of passengers that traveled in different passenger classes in the *Titanic* ship. To do so, first, we need to find the sum of passengers that traveled in each passenger class. These values can be found via value_counts() function, as shown below.

Script 23:

```
import pandas as pd
data = pd.read_csv(r"E:\Data Visualization with Python\
Datasets\titanic_data.csv")

pclass = data["Pclass"].value_counts()
print(pclass)
```

Here is an output.

Output:

```
3    491
1    216
2    184
Name: Pclass, dtype: int64
```

The output is a Pandas series, where index names contain the name of passenger class while values correspond to the sum of passengers traveling in each class. The output shows that 491 passengers traveled in the 3rd class, while 184 traveled in the 1st class. We know that to plot a pie chart, we need values and labels. The labels here can be fetched from index names, and values can be obtained via values of the series returned by **value_counts()** function as shown below:

Script 24:

```
print(pclass.index.values.tolist())
print(pclass.values.tolist())
```

Output:

```
[3, 1, 2]
[491, 216, 184]
```

Now that you have labels as well as their corresponding values, you can create a pie plot as follows:

Script 25:

```
labels = pclass.index.values.tolist()
values = pclass.values.tolist()
explode = (0.05, 0.05, 0.05)

plt.pie(values, explode=explode, labels=labels,
autopct='%1.1f%%', shadow=True, startangle=140)
plt.show()
```

Output:

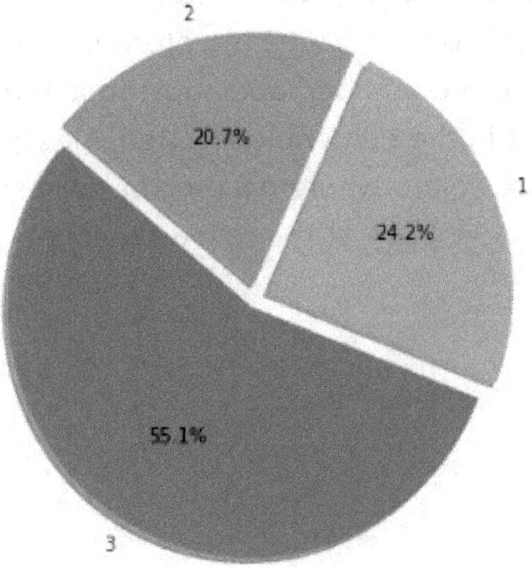

The output shows that around 55 percent of the passengers traveled in the 3rd class of the *Titanic*, while 20.7 percent and 24.2 percent of the passengers traveled in 2nd and 1st classes, respectively.

Further Readings - Matplotlib Pie Charts [5]

To study more about Matplotlib Pie Charts, please check Matplotlib's official documentation for Pie Charts. Get used to searching and reading this documentation. It is a great resource of knowledge.

2.10. Stack Plot

Stack plot is used to plot numeric information for multiple collections of items stacked on top of each other. To plot a stack plot, you need to call the **`stackplot()`** method. The first parameter to the **`stackplot()`** method is the list of labels. In script 26, the labels are the names of the seven days in a week. Next, you have to specify the collections that contain numeric values. In the script 26, the collections that contain numeric values are **`London, Tokyo, and Paris`**. The numeric values in these collections belong to temperature on each day of the week. Note that the number label must match the number of numeric values in the numeric collection. Finally, you need to specify a list of colors where each color corresponds to one numeric collection. Look at the following script.

Script 26:

```
import matplotlib.pyplot as plt

days= [“Monday”, “Tuesday”, “Wednesday”, “Thursday”,
“Friday”, “Saturday”, “Sunday”]

London = [25,26,32,19,28,39,24]

Tokyo = [20,29,23,35,32,26,18]

Paris= [18,21,28,35,29,25,22]


plt.plot([],[], color=’green’, label=’London’)
plt.plot([],[], color=’orange’, label=’Tokyo’)
plt.plot([],[], color=’yellow’, label=’Paris’)


plt.stackplot(days, London, Tokyo, Paris, colors=[‘green’,
‘orange’, ‘yellow’])

plt.legend()

plt.title(‘Days of Week vs Temperature’)
plt.xlabel(‘Days of Week’)
plt.ylabel(‘Temperature’)

plt.show()
```

Output:

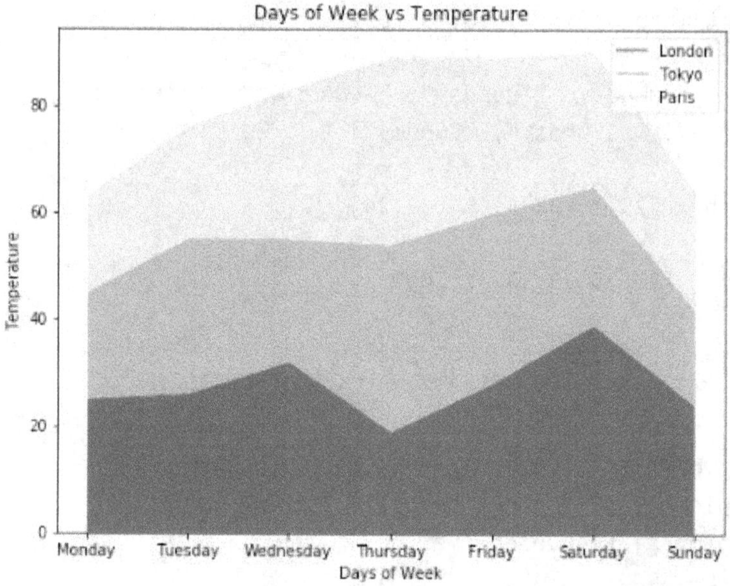

Further Readings - Matplotlib Stack Plots [6]

To study more about Matplotlib stack plots, please check Matplotlib's official documentation for Stack Plots. Get used to searching and reading this documentation. It is a great resource of knowledge.

Hands-on Time - Exercise

Now, it is your turn. Follow the instructions in **the exercises below** to check your understanding of the basic data visualization with Matplotlib. The answers to these questions are given at the end of the book.

Exercise 2.1

Question 1:

Which is one parameter that you must specify in order to make a scatter plot in Matplotlib?

A- color

B- c

C- r

D- None of the above

Question 2:

To create a legend, the value for which of the following parameter is needed to be specified?

A- title

B- label

C- axis

D- All of the above

Question 3:

How to show percentage values on a Matplotlib Pie Chart?

A - autopct = '%1.1f%%'

B - percentage = '%1.1f%%'

C - perc = '%1.1f%%'

D - None of the Above

Exercise 2.2

Create a Pie chart that shows the distribution of passengers with respect to their gender, in the unfortunate *Titanic* ship. You can use the Titanic dataset from *resources* for that purpose.

References

1. https://matplotlib.org/3.1.1/api/_as_gen/matplotlib.pyplot.plot.html
2. http://matplotlib.org/3.1.1/api/_as_gen/matplotlib.pyplot.scatter.html
3. https://matplotlib.org/3.1.1/api/_as_gen/matplotlib.pyplot.bar.html
4. https://matplotlib.org/3.1.1/api/_as_gen/matplotlib.pyplot.hist.html
5. https://matplotlib.org/3.1.1/api/_as_gen/matplotlib.pyplot.pie.html
6. https://matplotlib.org/3.1.1/gallery/lines_bars_and_markers/stackplot_demo.html

3

Advanced Plotting with Matplotlib

3.1. Introduction

In the second chapter, we started our discussion about the Matplotlib library and its basic plotting functions. In this chapter, you will strengthen the knowledge that you gained in the previous chapter. You will learn how to plot multiple plots using Matplotlib, how to plot subplots, and how to save Matplotlib plots to your local drive.

Requirements – Anaconda, Jupyter, and Matplotlib

- All the scripts in this book have been executed via the Jupyter notebook. Therefore, you should have the Jupyter notebook installed.
- Needless to say, we will be using the Matplotlib library.
- The Numpy and Pandas libraries should also be installed before this chapter.

Hands-on Time - Source Codes

All IPython notebooks for the source code of all the scripts in this chapter can be found in Resources/Chapter 3.ipynb. I would suggest that you write all the code in this chapter yourself and see if you can get the same output as mentioned in this chapter.

Before we start plotting anything, we need to import the **pyplot** module from the Matplotlib library. The following script does that:

```
import matplotlib.pyplot as plt
%matplotlib inline
```

3.2. Plotting Multiple Plots

All the plots that we plotted in the previous chapter were single plots or one axes containing two plots. In this section, you will see how to plot multiple standalone plots.

To do so, you need to first call the **subplot()** method and define the position where you want to plot your graph. The first argument to the **subplot()** method is the number of rows, and the second parameter is the number of columns. The third parameter is the cell number where you want to plot your graph. For instance, **subplot(2,2,1)** means that there will be two rows and 2 columns (hence, a total of 4 plots), and the next plot should be plotted in the first cell. The cell position starts from the top left, moves to the right, and then to the left for most of the new line. The following script plots four line plots, two on each row.

Script 1:

```
import matplotlib.pyplot as plt
import numpy as np
import math

plt.rcParams[“figure.figsize”] = [12,8]

x_vals = np.linspace(0, 20, 20)
y_vals = [math.sqrt(i) for i in x_vals]

plt.subplot(2,2,1)
plt.plot(x_vals, y_vals, ‘bo-’)

plt.subplot(2,2,2)
plt.plot(x_vals, y_vals, ‘rx-’)

plt.subplot(2,2,3)
plt.plot(x_vals, y_vals, ‘g*-’)

plt.subplot(2,2,4)
plt.plot(x_vals, y_vals, ‘g*-’)
```

Output:

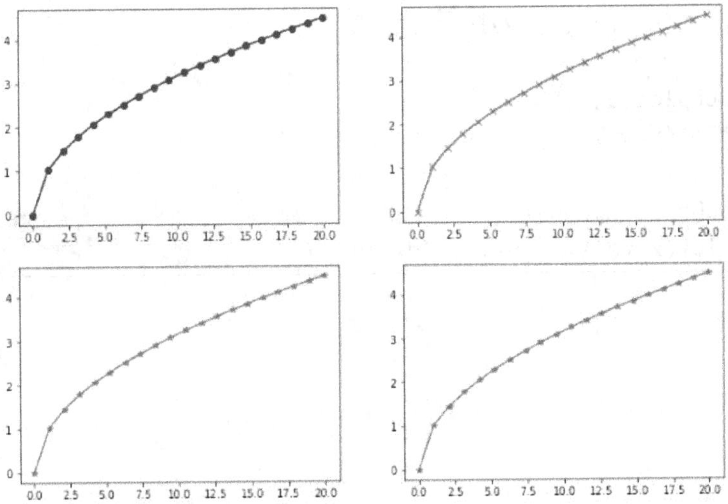

Let's see another example of how the **subplot()** method can be used to plot multiple plots. The following script plots six line plots in two rows and three columns.

Script 2:

```
import matplotlib.pyplot as plt
import numpy as np
import math

plt.rcParams["figure.figsize"] = [12,8]

x_vals = np.linspace(0, 20, 20)
y_vals = [math.sqrt(i) for i in x_vals]

plt.subplot(2,3,1)
plt.plot(x_vals, y_vals, 'bo-')

plt.subplot(2,3,2)
plt.plot(x_vals, y_vals, 'rx-')

plt.subplot(2,3,3)
plt.plot(x_vals, y_vals, 'g*-')

plt.subplot(2,3,4)
plt.plot(x_vals, y_vals, 'g*-')

plt.subplot(2,3,5)
plt.plot(x_vals, y_vals, 'bo-')

plt.subplot(2,3,6)
plt.plot(x_vals, y_vals, 'rx-')
```

Output:

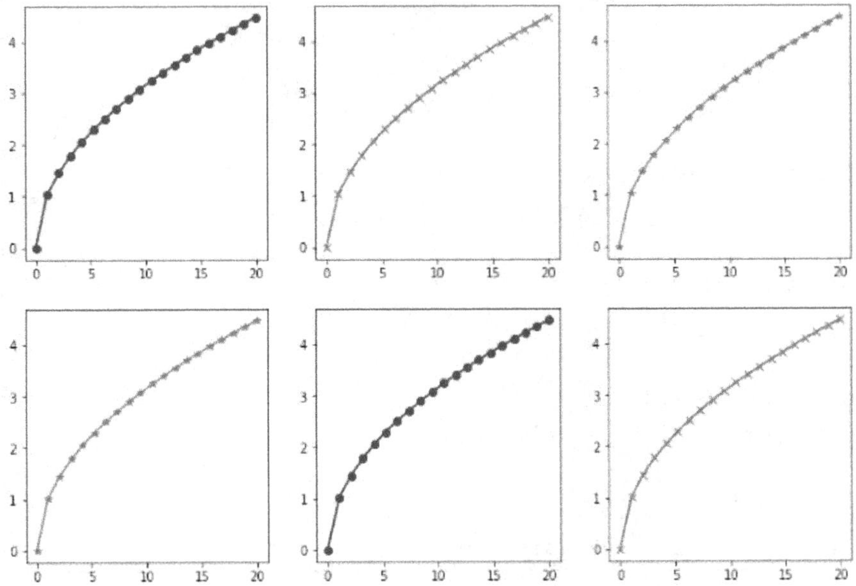

The idea of multiple plots is to show different information in each plot. The following script plots six line plots in two rows and three columns. The three line plots in the first row show the square root of 20 numbers between 0 and 20. The three line plots in the second row show the cube of the same 20 numbers.

Script 3:

```
import matplotlib.pyplot as plt
import numpy as np
import math

plt.rcParams["figure.figsize"] = [12,8]

x_vals = np.linspace(0, 20, 20)
y_vals = [math.sqrt(i) for i in x_vals]
y2_vals = x_vals ** 3
```

```
plt.subplot(2,3,1)
plt.plot(x_vals, y_vals, 'bo-')

plt.subplot(2,3,2)
plt.plot(x_vals, y_vals, 'rx-')

plt.subplot(2,3,3)
plt.plot(x_vals, y_vals, 'g*-')

plt.subplot(2,3,4)
plt.plot(x_vals, y2_vals, 'g*-')

plt.subplot(2,3,5)
plt.plot(x_vals, y2_vals, 'bo-')

plt.subplot(2,3,6)
plt.plot(x_vals, y2_vals, 'rx-')
```

Output:

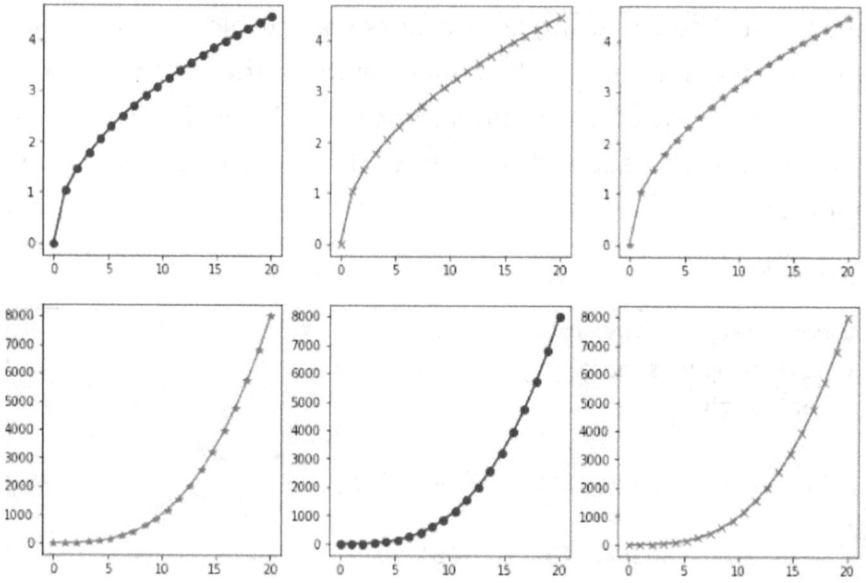

3.3. Plotting in Object-Oriented Way

In this section, you will see the object-oriented way of plotting Matplotlib plots. Look at the following script.

Script 4:

```
import matplotlib.pyplot as plt
import numpy as np
import math

plt.rcParams["figure.figsize"] = [12,8]

x_vals = np.linspace(0, 20, 20)
y_vals = [math.sqrt(i) for i in x_vals]

figure = plt.figure()

axes = figure.add_axes([0.5, 0.5, 0.5, 0.5])
```

In the script above, we first create the **figure()** object. Next, we add an axes to this figure object using the **add_axes()** method. You need to pass four numeric parameters to the **add_axes()** function. The parameters are the *distance* from the left and bottom axis, and then the *width* and *height* of the axis, respectively. The values passed are the fraction of the default values. The above script will create an empty figure since no plot has been added to it yet. Here is the output.

Output:

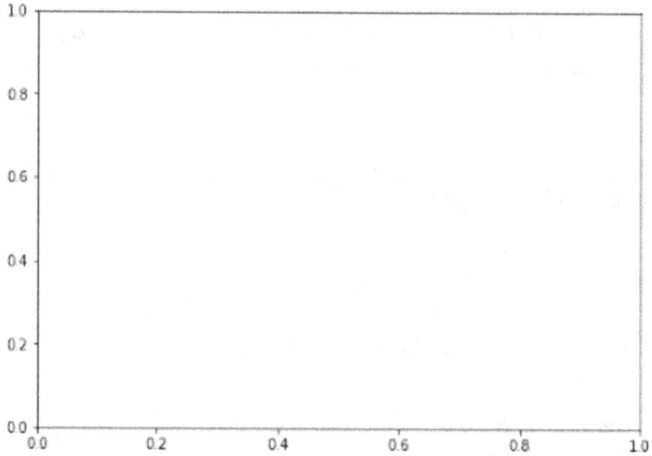

To add a plot to the above figure, all you have to do is call the **plot()** method using the axes object. This **plot()** is the same as the plot method of the **pyplot** module. Look at the following script.

Script 5:

```
import matplotlib.pyplot as plt
import numpy as np
import math

plt.rcParams["figure.figsize"] = [12,8]

x_vals = np.linspace(0, 20, 20)
y_vals = [math.sqrt(i) for i in x_vals]

figure = plt.figure()

axes = figure.add_axes([0.1, 0.1, 0.5, 0.5])

axes.plot(x_vals, y_vals)
axes.set_xlabel('X Axis')
axes.set_ylabel('Y Axis')
```

Output:

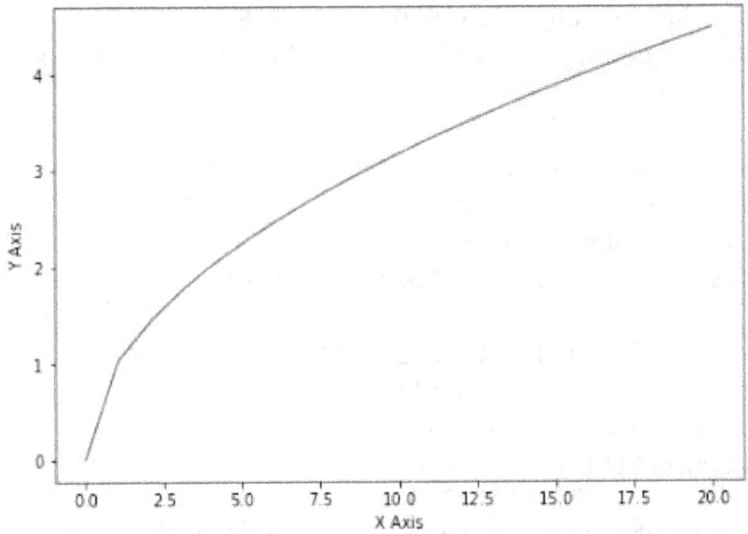

The best thing about the object-oriented way of plotting graphs is that you can plot a graph inside another graph. All you have to do is add one more axis using **figure.add_axes()** method and set its location to be inside the parent plot. The following script plots two plots. The outer plot displays the square root, while the inner plot displays the cube of 20 integers between 0 and 20.

Script 6:

```
import matplotlib.pyplot as plt
import numpy as np
import math

plt.rcParams["figure.figsize"] = [12,8]

x_vals = np.linspace(0, 20, 20)
y_vals = [math.sqrt(i) for i in x_vals]
y2_vals = x_vals ** 3
```

```
figure = plt.figure()

axes = figure.add_axes([0.0, 0.0, 0.8, 0.8])
axes2 = figure.add_axes([0.35, 0.07, 0.35, 0.3]) #
inset axes

axes.plot(x_vals, y_vals, 'g')
axes.set_xlabel('Values')
axes.set_ylabel('Square Root')
axes.set_title('Square Root Function')

axes2.plot(x_vals, y2_vals, 'b')
axes2.set_xlabel('Values')
axes2.set_ylabel('Cube')
axes2.set_title('Cube Function')
```

In the output below, you can see a line plot inside another plot.

Output:

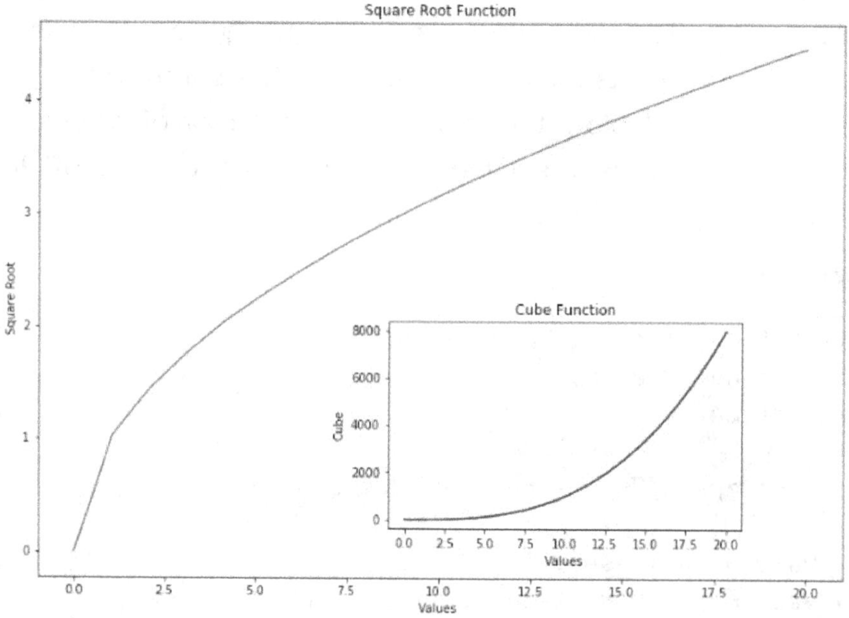

3.4. Using Subplots Function to Create Multiple Plots

In addition to using the **subplot()** function, again and again, to plot multiple plots as we did in section 3.1, you can also plot multiple plots via the subplots() function. The total number of plots is the multiple of the number of rows and columns. The **nrows** attribute of the axes function is used to specify the number of rows while the **ncols** attribute indicates the number of columns. The **subplots()** function returns multiple axes in a specified number of rows and columns.

Script 7:

```
import matplotlib.pyplot as plt
import numpy as np
import math

plt.rcParams["figure.figsize"] = [12,8]

x_vals = np.linspace(0, 20, 20)
y_vals = [math.sqrt(i) for i in x_vals]
y2_vals = x_vals ** 3

fig, axes = plt.subplots(nrows=4, ncols=2)
```

Output:

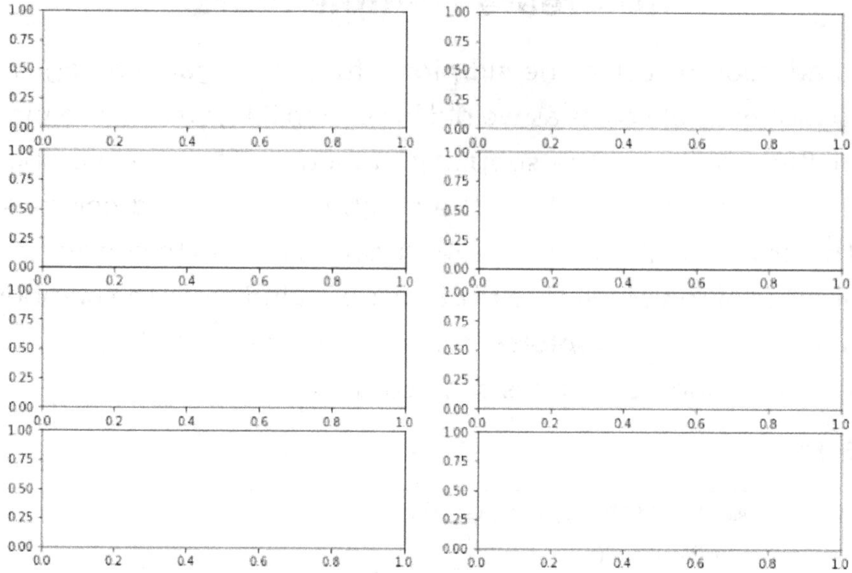

To add plots to the axes returned by the subplots() function, you need to iterate through each row and then each axes() in the row and then use the axes().plot() method to add your plot to the corresponding axis. The following script plots eight line plots in four rows and two columns.

Script 8:

```
import matplotlib.pyplot as plt
import numpy as np
import math

plt.rcParams[«figure.figsize»] = [12,8]

x_vals = np.linspace(0, 20, 20)
y_vals = [math.sqrt(i) for i in x_vals]
y2_vals = x_vals ** 3

fig, axes = plt.subplots(nrows=4, ncols=2)
```

```
for rows in axes:
    for ax1 in rows:
        ax1.plot(x_vals, y_vals, 'g')
        ax1.set_xlabel('Values')
        ax1.set_ylabel('Square Root')
        ax1.set_title('Square Root Function')
```

Output:

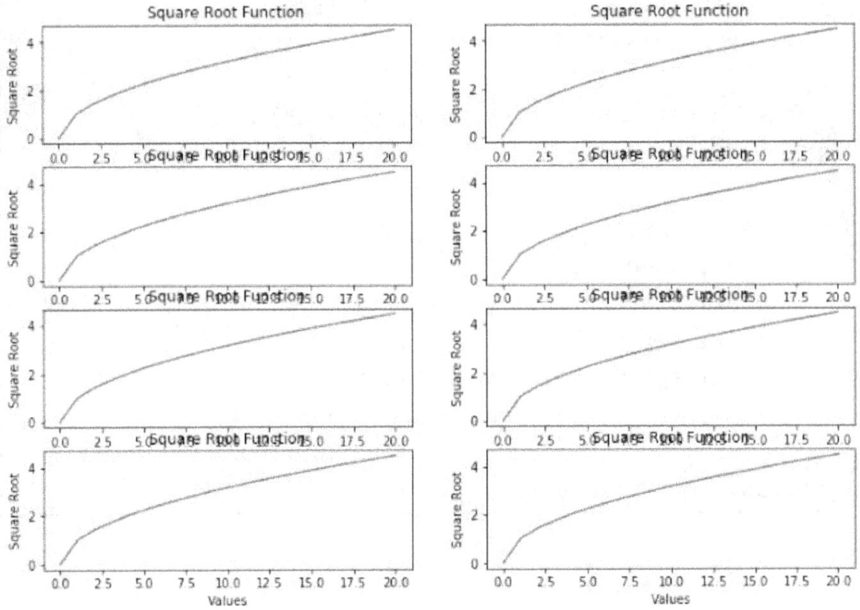

3.5. Saving a Matplotlib Plot

To save a Matplotlib graph, you need to call the savefig() method via the figure object. You simply need to pass the file location where you want to store your plot to the savefig() method. In the following script, the `subplots()` function is used to plot six plots in two rows and three columns.

Script 9:

```
import matplotlib.pyplot as plt
import numpy as np
import math

plt.rcParams[«figure.figsize»] = [12,8]

x_vals = np.linspace(0, 20, 20)
y_vals = [math.sqrt(i) for i in x_vals]
y2_vals = x_vals ** 3

fig, axes = plt.subplots(nrows=2, ncols=3)


for rows in axes:
    for ax1 in rows:
        ax1.plot(x_vals, y_vals, 'g')
        ax1.set_xlabel('Values')
        ax1.set_ylabel('Square Root')
        ax1.set_title('Square Root Function')

figure.savefig(r'E:/Subplots.jpg')
```

Output:

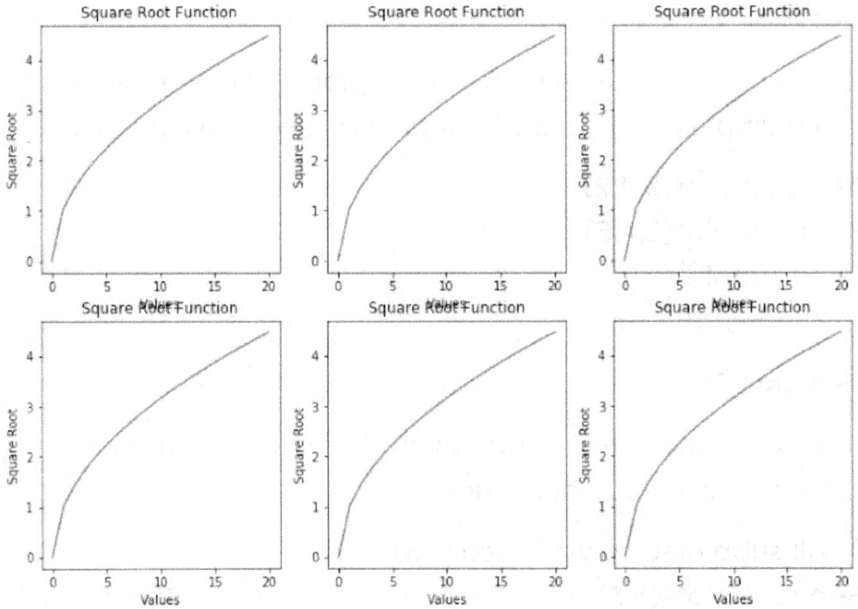

Further Readings – Matplotlib Subplots

To study more about the Matplotlib subplots, please check Matplotlib's official documentation for Subplots. Get used to searching and reading this documentation. It is a great resource of knowledge.

Hands-on Time – Exercise

Now, it is your turn. Follow the instructions in **the exercises below** to check your understanding of the advanced data visualization with Matplotlib. The answers to these questions are given at the end of the book.

Exercise 3.1

Question 1:

Which plot function will you use to plot a graph in the 5th cell of a multiple plot figure with four rows and two columns?

A- plt.subplot(5,4,2)

B- plt.subplot(2,4,5)

C- plt.subplot(4,2,5)

D- None of the Above

Question 2:

How will you create a subplot with five rows and three columns using subplots() function?

A- plt.subplots(nrows=5, ncols=3)

B- plt.subplots(5,3)

C- plt.subplots(rows=5, cols=3)

D- All of the Above

Question 3

Which function is used to save a graph?

A- figure.saveimage()

B- figure.savegraph()

C- figure.saveplot()

D- figure.savefig()

Exercise 3.2

Draw multiple plots with three rows and one column. Show the sine of any 30 integers in the first plot, the cosine of the same 30 integers in the second plot, and the tangent of the same 30 integers in the 3rd plot.

4

Introduction to the Python Seaborn Library

4.1. Introduction

In the previous two chapters, you saw how to plot different types of graphs using Python's Matplotlib library. In this chapter, you will see how to perform data visualization with Seaborn, which is yet another extremely handy Python library for data visualization. The Seaborn library is based on the Matplotlib library. Therefore, you will also need to import the Matplotlib library before you plot any Matplotlib graph.

To install the Seaborn library, you simply have to execute the following command at your command terminal:

```
$ pip install seaborn
```

Before you go and start plotting different types of plot, you need to import a few libraries. The following script does that:

```
import matplotlib.pyplot as plt
import seaborn as sns

plt.rcParams[«figure.figsize»] = [10,8]

tips_data = sns.load_dataset('tips')

tips_data.head()
```

The above script imports the Matplotlib and Seaborn libraries. Next, the default plot size is increased to 10 x 8. After that, the **load_dataset()** method of the Seaborn module is used to load the **tips** dataset. Finally, the first five records of the **tips** dataset have been displayed on the console. Here is the output.

Output:

	total_bill	tip	sex	smoker	day	time	size
0	16.99	1.01	Female	No	Sun	Dinner	2
1	10.34	1.66	Male	No	Sun	Dinner	3
2	21.01	3.50	Male	No	Sun	Dinner	3
3	23.68	3.31	Male	No	Sun	Dinner	2
4	24.59	3.61	Female	No	Sun	Dinner	4

The tips data set contains records of the bill paid by a customer at a restaurant. The dataset contains six columns: total_bill, tip, sex, smoker, day, time, and size. You do not have to download this dataset as it comes built-in with the Seaborn library. We will be using the **tips** dataset to plot some of the Seaborn plots. So, without any ado, let's start plotting with Seaborn.

Requirements – Anaconda, Jupyter, and Matplotlib

- All the scripts in this book have been executed via the Jupyter notebook. Therefore, you should have the Jupyter notebook installed.
- It goes without saying that we will be using the Matplotlib library.
- The Numpy and Pandas libraries should also be installed before this chapter.

Hands-on Time – Source Codes

All IPython notebooks for the source code of all the scripts in this chapter can be found in Resources/Chapter 4.ipynb. I would suggest that you write all the code in this chapter yourself and see if you can get the same output as mentioned in this chapter.

4.2. The Dist Plots

The dist plot, also known as the distributional plot, is used to plot the histogram of data for a specific column in the dataset. To plot a dist plot, you can use the **distplot()** function of the Seaborn library. The name of the column for which you want to plot a histogram is passed as a parameter to the **distplot()** function. The following script plots the dist plot for the **total_bill** column of the **tips** dataset.

Script 1:

```
plt.rcParams[«figure.figsize»] = [10,8]
sns.distplot(tips_data['total_bill'])
```

Output:

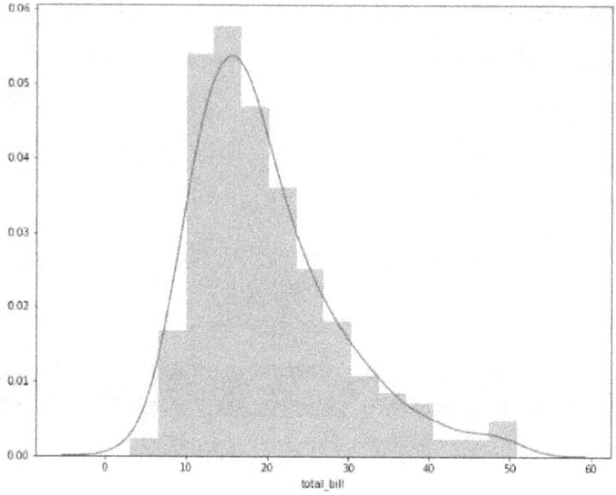

Similarly, the following script plots a dist plot for the **tip** column of the **tips** dataset.

Script 2:

```
sns.distplot(tips_data['tip'])
```

Output:

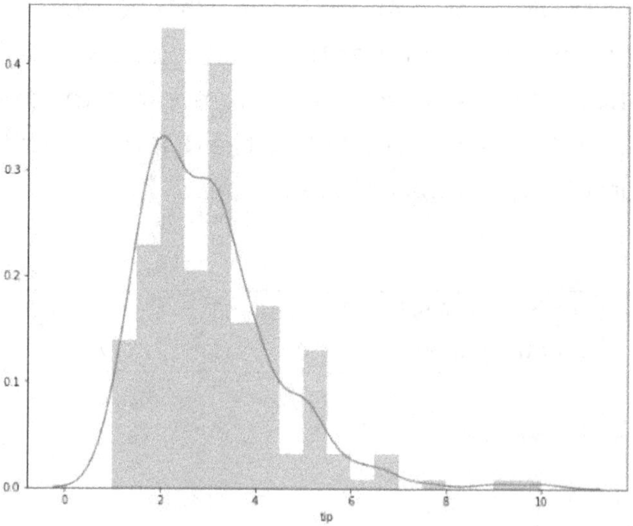

The line on top of the histogram shows the kernel density estimate for the histogram. The line can be removed by passing **False** as the value for the **kde** attribute of the **distplot()** function, as shown in the following example.

Script 3:

```
sns.distplot(tips_data['tip'], kde = False)
```

Output:

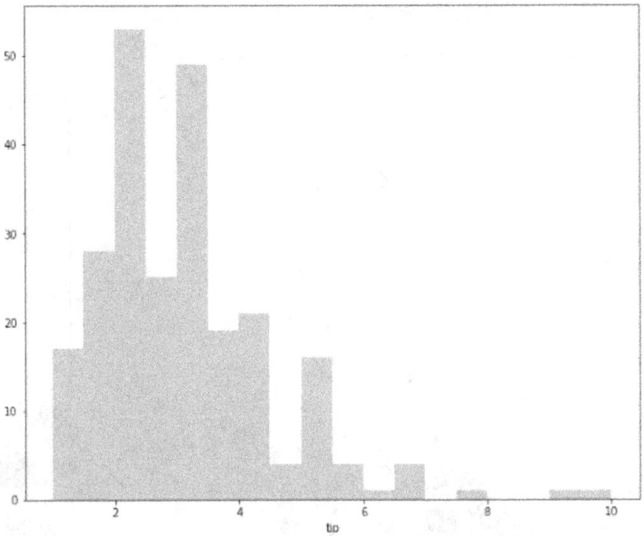

Further Readings - Seaborn Distributional Plots [1]

To study more about Seaborn distributional plots, please check Seaborn's official documentation for distributional plots. Try to plot distributional plots with a different set of attributes, as mentioned in the official documentation.

4.3. Joint Plot

The joint plot is used to plot the histogram distribution of two columns, one on the x-axis and the other on the y-axis. A scatter plot is by default drawn for the points in the two columns. To plot a joint plot, you need to call the **jointplot()** function. The following script plots a joint plot for the **total_bill** and **tip** columns of the **tips** dataset.

Script 4:

```
sns.jointplot(x='total_bill', y='tip', data=tips_data)
```

Output:

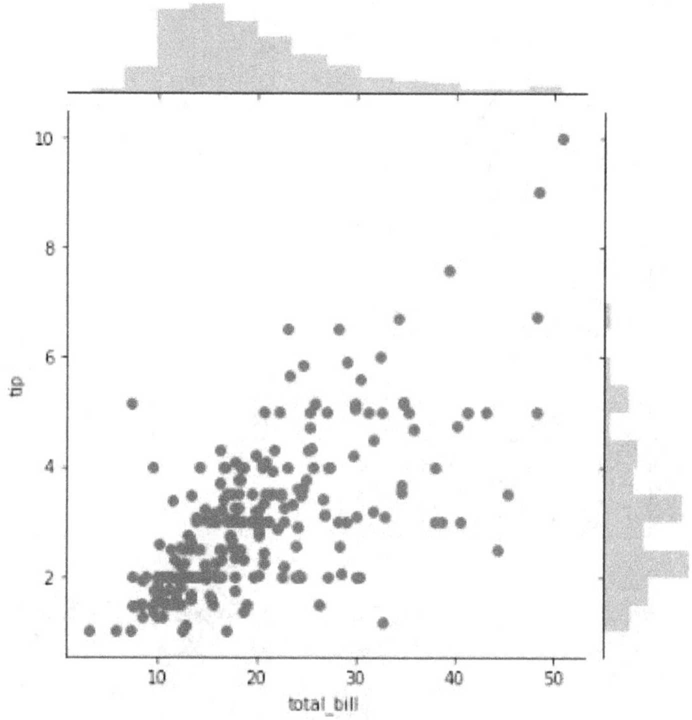

The scatter plot can be replaced by a regression line in a joint plot. To do so, you need to pass **reg** as the value for the kind parameter of the **jointplot()** function.

Script 5:

```
sns.jointplot(x='size', y='total_bill', data=tips_data,
kind = 'reg')
```

Output:

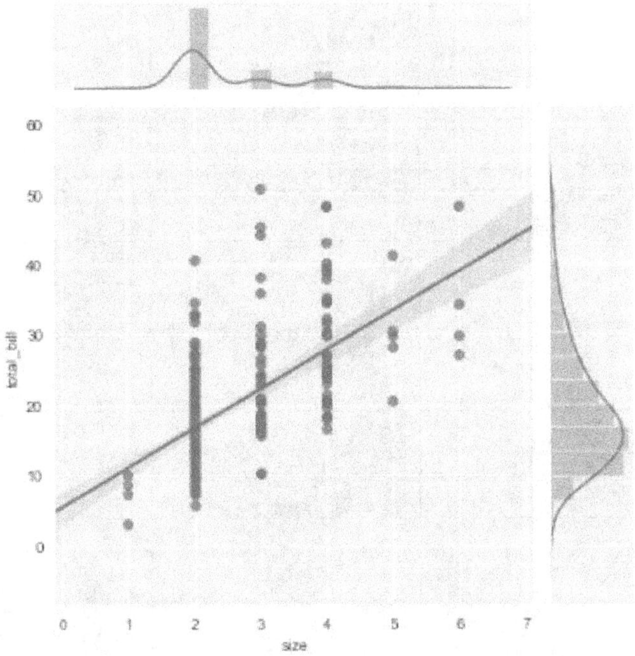

Further Readings - Seaborn Joint Plots [2]

To study more about Seaborn joint plots, please check Seaborn's official documentation for joint plots. Try to plot joint plots with a different set of attributes, as mentioned in the official documentation.

4.4. Pair Plot

The pair plot is used to plot a joint plot for all the combinations of numeric and Boolean columns in a dataset. To plot a pair plot, you need to call the **pairplot()** function and pass it to your dataset.

Script 6:

```
sns.pairplot(data=tips_data)
```

Output:

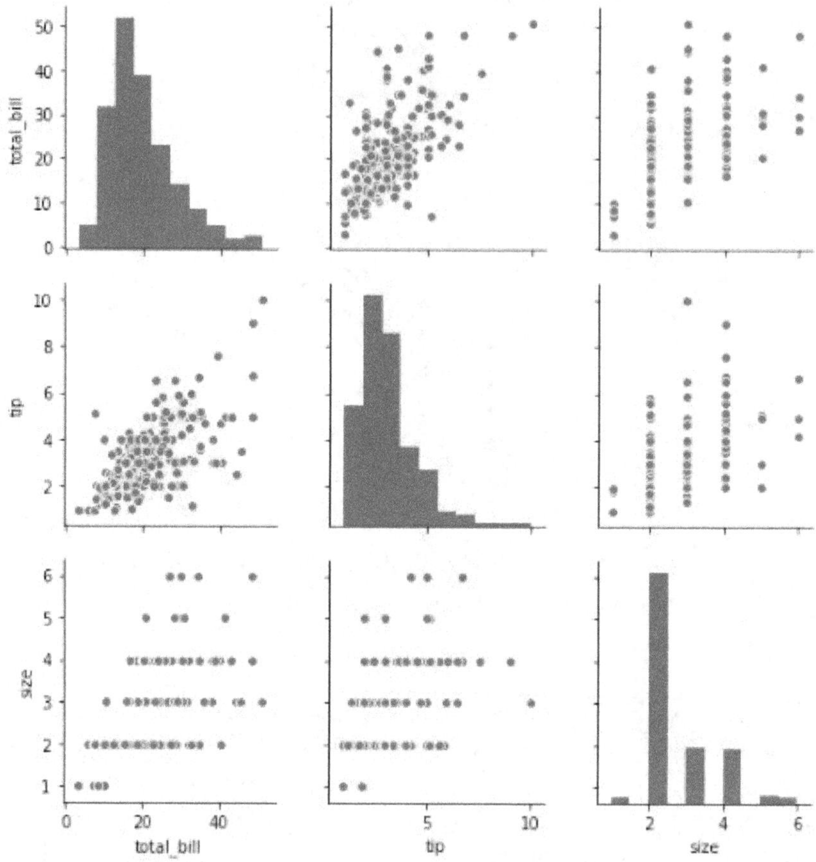

You can also plot multiple pair plots per value in a categorical column. To do so, you need to pass the name of the categorical column as the value for the **hue** parameter. The following script plots two pair plots (one for lunch and one for dinner) for every combination of numeric or Boolean columns.

Script 7:

```
sns.pairplot(data=tips_data, hue = 'time')
```

Output:

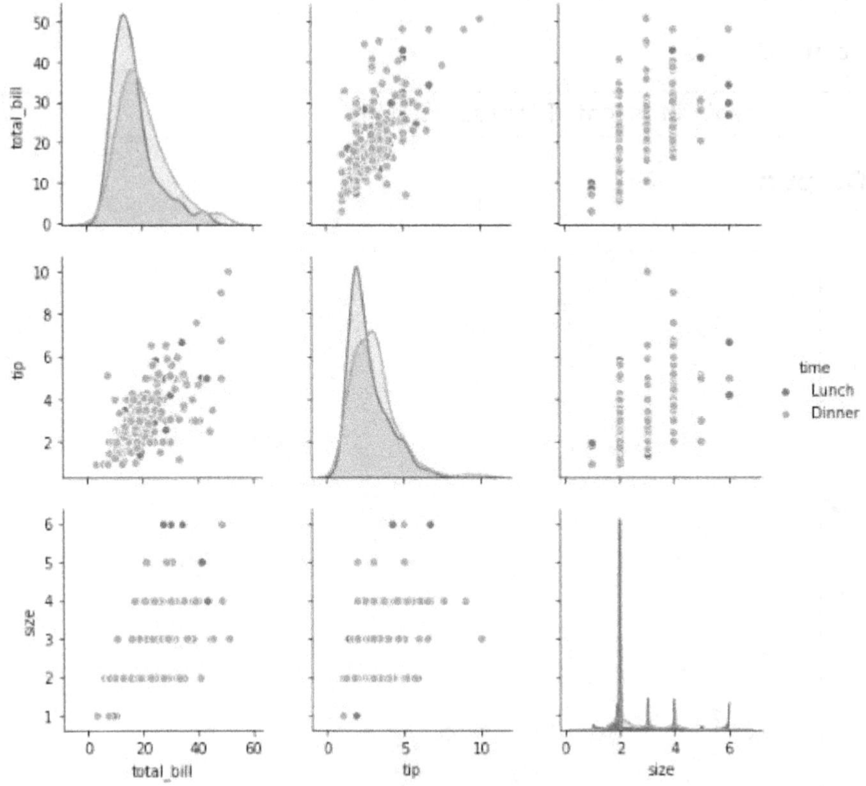

Further Readings – Seaborn Pair Plot [3]

To study more about Seaborn pair plots, please check Seaborn's official documentation for pair plots. Try to plot pair plots with a different set of attributes, as mentioned in the official documentation.

4.5. Rug Plot

The rug plot is the simplest of all the Seaborn plots. The rug plot basically plots small rectangles for all the data points in a specific column. The **`rugplot()`** function is used to plot a rug plot in Seaborn. The following script plots a **rugplot()** for the **total_bill** column of the tips dataset.

Script 8:

```
sns.rugplot(tips_data['total_bill'])
```

Output:

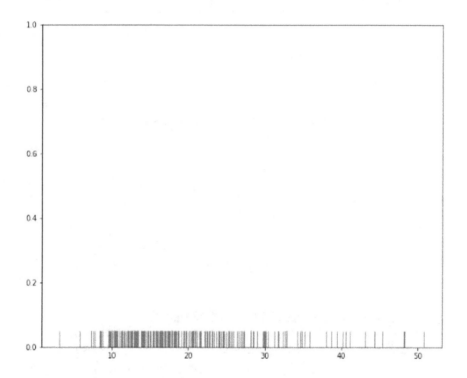

You can see a high concentration of rectangles between 10 and 20, which shows that the total bill amount for most of the bills is between 10 and 20.

Further Readings – Seaborn Rug Plot [4]

To study more about Seaborn rug plots, please check Seaborn's official documentation for rug plots. Try to plot rug plots with a different set of attributes, as mentioned in the official documentation.

4.6. Bar Plot

The bar plot is used to capture the relationship between a categorical and numerical column. For each unique value in a categorical column, a bar is plotted, which by default, displays the mean value for the data in a numeric column specified by the bar plot.

In the following script, we first import the built-in Titanic dataset from the Seaborn library via the **load_dataset()** function. You can also read the CSV file named titanic_data.csv from the *resources* folder, as mentioned in chapter 2.

Script 9:

```
import matplotlib.pyplot as plt
import seaborn as sns

plt.rcParams[«figure.figsize»] = [8,6]
sns.set_style(«darkgrid»)

titanic_data = sns.load_dataset('titanic')

titanic_data.head()
```

Here are the first five rows of the Titanic dataset.

Output:

	survived	pclass	sex	age	sibsp	parch	fare	embarked	class	who	adult_male	deck	embark_town	alive	alone
0	0	3	male	22.0	1	0	7.2500	S	Third	man	True	NaN	Southampton	no	False
1	1	1	female	38.0	1	0	71.2833	C	First	woman	False	C	Cherbourg	yes	False
2	1	3	female	26.0	0	0	7.9250	S	Third	woman	False	NaN	Southampton	yes	True
3	1	1	female	35.0	1	0	53.1000	S	First	woman	False	C	Southampton	yes	False
4	0	3	male	35.0	0	0	8.0500	S	Third	man	True	NaN	Southampton	no	True

Next, we will call the **barplot()** function from the Seaborn library to plot a bar plot that displays the average age of passengers traveling in different classes of the *Titanic* ship.

Script 10:

```
sns.barplot(x='pclass', y='age', data=titanic_data)
```

Output:

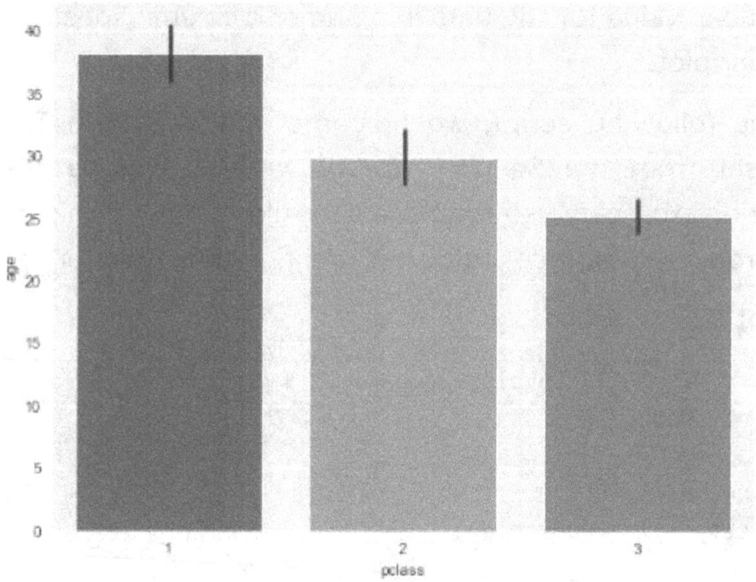

The output shows that the average age of the passengers traveling in the first class is between 35 and 40. The average age of the passengers traveling in the second class is around 30, while the passengers traveling in the 3rd class have an average age of 25.

You can further categorize the bar plot using the **hue** attribute. For example, the following bar plot plots the average ages of passengers traveling in different classes and further categorized based on their genders.

Script 11:

```
sns.barplot(x='pclass', y='age', hue ='sex', data=titanic_
data)
```

Output:

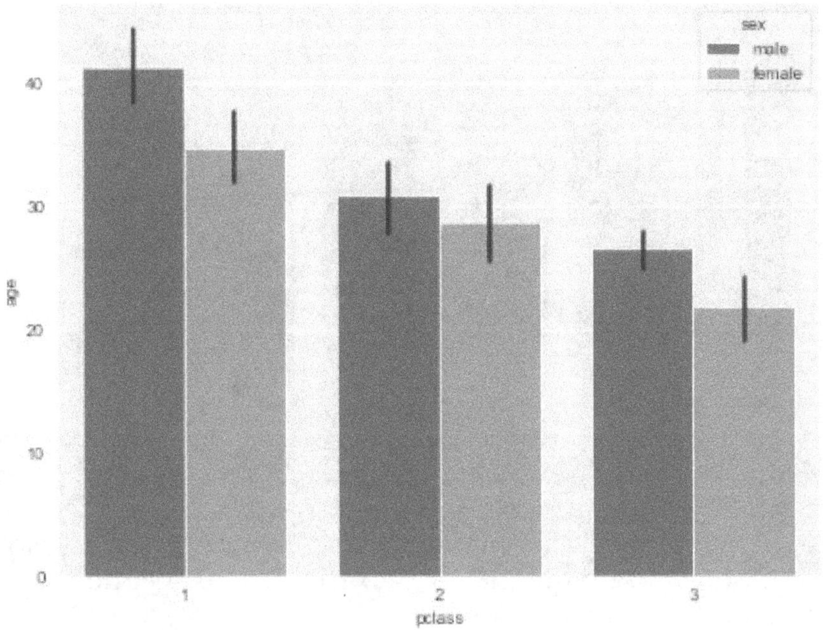

The output shows that irrespective of the gender, the passengers traveling in upper classes are on average older than the passengers traveling in lower classes.

You can also plot multiple bar plots depending upon the number of unique values in a categorical column. To do so, you need to call the **catplot()** function and pass the categorical column name as the value for the **col** attribute column. The following script plots two bar plots—one for the passengers who survived the *Titanic* accident and one for those who didn't survive.

Script 12:

```
sns.catplot(x=»pclass», y=»age», hue=»sex», col=»survived»,
data=titanic_data, kind=»bar»);
```

Output:

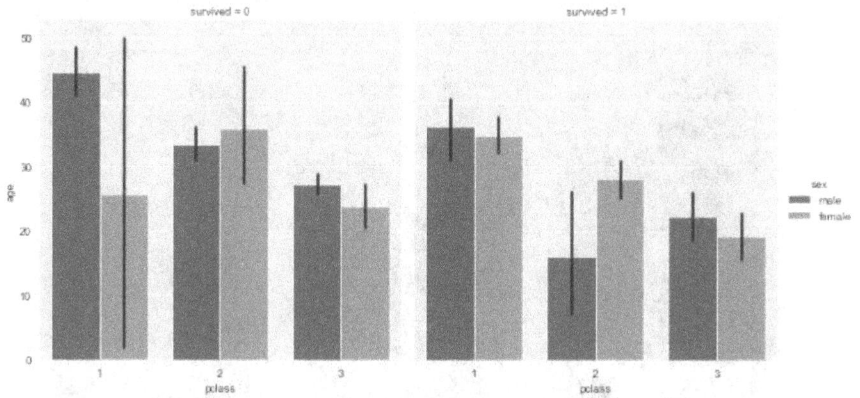

Further Readings –Seaborn Bar Plot [5]

To study more about Seaborn bar plots, please check Seaborn's official documentation for bar plots. Try to plot bar plots with a different set of attributes, as mentioned in the official documentation.

4.7. Count Plot

The count plot plots plot like a bar plot. However, unlike the bar plot, which plots average values, the count plot simply displays the counts of the occurrences of records for each unique value in a categorical column. The **countplot()** function is used to plot a count plot with Seaborn. The following script plots a count plot for the **pclass** column of the **Titanic** dataset.

Script 13:

```
sns.countplot(x='pclass', data=titanic_data)
```

The output shows that around 200 passengers traveled in the first class while an overwhelming majority of passengers traveled in the 3rd class of the *Titanic* ship.

Output:

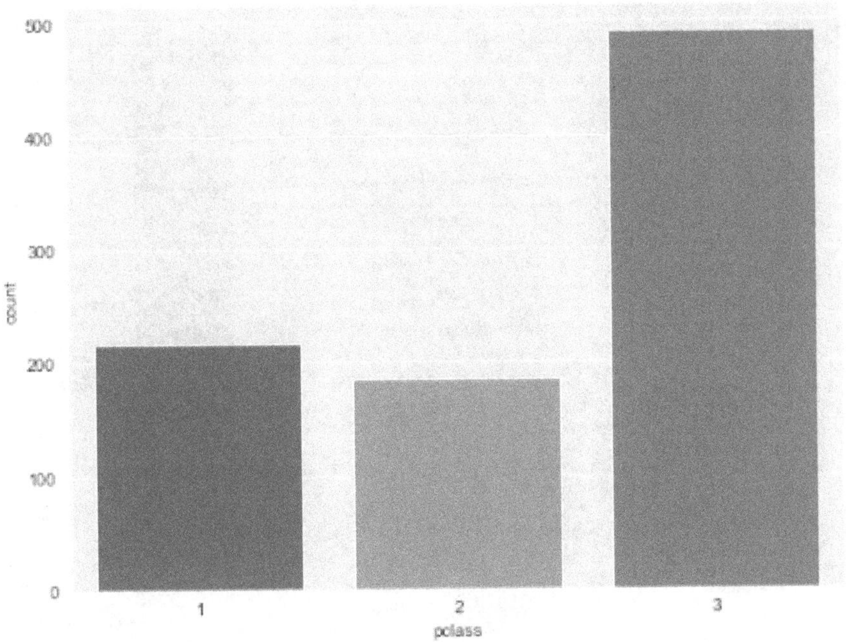

Like a bar plot, you can also further categorize the count plot by passing a value for the hue parameter. The following script plots a count plot for the passengers traveling in different classes of the *Titanic* ship categorized further by their genders.

Script 14:

```
sns.countplot(x='pclass', hue='sex', data=titanic_data)
```

Output:

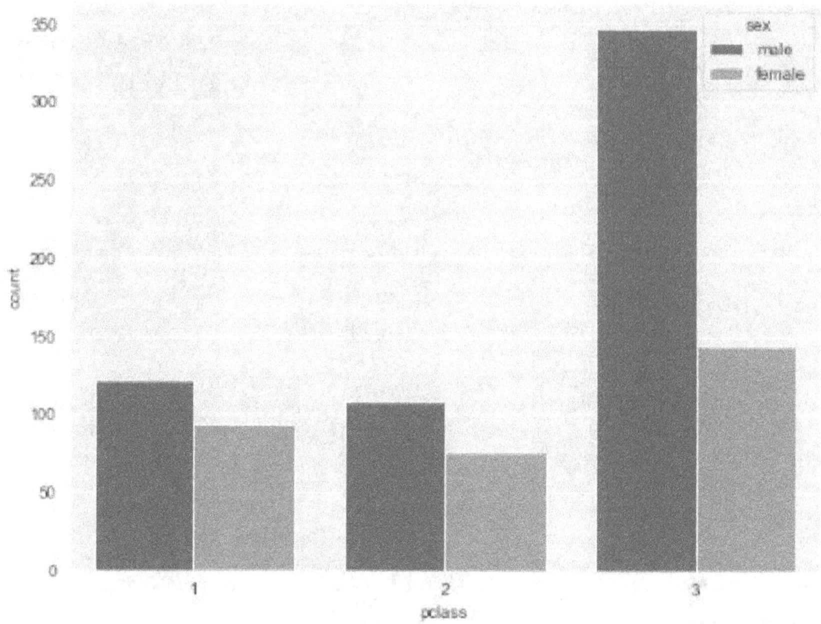

Further Readings – Seaborn Count Plot [6]

To study more about Seaborn count plots, please check Seaborn's official documentation for count plots. Try to plot count plots with a different set of attributes, as mentioned in the official documentation.

4.8. Box Plot

The box plot is used to plot quartile information for data in a numeric column. To plot a box plot, the **boxplot()** method is used. To plot a horizontal box plot, the column name of the dataset is passed to the x-axis. The following script plots a box plot for the **fare** column of the **Titanic** dataset.

Script 15:

```
sns.boxplot(x=titanic_data[«fare»])
```

Output:

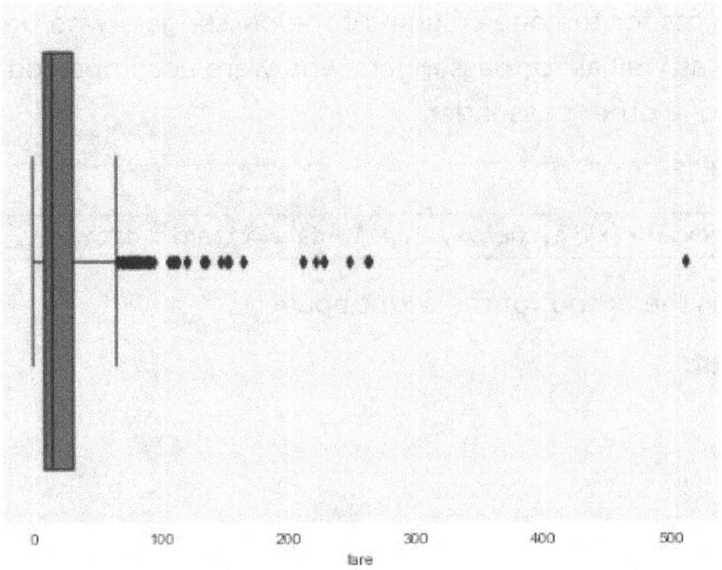

Similarly, the following script plots the vertical box plot for the fare column of the Titanic dataset.

Script 16:

```
sns.boxplot(y=titanic_data[«fare»])
```

Output:

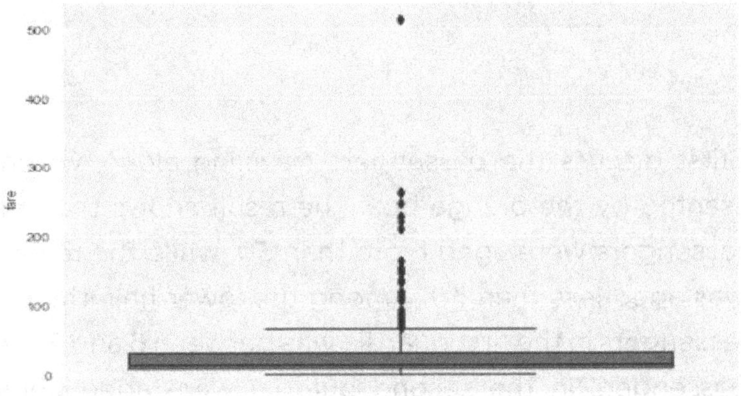

You can also plot multiple box plots for every unique value in a categorical column. For instance, the following script plots box plots for the age column of the passengers who traveled alone as well as for passengers who were accompanied by at least one other passenger.

Script 17:

```
sns.boxplot(x='alone', y='age', data=titanic_data)
```

Here is the output of the script above.

Output:

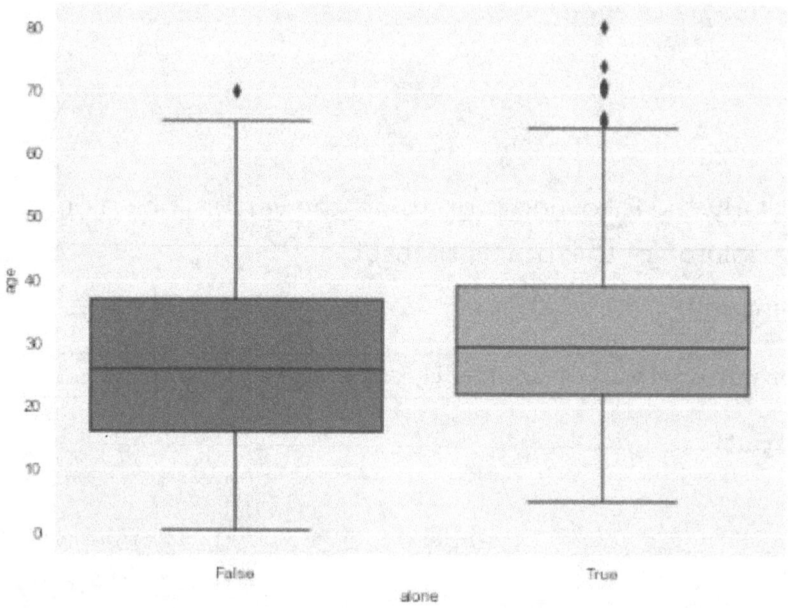

Let's first discuss the passengers traveling alone, which are represented by the orange box. The result shows that half of the passengers were aged more than 30, while the remaining half was aged less than 30. Among the lower half, the age of the passengers in the first quartile was between 6 and 23, while the passengers in the second quartile were aged between

24 and 30. In the same way, you can get information about the 3rd and 4th age quartile of the passengers traveling alone. A comparison of the two box plots reveals that the median age of the passengers traveling alone is slightly greater than the median age of the passengers accompanied by other passengers.

Like bar and count plots, the hue attribute can also be used to categorize box plots.

For instance, the following script plots box plots for the passengers traveling alone and along with other passengers, further categorized based on their genders.

Script 18:

```
sns.boxplot(x='alone', y='age', hue='sex',data=titanic_
data)
```

Output:

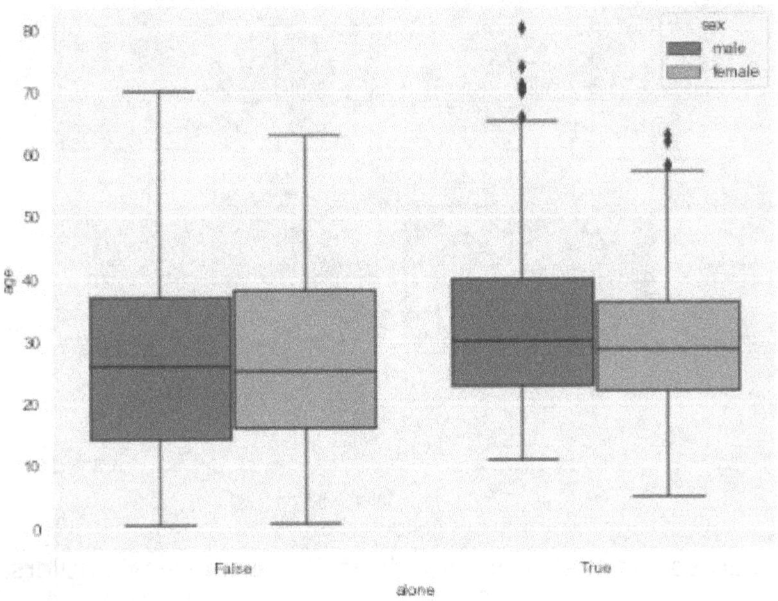

The two box plots on the left correspond to the passengers not traveling alone, while the two box plots on the right correspond to the passengers traveling alone. The output shows that the median value of age for male passengers is higher for both types of passengers, i.e., passengers traveling alone or not. Furthermore, male passengers who are traveling alone have the overall highest median age value.

By default, the box plot draws outliers. To remove outliers from a box plot, you have to pass **False** as the value for the **showfliers** attribute of the **boxplot()** function. Here is an example.

Script 19:

```
sns.boxplot(x='alone', y='age', hue='sex',data=titanic_
data, showfliers=False)
```

Output:

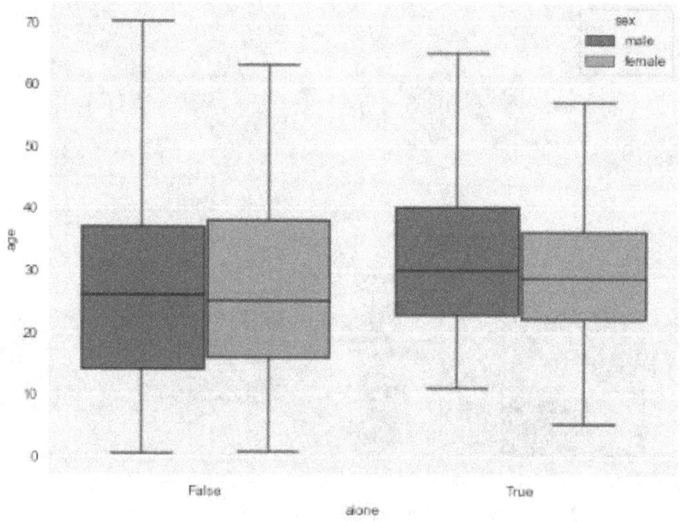

You can see that the output doesn't contain any outliers for the box plots.

Further Readings –Seaborn Box Plot [7]

To study more about Seaborn box plots, please check Seaborn's official documentation for box plots. Try to plot box plots with a different set of attributes, as mentioned in the official documentation.

4.9. Violin Plot

Violin plots are similar to box plots. However, unlike box plots that plot quartile information, violin plots plot the overall distribution of values in numeric columns. The following script plots two violin plots for the passengers traveling alone and along with another passenger. The **violinplot()** function is used to plot a swarm plot with Seaborn.

Script 20:

```
sns.violinplot(x='alone', y='age', data=titanic_data)
```

Here is the output of the above script.

Output:

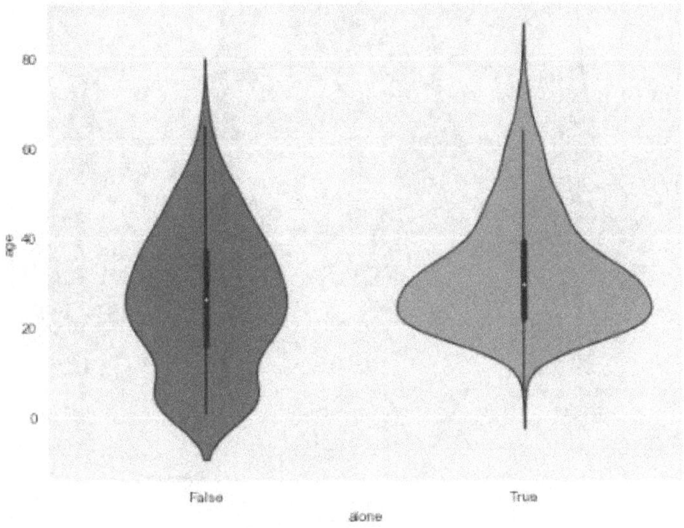

The output shows that among the passengers traveling alone, the passengers whose age is less than 15 are very few as shown by the orange violin plot on the right. This behavior is understandable as children are normally accompanied by someone. This can be further verified by looking at the blue violin plot on the left that corresponds to the passengers accompanied by other passengers.

The hue attribute can also be used to categorize the violin plot further.

The following script plots a violin plot, first categorized by whether or not the passengers travel alone, and then by their gender.

Script 21:

```
sns.violinplot(x='alone', y='age', hue='sex',data=titanic_
data)
```

Output:

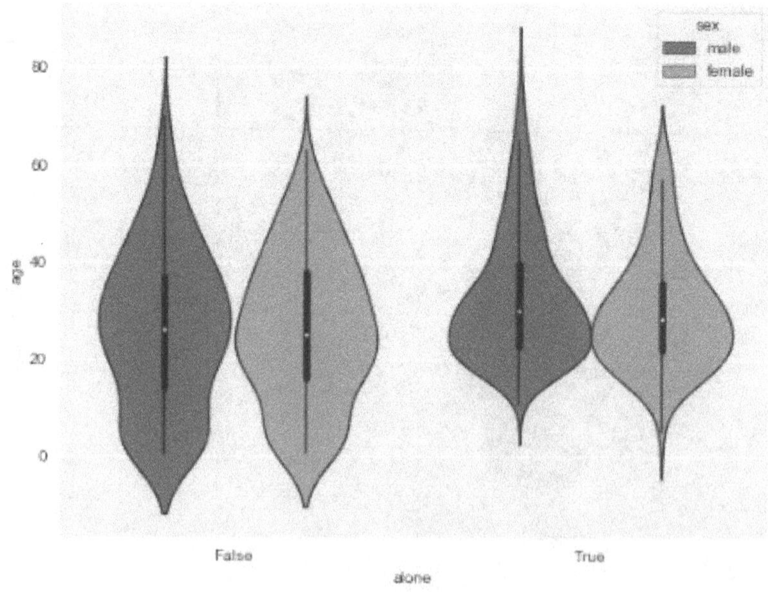

The output shows that among the passengers traveling alone, the number of female passengers with age greater than 80 is less compared to male passengers. And the trend that younger passengers did not travel alone stays the same for both genders.

For a better comparison and to save space, you can also plot split violin plots. In split violin plots, each half corresponds to one value in a category column. For instance, the following script plots two violin plots—one each for the passengers traveling alone and for the passengers not traveling alone. Each plot is further split into two parts based on the genders of the passengers.

Script 22:

```
sns.violinplot(x='alone', y='age', hue='sex',data=titanic_
data, split=True)
```

Output:

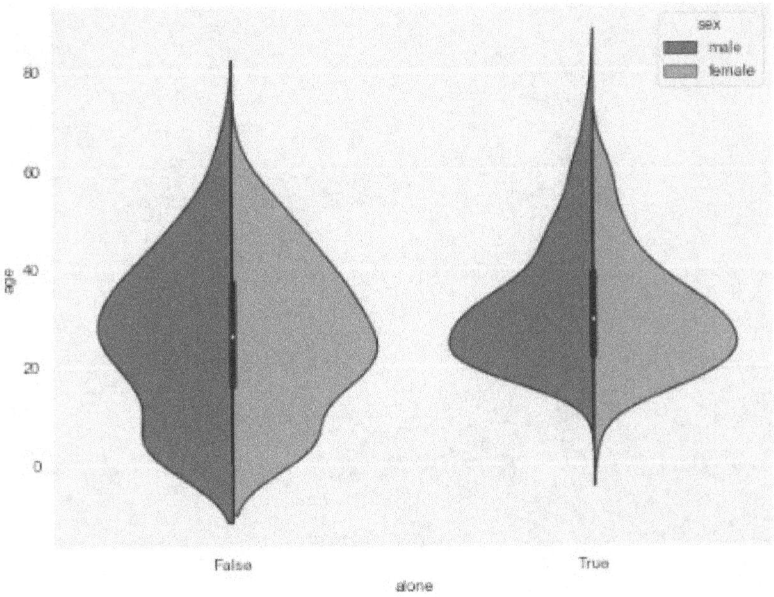

Further Readings –Seaborn Violin Plot [8]

To study more about Seaborn violin plots, please check Seaborn's official documentation for Violin plots. Try to plot violin plots with a different set of attributes, as mentioned in the official documentation.

4.10. Strip Plot

Strip plot in Seaborn is used to draw a scatter plot in the form of strips for all the unique values in the categorical column. For instance, the following strip plot plots the ages of the passengers traveling alone and passengers accompanied by someone. The **stripplot()** function is used to plot a swarm plot with Seaborn.

Script 23:

```
sns.stripplot(x='alone', y='age', data=titanic_data)
```

Output:

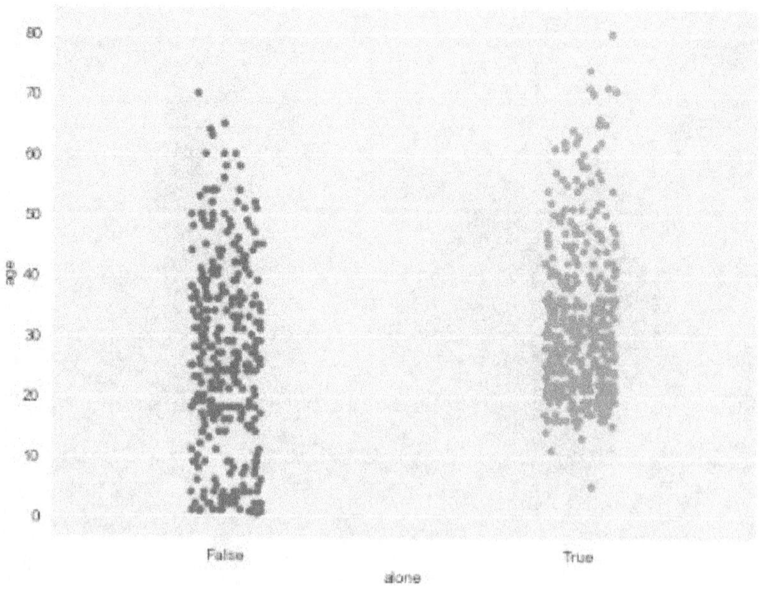

The hue parameter can be used here again to further categorize strip plots, as shown in the following example.

Script 24:

```
sns.stripplot(x='alone', y='age', hue='sex',data=titanic_
data)
```

Output:

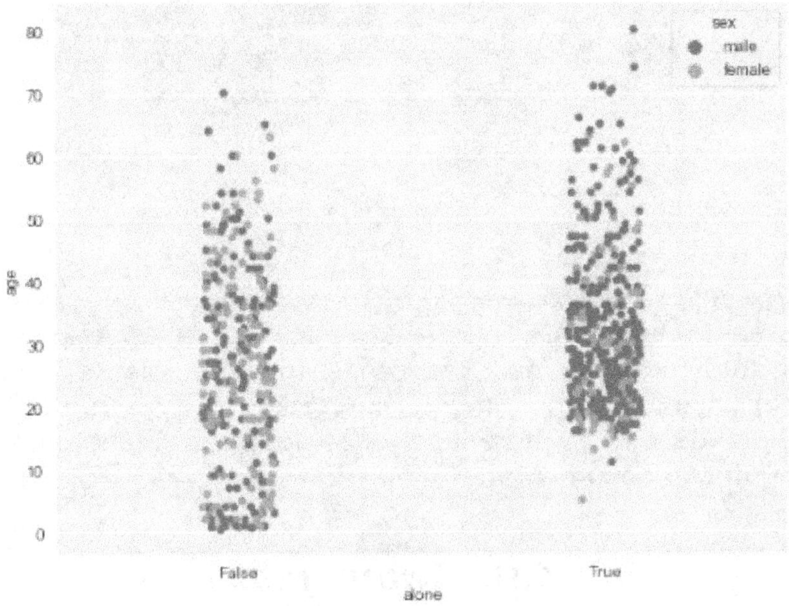

Finally, like violin plots, you can also split strip plots, as demonstrated by the following example.

Script 25:

```
sns.stripplot(x='alone', y='age', hue='sex',data=titanic_
data, split = True)
```

Output:

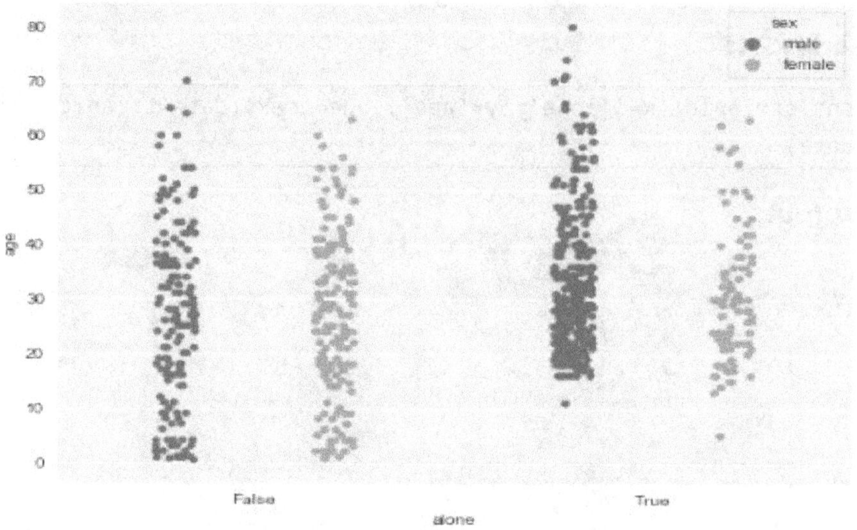

Further Readings –Seaborn Strip Plot [9]

To study more about Seaborn strip plots, please check Seaborn's official documentation for strip plots. Try to plot strip plots with a different set of attributes, as mentioned in the official documentation.

4.11. Swarm Plot

Swarm plots are a combination of violin plot and strip plots. While the swarm plots plot the distribution of data in the form of a violin, the actual data points within the violin plots are displayed in the form of a scatter plot. The final plot looks like a swarm of bees.

Let's plot a swarm plot that displays the passengers traveling alone and with other passengers. The **`swarmplot()`** function is used to plot a swarm plot with Seaborn.

Script 26:

```
sns.swarmplot(x='alone', y='age', data=titanic_data)
```

Output:

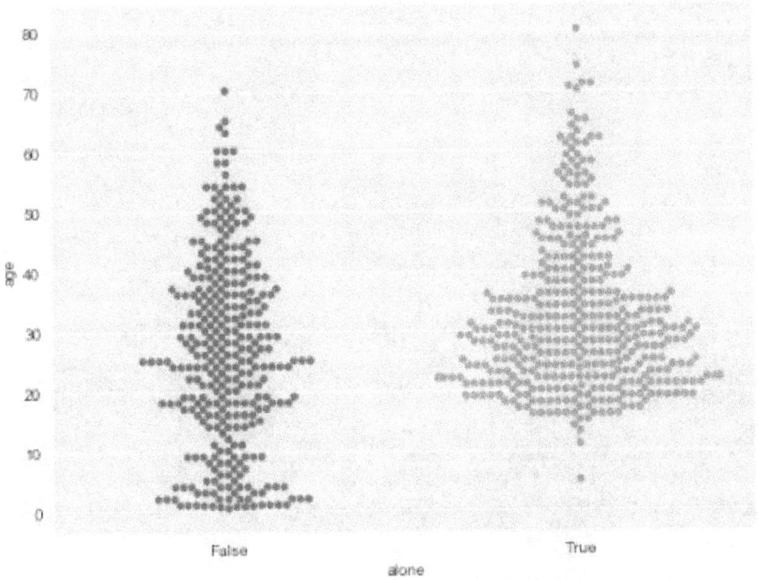

The output of script 26 is quite similar to the output of script 20. However, in the output of script 26, each data point is explicitly displayed. You can even count the number of passengers for each age group looking at the swarm plot. For instance, the above plot shows that among the passengers traveling alone, there is only one passenger with age less than 10 as there is only one orange dot in the range of 0–10. On the other hand, if you look at the blue swarm plot, you can see multiple blue dots in the range of 0-10. Hence, you can conclude that passengers in the age group 0–10 were mostly accompanied by someone.

With the hue parameter, you can further categorize the swarm plot, as shown in the following script.

Script 27:

```
sns.swarmplot(x='alone', y='age', hue='sex',data=titanic_
data)
```

Output:

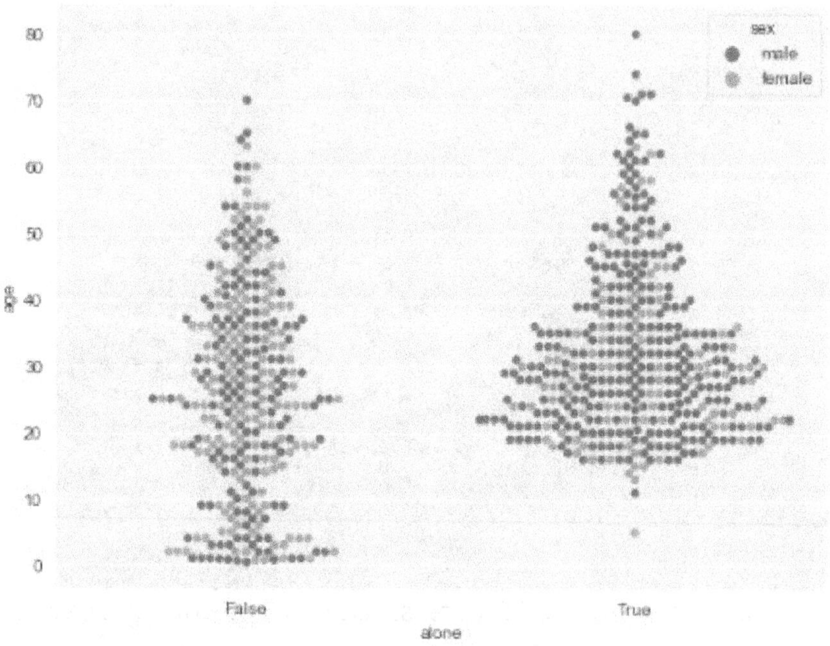

The output shows that among the passengers traveling alone, there was no male passenger aged less than 10 while there was only one female passenger aged less than10 who traveled alone.

Finally, you can split swarm plots by setting the value of the **split** attribute to **True,** as shown below.

Script 28:

```
sns.swarmplot(x='alone', y='age', hue='sex',data=titanic_
data, split = True)
```

Output:

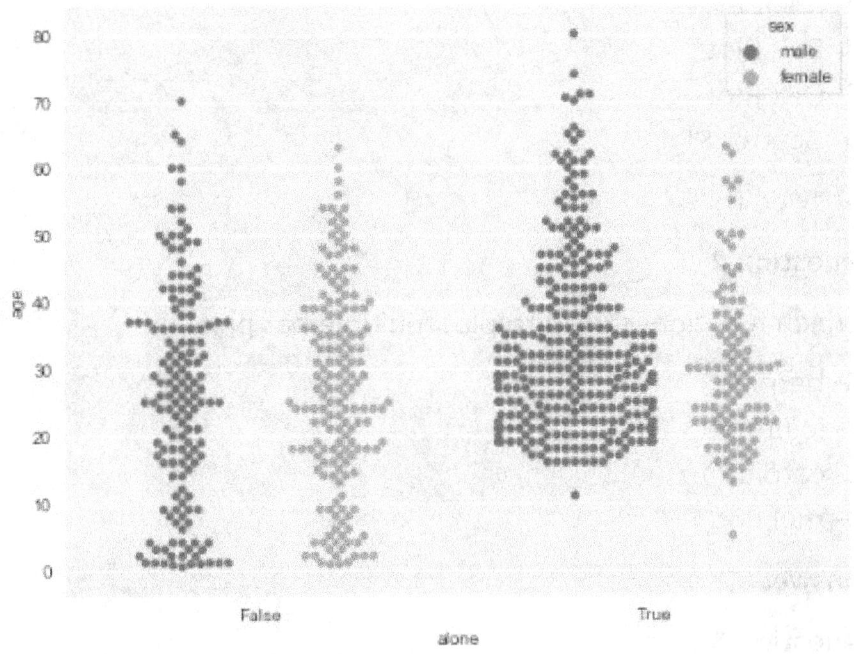

Further Readings - Seaborn Swarm Plot [10]

To study more about Seaborn swarm plots, please check Seaborn's official documentation for swarm plots. Try to plot swarm plots with a different set of attributes, as mentioned in the official documentation.

Hands-on Time - Exercise

Now, it is your turn. Follow the instructions in **the exercises below** to check your understanding of the advanced data visualization with the Seaborn library. The answers to these questions are given at the end of the book.

Exercise 4.1

Question 1

Which plot is used to plot multiple joint plots for all the combinations of numeric and Boolean columns in a dataset?

A- Joint Plot

B- Pair Plot

C- Dist Plot

D- Scatter Plot

Answer: B

Question 2

Which function is used to plot multiple bar plots?

A- barplot()

B- jointplot()

C- catplot()

D- mulplot()

Answer: C

Question 3

Which attribute is used to set the default type of a joint plot?

A- kind

B- type

C- hue

D- col

Answer: A

Exercise 4.2

Plot a swarm violin plot using Titanic data that displays the fare paid by male and female passengers.

Further, categorize the plot by passengers who survived and by those who didn't.

References

1. https://seaborn.pydata.org/generated/seaborn.distplot.html
2. https://seaborn.pydata.org/generated/seaborn.jointplot.html
3. https://seaborn.pydata.org/generated/seaborn.pairplot.html
4. https://seaborn.pydata.org/generated/seaborn.rugplot.html
5. https://seaborn.pydata.org/generated/seaborn.barplot.html
6. https://seaborn.pydata.org/generated/seaborn.countplot.html
7. https://seaborn.pydata.org/generated/seaborn.boxplot.html
8. https://seaborn.pydata.org/generated/seaborn.violinplot.html
9. https://seaborn.pydata.org/generated/seaborn.stripplot.html
10. https://seaborn.pydata.org/generated/seaborn.swarmplot.html

5

Advanced Plotting with Seaborn

In the previous chapter, you examined how to plot some of the basic plots with Python's Seaborn library. In this chapter, you will see some of the advanced Seaborn plots in action.

Requirements – Anaconda, Jupyter, and Matplotlib

- All the scripts in this book have been executed via the Jupyter notebook. Therefore, you should have the Jupyter notebook installed.
- Needless to say, we will be using the Matplotlib library.
- The Numpy and Pandas libraries should also be installed before this chapter.
- Finally, you will need to install and import Python's Seaborn library to execute scripts in this chapter. To install the Seaborn library, please refer to Chapter 4.

Hands-on Time – Source Codes

All IPython notebooks for the source code of all the scripts in this chapter can be found in Resources/Chapter 5.ipynb. I would suggest that you write all the code in this chapter yourself and see if you can get the same output, as mentioned in this chapter.

5.1. Scatter Plot

In chapter 2, you saw how to plot a scatter plot with Matplotlib. In this section, you will see how to plot a scatter plot with Python's Seaborn library.

Let's first import the **tips** dataset from the Seaborn library.

Script 1:

```
import matplotlib.pyplot as plt
import seaborn as sns

plt.rcParams[«figure.figsize»] = [10,8]

tips_data = sns.load_dataset('tips')

tips_data.head()
```

Output:

	total_bill	tip	sex	smoker	day	time	size
0	16.99	1.01	Female	No	Sun	Dinner	2
1	10.34	1.66	Male	No	Sun	Dinner	3
2	21.01	3.50	Male	No	Sun	Dinner	3
3	23.68	3.31	Male	No	Sun	Dinner	2
4	24.59	3.61	Female	No	Sun	Dinner	4

Let's now plot a scatter plot with the values from the **total_bill** column of the **tips** dataset on the x-axis and values from the tips column on the y-axis. To plot a scatter plot, you need to call the **scatterplot()** method of the Seaborn library.

Script 2:

```
sns.scatterplot(x=»total_bill», y=»tip», data=tips_data)
```

Output:

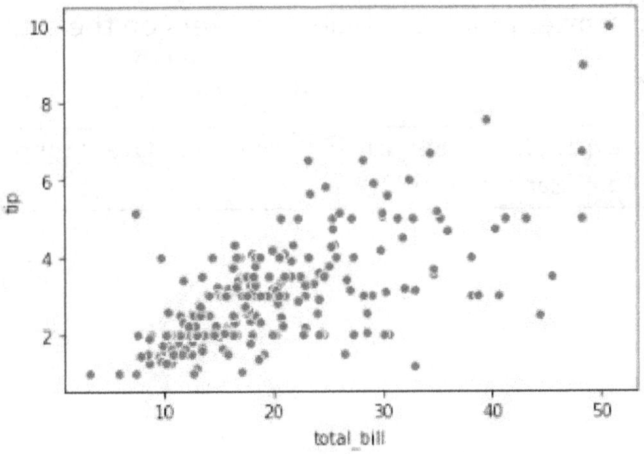

To change the color of the scatter plot, simply pass the first letter of any color to the **color** attribute of the **scatterplot()** function.

Script 3:

```
sns.scatterplot(x=»total_bill», y=»tip», data=tips_data,
color = 'r')
```

Output:

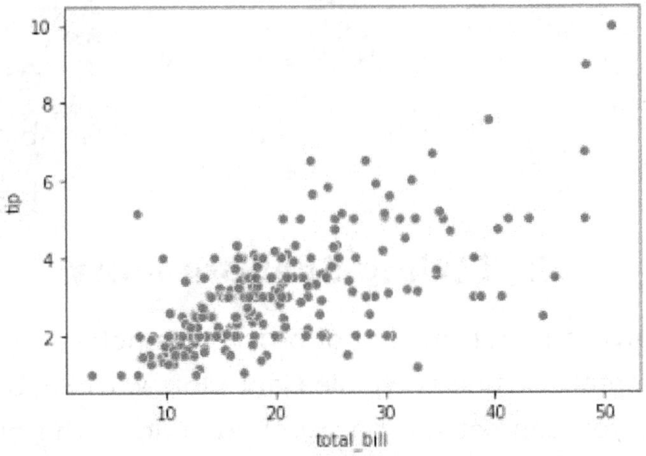

Finally, to change the marker shape for the scatter plot, you need to pass a value for the marker attribute. For example, the following scatter plot plots blue x markers on the scatter plot.

Script 4:

```
sns.scatterplot(x=»total_bill», y=»tip», data=tips_data,
color = 'b', marker = 'x')
```

Output:

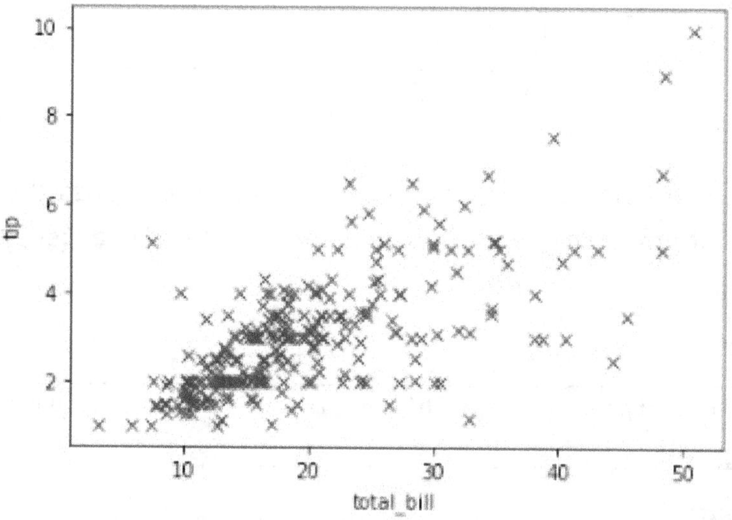

Further Readings – Seaborn Scatter Plots [1]

To study more about Seaborn scatter plots, please check Seaborn's official documentation for Scatter plots. Try to plot scatter plots with a different set of attributes, as mentioned in the official documentation.

5.2. Styling Seaborn Plots

While Matplotlib plots might not be that aesthetically pleasing, you can create aesthetically pleasant plots with Seaborn. For instance, you can set the background style of the plot with

set_style() function. You can pass one of the **darkgrid, whitegrid, white,** and **ticks** as a value to the **set_style**() function. Here is an example of the **set_style()** function.

Script 5:

```
sns.set_style('darkgrid')
sns.scatterplot(x=»total_bill», y=»tip», data=tips_data,
color = 'b', marker = 'x')
```

Output:

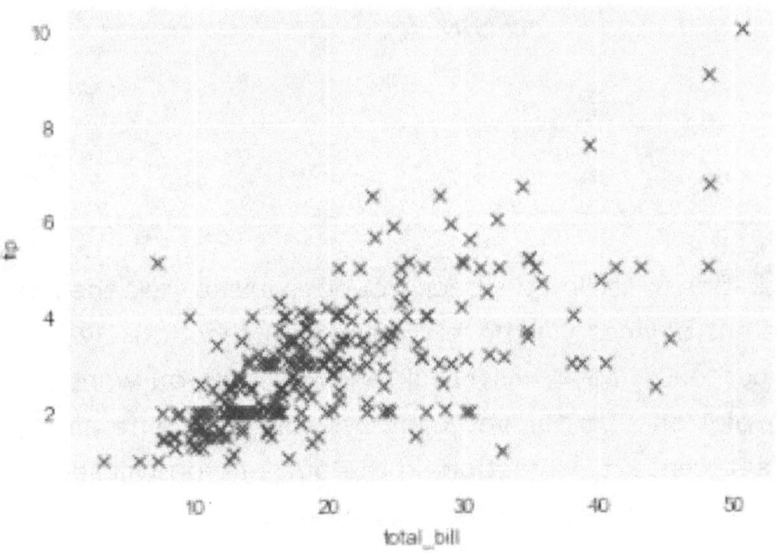

Similarly, if you pass **whitegrid** as a value to the **set_style()** function, you will see grids with a white background. Here is an example.

Script 6:

```
sns.set_style('whitegrid')
sns.scatterplot(x=»total_bill», y=»tip», data=tips_data,
color = 'b', marker = 'x')
```

Output:

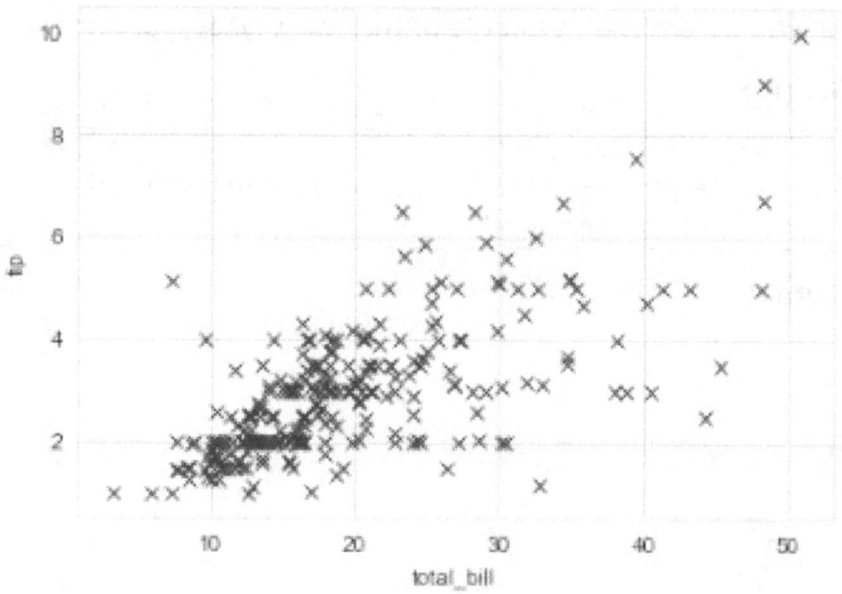

In addition to styling the background, you can style the plot for different devices via the **set_context()** function. By default, the context is set to **notebook.** However, if you want to plot your plot on a poster, you can pass **poster** as a parameter to the **set_context()** function. In the output, you will see a plot with bigger annotations, as shown below.

Script 7:

```
sns.set_context('poster')
sns.scatterplot(x=»total_bill», y=»tip», data=tips_data,
color = 'b', marker = 'x')
```

Output:

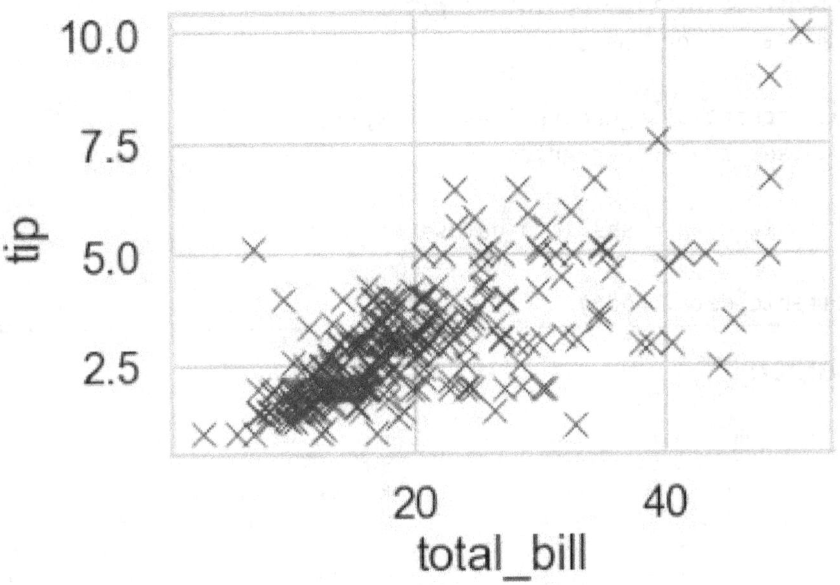

Further Readings – Styling Seaborn Plots [2]

To study more about how to style seaborn plots, please check Seaborn's official documentation for styling Seaborn plots. Try to Apply Seaborn styles with a different set of attributes, as mentioned in the official documentation.

5.3. Heat Maps

A heat map is a type of matrix plot and is used to plot the correlation between numeric columns in a dataset in the form of a matrix. To plot a heat map, both columns and rows should have meaningful information. To plot a heat map, we will use the Titanic dataset. Let's first import the Titanic dataset.

Script 8:

```
import matplotlib.pyplot as plt
import seaborn as sns

plt.rcParams[«figure.figsize»] = [8,6]
sns.set_style(«darkgrid»)

titanic_data = sns.load_dataset('titanic')

titanic_data.head()
```

Output:

	survived	pclass	sex	age	sibsp	parch	fare	embarked	class	who	adult_male	deck	embark_town	alive	alone
0	0	3	male	22.0	1	0	7.2500	S	Third	man	True	NaN	Southampton	no	False
1	1	1	female	38.0	1	0	71.2833	C	First	woman	False	C	Cherbourg	yes	False
2	1	3	female	26.0	0	0	7.9250	S	Third	woman	False	NaN	Southampton	yes	True
3	1	1	female	35.0	1	0	53.1000	S	First	woman	False	C	Southampton	yes	False
4	0	3	male	35.0	0	0	8.0500	S	Third	man	True	NaN	Southampton	no	True

The above output shows that we have meaningful information along columns only. To plot a heat map, we need meaningful information on rows as well. One of the ways to get meaningful information among rows is to call the corr() function on a Pandas dataframe. Let's see what the corr() function does to the Pandas dataframe that contains the Titanic dataset.

Script 9:

```
titanic_data.corr()
```

Output:

	survived	pclass	age	sibsp	parch	fare	adult_male	alone
survived	1.000000	-0.338481	-0.077221	-0.035322	0.081629	0.257307	-0.557080	-0.203367
pclass	-0.338481	1.000000	-0.369226	0.083081	0.018443	-0.549500	0.094035	0.135207
age	-0.077221	-0.369226	1.000000	-0.308247	-0.189119	0.096067	0.280328	0.198270
sibsp	-0.035322	0.083081	-0.308247	1.000000	0.414838	0.159651	-0.253586	-0.584471
parch	0.081629	0.018443	-0.189119	0.414838	1.000000	0.216225	-0.349943	-0.583398
fare	0.257307	-0.549500	0.096067	0.159651	0.216225	1.000000	-0.182024	-0.271832
adult_male	-0.557080	0.094035	0.280328	-0.253586	-0.349943	-0.182024	1.000000	0.404744
alone	-0.203367	0.135207	0.198270	-0.584471	-0.583398	-0.271832	0.404744	1.000000

From the output above, you can see that we now have meaningful information across rows as well. In the following script, we first increase the default plot size and then pass the correlation matrix of the Titanic dataset to the heatmap() function to create a heat map.

Script 10:

```
plt.rcParams[«figure.figsize»] = [10,8]
corr_values = titanic_data.corr()
sns.heatmap(corr_values, annot= True)
```

You can see a heat map in the output, as shown below. The higher the correlation is, the darker the cell containing the correlation.

Output:

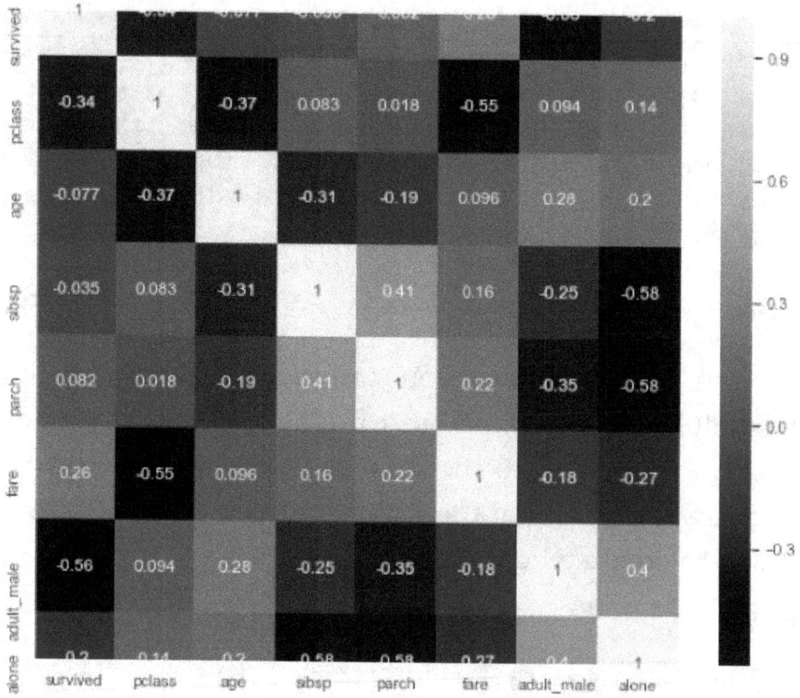

You can see that the above plot is cropped from the top and bottom. The following script plots the uncropped plot. In the following script, we use the **set_ylim()** method to increase the plot size from top and bottom cell by 0.5 percent.

Script 11:

```
plt.rcParams[«figure.figsize»] = [10,8]
corr_values = titanic_data.corr()
ax = sns.heatmap(corr_values, annot= True)
bottom, top = ax.get_ylim()
ax.set_ylim(bottom + 0.5, top - 0.5)
```

Output:

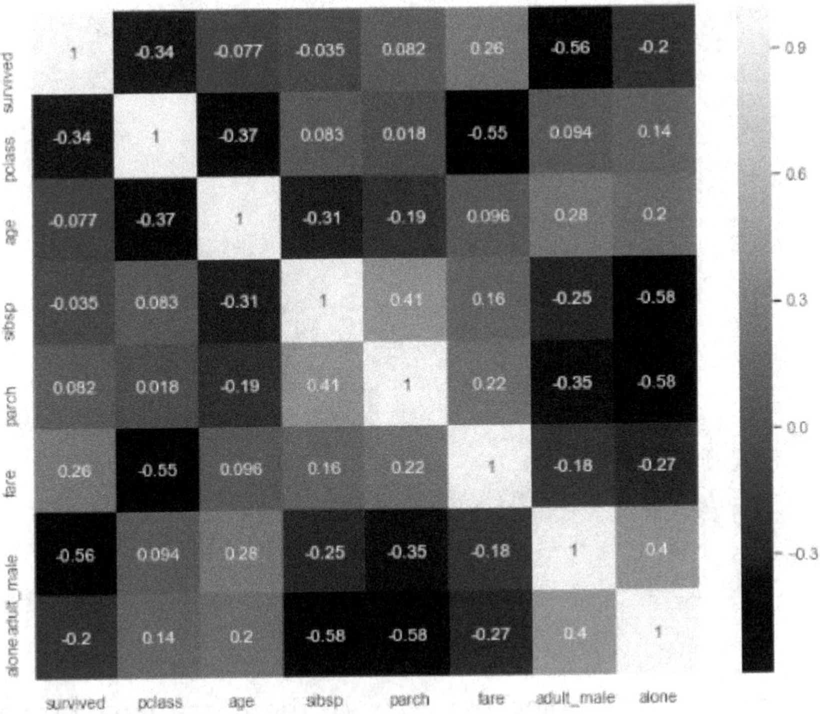

You can also change the default color of the heatmap. To do so, you need to pass a value for the **cmap** attribute of the **heatmap()** function. Look at the script below:

Script 12:

```
plt.rcParams[«figure.figsize»] = [10,8]
corr_values = titanic_data.corr()
ax = sns.heatmap(corr_values, annot= True, cmap =
'coolwarm')
bottom, top = ax.get_ylim()
ax.set_ylim(bottom + 0.5, top - 0.5)
```

Output:

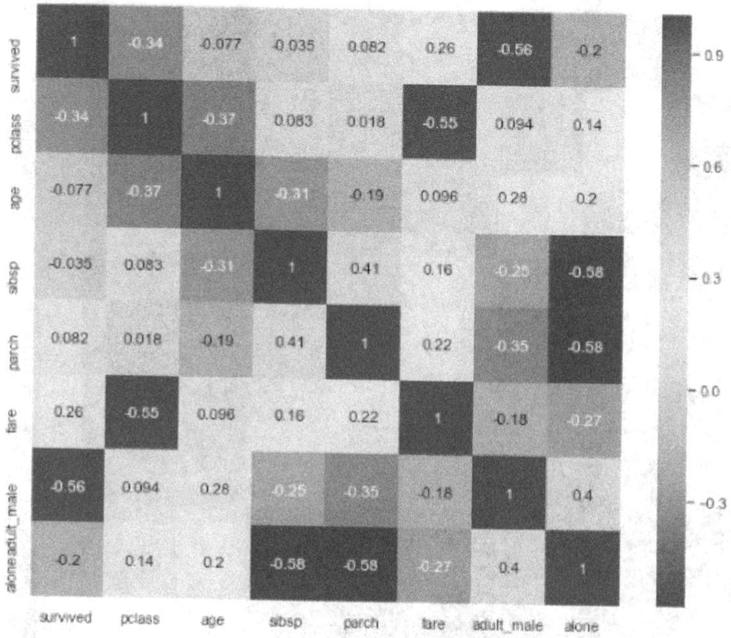

In addition to changing the color of the heat map, you can also specify the line color and width that separates cells in a heat map.

Let's import the flights dataset from the Seaborn library. The flights dataset contains records of the passengers traveling each month from 1949 to 1960.

Script 13:

```
import matplotlib.pyplot as plt
import seaborn as sns

plt.rcParams[«figure.figsize»] = [10,8]

flights_data = sns.load_dataset('flights')

flights_data.head()
```

Output:

	year	month	passengers
0	1949	January	112
1	1949	February	118
2	1949	March	132
3	1949	April	129
4	1949	May	121

In addition to the **corr()** function, which returns the correlation between the numeric columns, you can also use the **pivot_table()** function to get a matrix with meaningful rows and color. For instance, the **pivot_table()** function in the following script returns a matrix where rows represent months, columns represent years from 1949 to 1960, and each cell contains the number of passengers traveling in a specific month of a specific year. The matrix created via the **pivot_table()** method can then be plotted via the **heatmap()** function.

Script 14:

```
flights_data_pivot =flights_data.pivot_table(index='month',
columns='year', values='passengers')
ax = sns.heatmap(flights_data_pivot,  cmap = 'coolwarm',
linecolor='black', linewidth=1)
bottom, top = ax.get_ylim()
ax.set_ylim(bottom + 0.5, top - 0.5)
```

Output:

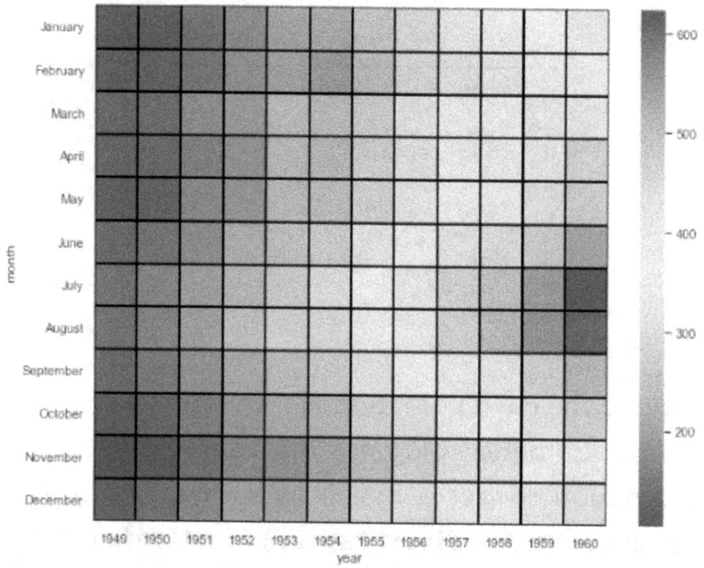

Further Readings – Seaborn Heatmaps [3]

To study more about Seaborn heatmaps, please check Seaborn's official documentation for heat maps. Try to plot heat maps with a different set of attributes, as mentioned in the official documentation.

5.4. Cluster Maps

A cluster map is also a type of matrix plot. Cluster map clusters data on the base of hierarchical clustering. To plot a cluster map, you need to call the **cluster_map()** function. The following script plots a cluster map that clusters the number of passengers with respect to years and months.

Script 15:

```
flights_data_pivot =flights_data.pivot_table(index='month',
columns='year', values='passengers')
ax = sns.clustermap(flights_data_pivot, cmap = 'coolwarm')
```

Here is the output. The output clearly shows that passengers traveling from 1949 to 1954 have been clustered together, while those traveling from 1955 to 1960 have been clustered together in an outer hierarchical cluster. This is due to the fact that the number of passengers increased rapidly. Hence, the first half of the years is clustered together, while the second half is clustered together.

Output:

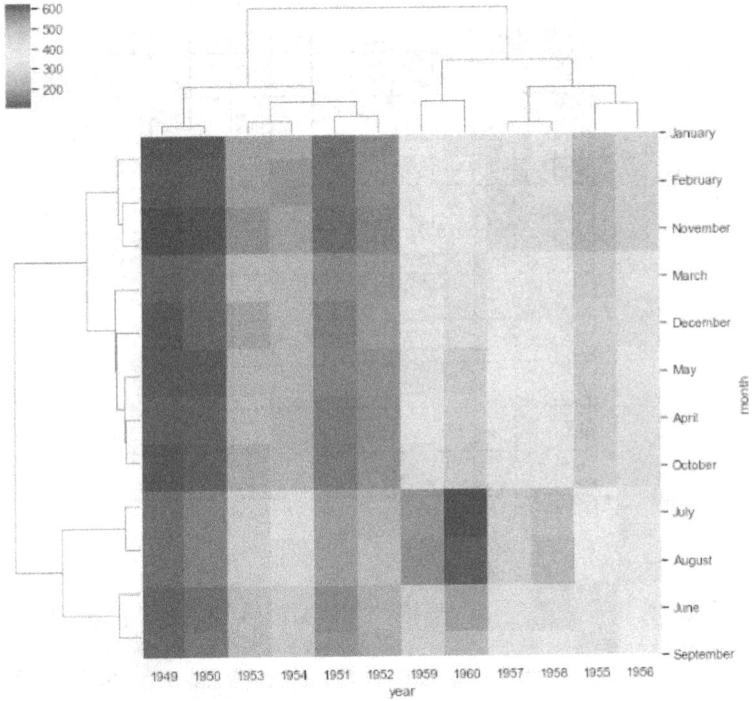

With respect to months, June to September has been clustered together. This behavior can be justified by the fact that in most countries, the summer holiday period lies between June and September.

Like heat map, you can also specify line color and width separating cells in a cluster map. Here is an example:

Script 16:

```
flights_data_pivot =flights_data.pivot_table(index='month',
columns='year', values='passengers')
ax = sns.clustermap(flights_data_pivot,  cmap = 'coolwarm',
linecolor='black', linewidth=1)
```

Output:

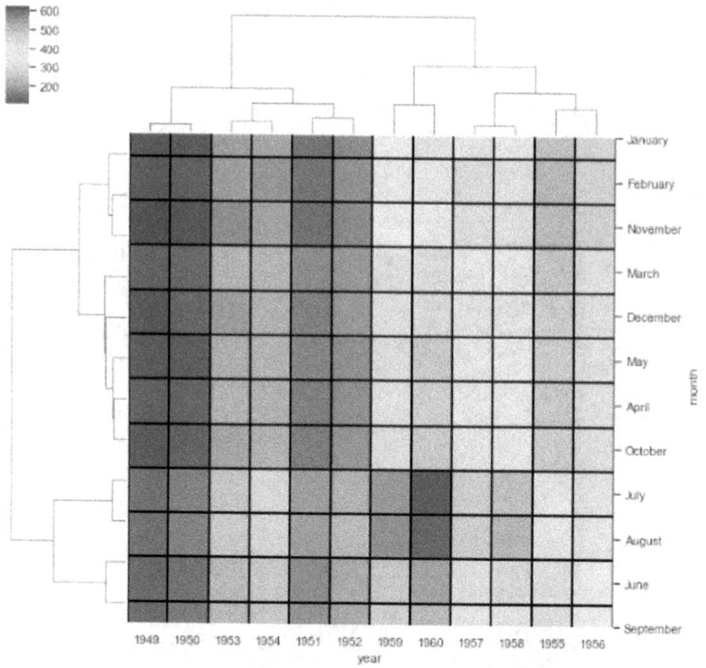

Further Readings – Seaborn Cluster Maps [4]

To study more about Seaborn cluster maps, please check Seaborn's official documentation for cluster maps. Try to plot cluster maps with a different set of attributes, as mentioned in the official documentation.

5.5. Pair Grids

In the previous chapter, you saw how the pair plot can be used to plot relationships between numeric columns of a dataset.

Before we see pair grids in action, let's revise how the pair plot works. The following script plots the pair plot for the **tips** dataset.

Script 17:

```
import matplotlib.pyplot as plt
import seaborn as sns

plt.rcParams[«figure.figsize»] = [10,8]

tips_data = sns.load_dataset('tips')

sns.pairplot(tips_data)
```

Output:

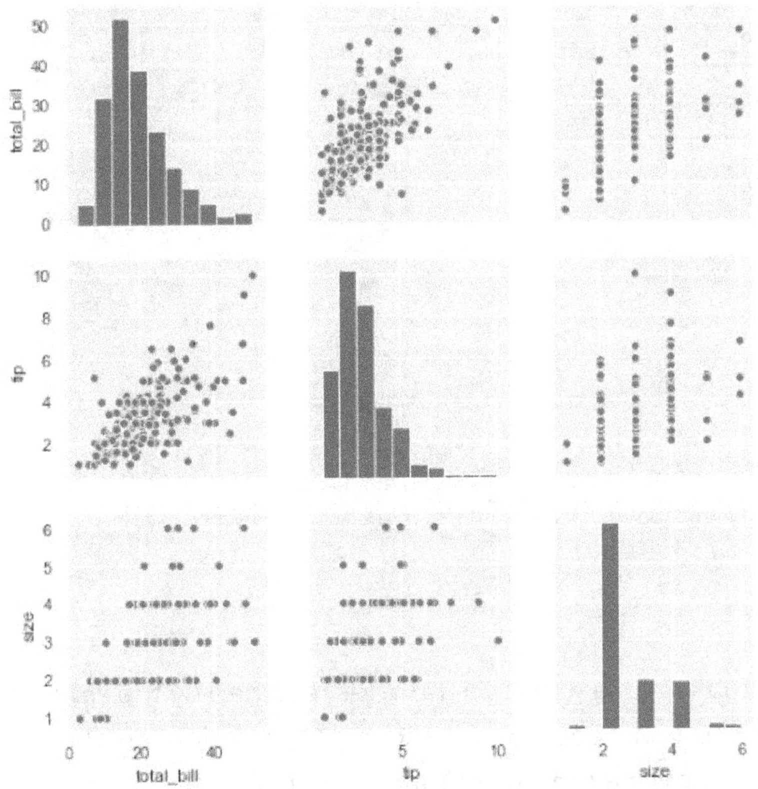

Let's now plot a pair grid for the tips dataset. To do so, you have to pass the Pandas dataframe containing the tips dataset to the PairGrid() function, as shown below.

Script 18:

```
sns.PairGrid(tips_data)
```

In the output, you should see the empty grids as follows.

Output:

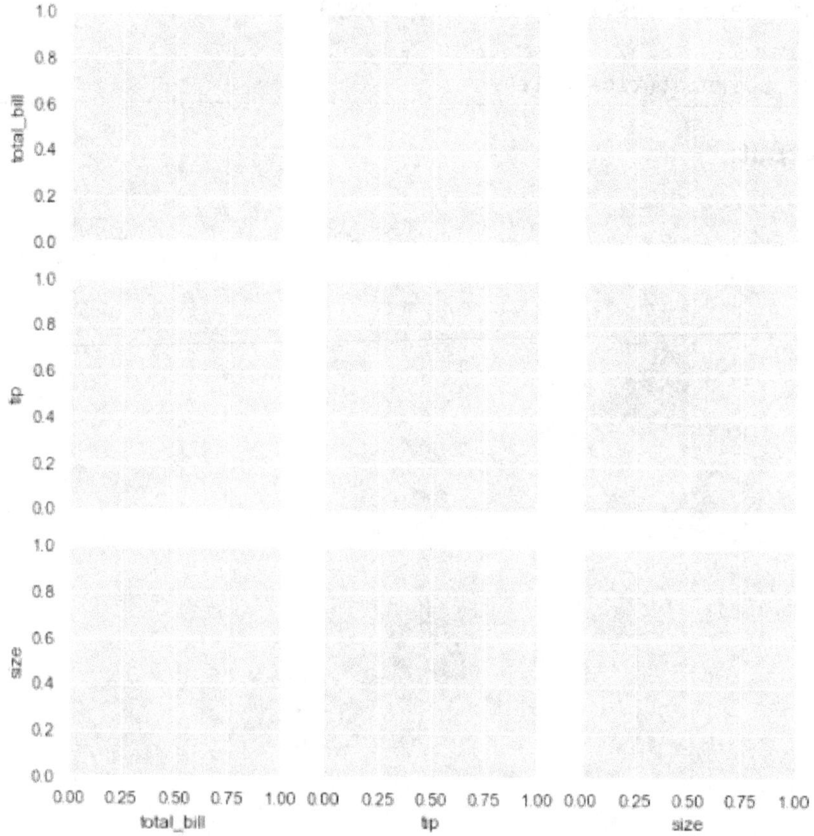

To actually plot a graph on the grids returned by the **`PairGrid()`** function, you need to call the **`map()`** function on the object returned by the **`PairGrid()`** function. Inside the map function, the type of plot is passed as a parameter. For instance, the following **PairGrid()** function plots a scatter plot for all the pairs of numerical columns in the tips dataset.

Script 19:

```
pgrids = sns.PairGrid(tips_data)
pgrids.map(plt.scatter)
```

Output:

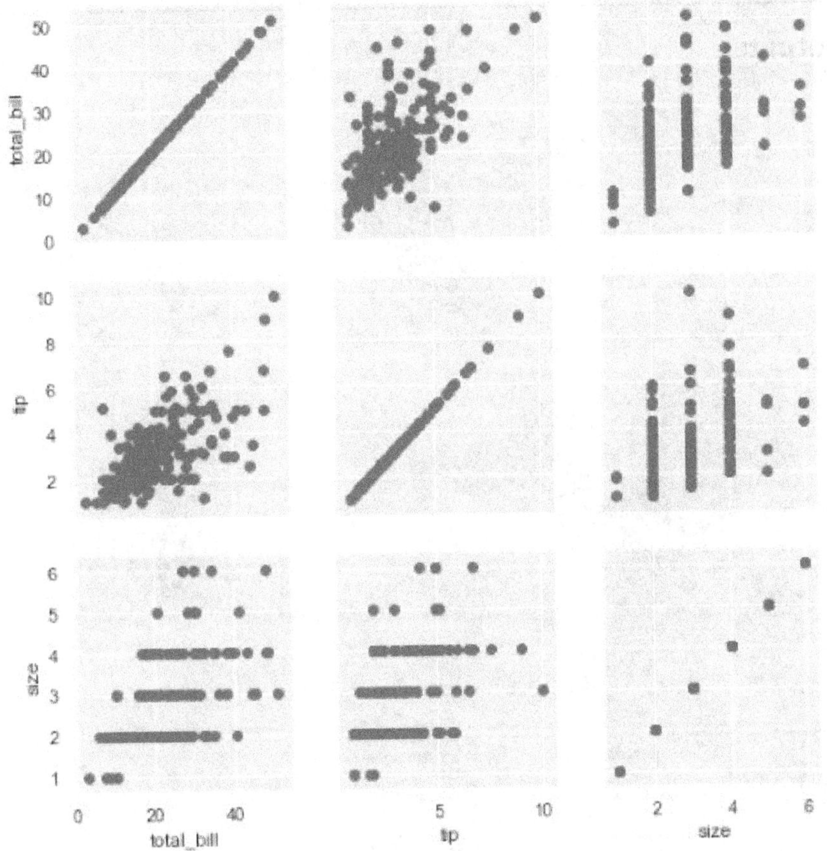

With a pair grid, you can plot different types of plots on the diagonal, upper portion from the diagonal, and the lower portion from a diagonal. For instance, the following pair grid plots a kernel density estimation plots on diagonal, distributional plots on the upper part of the diagonal, and scatter plots on the lower side of the diagonal.

Script 20:

```
pgrids = sns.PairGrid(tips_data)

pgrids.map_diag(sns.distplot)
pgrids.map_upper(sns.kdeplot)
pgrids.map_lower(plt.scatter)
```

Output:

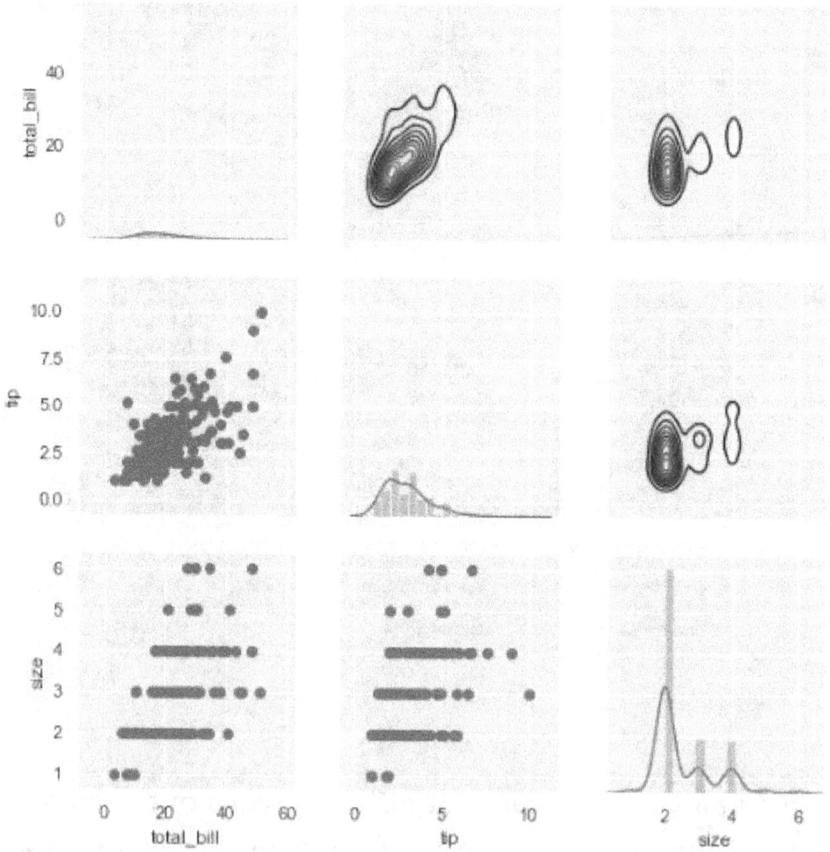

Further Readings - Seaborn Pair Grids [5]

To study more about Seaborn pair grids, please check Seaborn's official documentation for pair grids. Try to plot pair grids with a different set of attributes, as mentioned in the official documentation.

5.6. Facet Grids

Facet grids in Seaborn are used to plot two categorical columns against two numerical columns. For instance, if you want to plot the distributional plots for the total_bill column of the tips dataset with respect to sex and time, you can plot facet grids as follows.

Script 21:

```
fgrid = sns.FacetGrid(data=tips_data, col='sex',
row='time')
fgrid.map(sns.distplot, 'total_bill')
```

You can see gender across columns and time across rows as respectively, specified by the **FacetGrid()** function's **col** and **row** attributes.

Output:

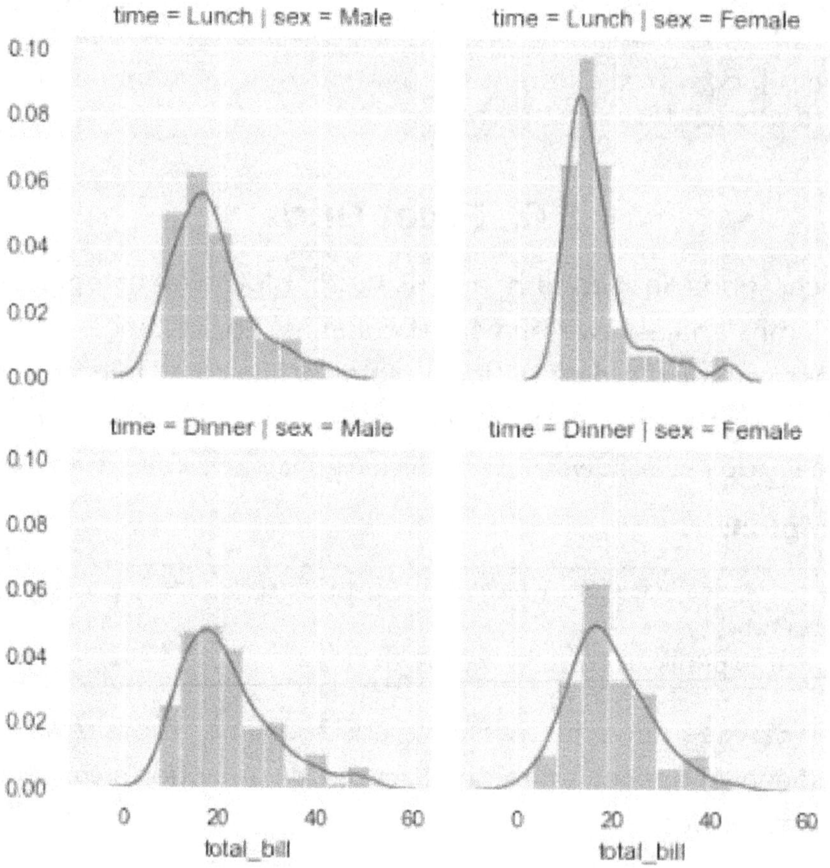

Similarly, you can use the facet grid to plot scatter plots for the **total_bill** and **tips** columns, with respect to sex and time columns.

Script 22:

```
fgrid = sns.FacetGrid(data=tips_data, col='sex',
row='time')
fgrid.map(plt.scatter, 'total_bill', 'size')
```

Output:

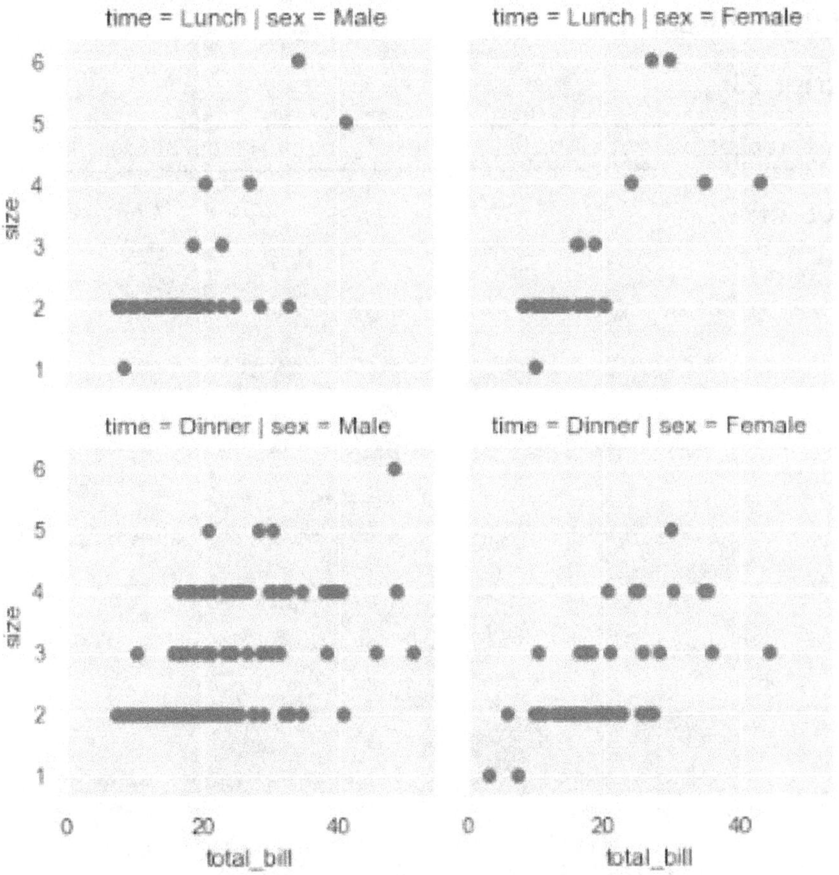

Further Readings - Seaborn Facet Grid [6]
To study more about Seaborn facet grids, please check Seaborn's official documentation for facet grids. Try to plot facet grids with a different set of attributes, as mentioned in the official documentation.

5.7. Regression Plots

Regression plots are used to plot a scatter plot for two columns along with the regression lines. To plot a regression plot with

Seaborn, you need to call the **lmplot()** method. The following script plots a regression plot for **total_bill** and **tips** columns of the **tips** dataset.

Script 23:

```
sns.lmplot(x='total_bill', y='tip', data =tips_data)
```

Output:

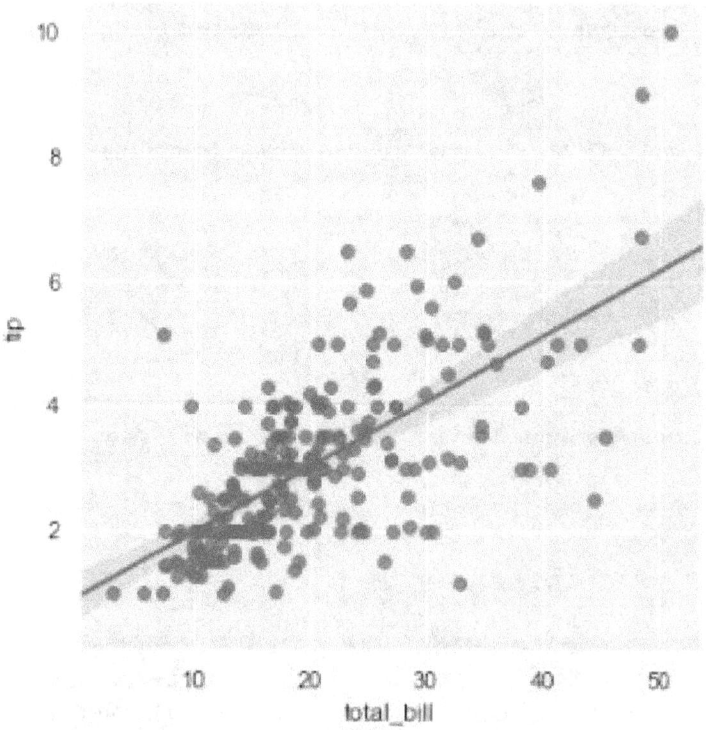

You can plot regression plots for two columns on the y-axis. To do so, you need to pass a column name for the **hue** parameter of the **lmplot()** function.

Script 24:

```
sns.lmplot(x='total_bill', y='tip', data =tips_data,
hue='time')
```

Output:

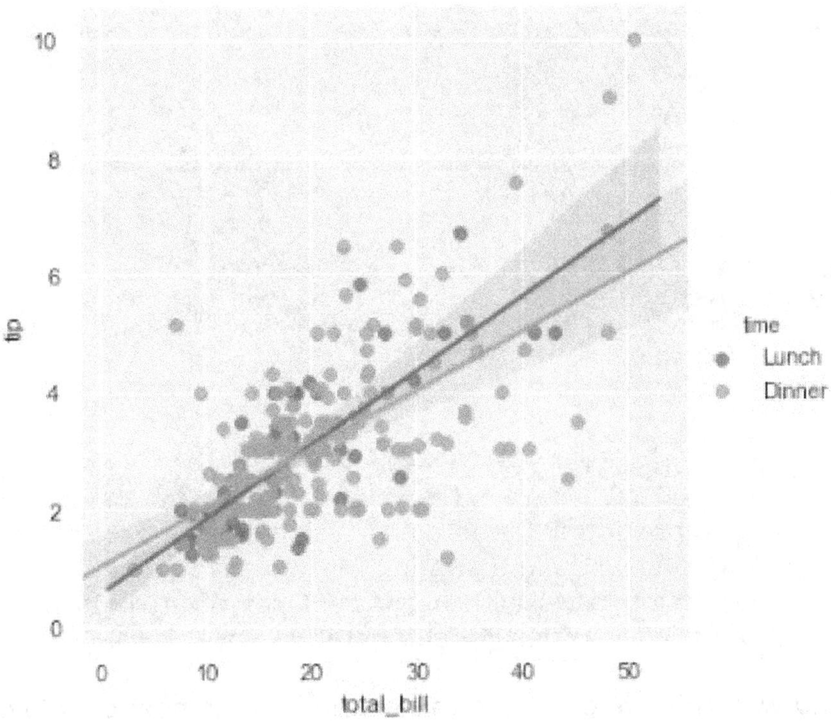

The output shows that there is a higher variation in the number of bills paid during lunchtime as compared to the number of bills paid during dinner.

In addition to having on plot for both the columns on the x-axis, you can create two different plots via **col** parameter as shown below:

Script 25:

```
sns.lmplot(x='total_bill', y='tip', data =tips_data,
col='time')
```

Output:

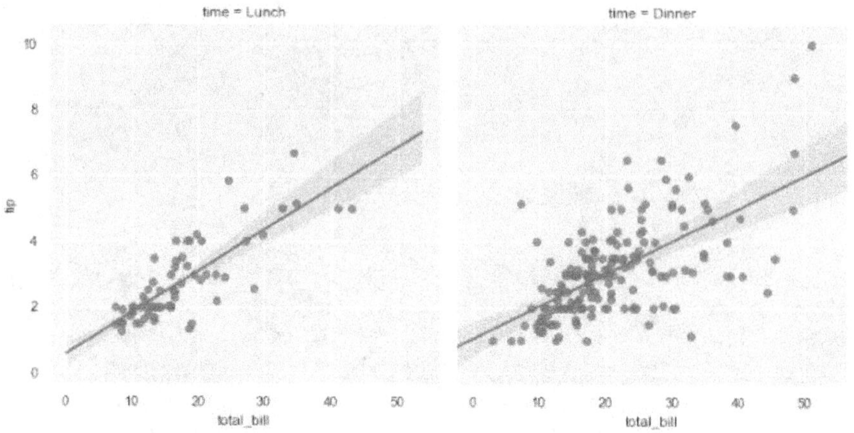

Further Readings – Seaborn Regression Plots [7]

To study more about Seaborn regression plots, please check Seaborn's official documentation for régression plots. Try to plot regression plots with a different set of attributes, as mentioned in the official documentation.

And with this, we conclude this chapter. In the next couple of chapters, you will see how to work with the Pandas library, and how to plot different types of plots with Python Pandas library.

Hands-on Time – Exercise

Now, it is your turn. Follow the instructions in **the exercises below** to check your understanding of the advanced data visualization with the Seaborn library. The answers to these questions are given at the end of the book.

Exercise 5.1

Question 1

Which seaborn function allows you to plot a graph that can be printed as a poster?

A- set_style ('darkgrid')

B- set_style ('whitegrid')

C- set_style ('poster')

D- set_context ('poster')

Question 2

Which function can be used to find the correlation between all the numeric columns of a Pandas dataframe?

A- correlation()

B- corr()

C- heatmap()

D- none of the above

Question 3

Which function is used to annotate a heat map?

A- annotate()

B- annot()

C- mark()

D- display()

Exercise 5.2

Plot two scatter plots on the same graph using the tips_ dataset. In the first scatter plot, display values from the total_ bill column on the x-axis and from the tip column on the y-axis. The color of the first scatter plot should be green. In the second scatter plot, display values from the total_bill column on the x-axis and from the size column on the y-axis. The color of the second scatter plot should be blue, and markers should be x.

References

1. https://seaborn.pydata.org/generated/seaborn.scatterplot.html
2. https://seaborn.pydata.org/tutorial/aesthetics.html
3. https://seaborn.pydata.org/generated/seaborn.heatmap.html
4. https://seaborn.pydata.org/generated/seaborn.clustermap.html
5. https://seaborn.pydata.org/generated/seaborn.PairGrid.html
6. https://seaborn.pydata.org/generated/seaborn.FacetGrid.html
7. https://seaborn.pydata.org/generated/seaborn.lmplot.html

6

Introduction to Pandas Library for Data Analysis

6.1. Introduction

In this chapter, you will see how to use Python's Pandas library for data analysis. In the next chapter, you will see how to use the Pandas library for data visualization by plotting different types of plots.

Execute the following script on your command prompt to download the Pandas library.

```
$ pip install pandas
```

The following script imports the Pandas library in your application. Execute the script at the type of all Python codes that are provided in this chapter.

```
import pandas as pd
```

Furthermore, the following are the libraries that you need to install before running the scripts in this chapter.

Requirements – Anaconda, Jupyter, and Matplotlib

- All the scripts in this book have been executed via the Jupyter notebook. Therefore, you should have the Jupyter notebook installed.
- It goes without saying that we will be using the Matplotlib library.
- The Numpy and Pandas libraries should also be installed before this chapter.

Hands-on Time – Source Codes

All IPython notebooks for the source code of all the scripts in this chapter can be found in Resources/Chapter 6.ipynb. I would suggest that you write all the code in this chapter yourself and see if you can get the same output as mentioned in this chapter.

6.2. Reading Data into the Pandas Dataframe

In the second chapter of this book, you saw how the Pandas library can be used to read CSV and TSV files. Here, we will just briefly recap how to read CSV files with Pandas. The following script reads the "titanic_data.csv" file from the *Datasets* folders in the *Resources*. The beginning five rows of the Titanic dataset have been printed via the **head()** method of the Pandas dataframe containing the Titanic dataset.

Script 1:

```
import pandas as pd
titanic_data = pd.read_csv(r»E:\Data Visualization with
Python\Datasets\titanic_data.csv»)
titanic_data.head()
```

Output:

	PassengerId	Survived	Pclass	Name	Sex	Age	SibSp	Parch	Ticket	Fare	Cabin	Embarked
0	1	0	3	Braund, Mr. Owen Harris	male	22.0	1	0	A/5 21171	7.2500	NaN	S
1	2	1	1	Cumings, Mrs. John Bradley (Florence Briggs Th...	female	38.0	1	0	PC 17599	71.2833	C85	C
2	3	1	3	Heikkinen, Miss. Laina	female	26.0	0	0	STON/O2. 3101282	7.9250	NaN	S
3	4	1	1	Futrelle, Mrs. Jacques Heath (Lily May Peel)	female	35.0	1	0	113803	53.1000	C123	S
4	5	0	3	Allen, Mr. William Henry	male	35.0	0	0	373450	8.0500	NaN	S

The **read_csv()** method reads data from a CSV or TSV file and stores it in a Pandas dataframe, which is a special object that stores data in the form of rows and columns.

6.3. Filtering Rows

One of the most common tasks that you need to perform while handling the Pandas dataframe is to filter rows based on the column values.

To filter rows, first, you have to identify the indexes of the rows to filter. For those indexes, you need to pass True to the opening and closing square brackets that follow the Pandas dataframe name.

The following script returns a series of True and False. True will be returned for indexes where the Pclass column has a value of 1.

Script 2:

```
titanic_pclass1= (titanic_data.Pclass == 1)
titanic_pclass1
```

Output:

```
0      False
1       True
2      False
3       True
4      False
       ...
886    False
887     True
888    False
889     True
890    False
Name: Pclass, Length: 891, dtype: bool
```

Now the **titanic_pclass1** series, which contains True or False, can be passed inside the opening and closing square brackets that follow the **titanic_data** dataframe. The result will be the Titanic dataset, containing only those records where the Pclass column contains 1.

Script 3:

```
titanic_pclass1= (titanic_data.Pclass == 1)
titanic_pclass1_data = titanic_data[titanic_pclass1]
titanic_pclass1_data.head()
```

Output:

	PassengerId	Survived	Pclass	Name	Sex	Age	SibSp	Parch	Ticket	Fare	Cabin	Embarked
1	2	1	1	Cumings, Mrs. John Bradley (Florence Briggs Th...	male	38.0	1	0	PC 17599	71.2833	C85	C
3	4	1	1	Futrelle, Mrs. Jacques Heath (Lily May Peel)	male	35.0	1	0	113803	53.1000	C123	S
6	7	0	1	McCarthy, Mr. Timothy J	male	54.0	0	0	17463	51.8625	E46	S
11	12	1	1	Bonnell, Miss. Elizabeth	male	58.0	0	0	113783	26.5500	C103	S
23	24	1	1	Sloper, Mr. William Thompson	male	28.0	0	0	113788	35.5000	A6	S

The comparison between the column values and filtering of rows can be made in a single line, as shown below.

Script 4:

```
titanic_pclass_data = titanic_data[titanic_data.Pclass == 1]
titanic_pclass_data.head()
```

Output:

	PassengerId	Survived	Pclass	Name	Sex	Age	SibSp	Parch	Ticket	Fare	Cabin	Embarked
1	2	1	1	Cumings, Mrs. John Bradley (Florence Briggs Th...	male	38.0	1	0	PC 17599	71.2833	C85	C
3	4	1	1	Futrelle, Mrs. Jacques Heath (Lily May Peel)	male	35.0	1	0	113803	53.1000	C123	S
6	7	0	1	McCarthy, Mr. Timothy J	male	54.0	0	0	17463	51.8625	E46	S
11	12	1	1	Bonnell, Miss. Elizabeth	male	58.0	0	0	113783	26.5500	C103	S
23	24	1	1	Sloper, Mr. William Thompson	male	28.0	0	0	113788	35.5000	A6	S

Another commonly used operator to filter rows is the **isin** operator. The **isin** operator takes a list of values and returns only those rows where the column used for comparison contains values from the list passed to **isin** operator as a parameter. For instance, the following script filters those rows where age is in 20, 21, or 22.

Script 5:

```
ages = [20,21,22]
age_dataset = titanic_data[titanic_data[«Age»].isin(ages)]
age_dataset.head()
```

Output:

	PassengerId	Survived	Pclass	Name	Sex	Age	SibSp	Parch	Ticket	Fare	Cabin	Embarked
0	1	0	3	Braund, Mr. Owen Harris	male	22.0	1	0	A/5 21171	7.25	NaN	S
12	13	0	3	Saundercock, Mr. William Henry	male	20.0	0	0	A/5. 2151	8.05	NaN	S
37	38	0	3	Cann, Mr. Ernest Charles	male	21.0	0	0	A./5. 2152	8.05	NaN	S
51	52	0	3	Nosworthy, Mr. Richard Cater	male	21.0	0	0	A/4. 39886	7.80	NaN	S
56	57	1	2	Rugg, Miss. Emily	male	21.0	0	0	C.A. 31026	10.50	NaN	S

You can filter rows in a Pandas dataframe based on multiple conditions using logical and (&) and or (|) operators. The following script returns those rows from the Pandas dataframe where passenger class is 1 and passenger age is in 20, 21, and 22.

Script 6:

```
ages = [20,21,22]
ageclass_dataset = titanic_data[titanic_data[«Age»].
isin(ages) & (titanic_data[«Pclass»] == 1) ]
ageclass_dataset.head()
```

Output:

	PassengerId	Survived	Pclass	Name	Sex	Age	SibSp	Parch	Ticket	Fare	Cabin	Embarked
102	103	0	1	White, Mr. Richard Frasar	male	21.0	0	1	35281	77.2875	D26	S
151	152	1	1	Pears, Mrs. Thomas (Edith Wearne)	male	22.0	1	0	113776	66.6000	C2	S
356	357	1	1	Bowerman, Miss. Elsie Edith	male	22.0	0	1	113505	55.0000	E33	S
373	374	0	1	Ringhini, Mr. Sante	male	22.0	0	0	PC 17760	135.6333	NaN	C
539	540	1	1	Frolicher, Miss. Hedwig Margaritha	male	22.0	0	2	13568	49.5000	B39	C

6.4. Filtering Columns

To filter columns from a Pandas dataframe, you can use the **filter()** method. The list of columns that you want to filter is passed to the filter() method. The following script filters Name, Sex, and Age columns from the Titanic dataset and ignores all the other columns.

Script 7:

```
titanic_data_filter  = titanic_data.filter([«Name», «Sex»,
«Age»])
titanic_data_filter.head()
```

The output below shows that the dataset now contains only Name, Sex, and Age columns.

Output:

	Name	Sex	Age
0	Braund, Mr. Owen Harris	male	22.0
1	Cumings, Mrs. John Bradley (Florence Briggs Th...	female	38.0
2	Heikkinen, Miss. Laina	female	26.0
3	Futrelle, Mrs. Jacques Heath (Lily May Peel)	female	35.0
4	Allen, Mr. William Henry	male	35.0

In addition to filtering columns, you can also drop columns that you don't want in the dataset. To do so, you need to call the **drop()** method and pass it the list of columns that you want to drop. For instance, the following script drops the Name, Age, and Sex columns from the Titanic dataset and returns the remaining columns.

Script 8:

```
titanic_data_filter  = titanic_data.drop([«Name», «Sex»,
«Age»], axis = 1)
titanic_data_filter.head()
```

Output:

	PassengerId	Survived	Pclass	SibSp	Parch	Ticket	Fare	Cabin	Embarked
0	1	0	3	1	0	A/5 21171	7.2500	NaN	S
1	2	1	1	1	0	PC 17599	71.2833	C85	C
2	3	1	3	0	0	STON/O2. 3101282	7.9250	NaN	S
3	4	1	1	1	0	113803	53.1000	C123	S
4	5	0	3	0	0	373450	8.0500	NaN	S

Further Readings – Pandas Filter [1]

To study more about the Pandas Filter method, please check Pandas' official documentation for the filter method. Try to execute the filter method with a different set of attributes, as mentioned in the official documentation.

6.5. Concatenating Dataframes

Often times, you need to concatenate or join multiple Pandas dataframes horizontally or vertically. Let's first see how to concatenate or join Pandas dataframes vertically. We will first create two Pandas dataframes using Titanic data. The first dataframe contains rows where the passenger class is 1, while the second dataframe contains rows where the passenger class is 2.

Script 9:

```
titanic_pclass1_data = titanic_data[titanic_data.Pclass == 1]
print(titanic_pclass1_data.shape)

titanic_pclass2_data = titanic_data[titanic_data.Pclass == 2]
print(titanic_pclass2_data.shape)
```

Output:

(216, 12)

(184, 12)

The output shows that both the newly created dataframes have 12 columns. It is important to mention that while concatenating data vertically, both the dataframes should have an equal number of columns.

There are two ways to concatenate datasets horizontally. You can call the **append()** method via the first dataframe and pass the second dataframe as a parameter to the **append()** method. Look at the following script.

Script 10:

```
final_data = titanic_pclass1_data.append(titanic_pclass2_
data, ignore_index=True)
print(final_data.shape)
```

Output:

(400, 12)

The output now shows that the total number of rows is 400, which is the sum of the number of rows in the two dataframes that we concatenated.

Further Readings – Pandas append [2]

To study more about the Pandas append method, please check Pandas' official documentation for the append method. Try to execute the append method with a different set of attributes, as mentioned in the official documentation.

The other way to concatenate two dataframes is by passing both the dataframes as parameters to the **concat()** method of the Pandas module. The following script shows how to do that.

Script 11:

```
final_data = pd.concat([titanic_pclass1_data, titanic_
pclass2_data])
print(final_data.shape)
```

Output:

(400, 12)

To concatenate dataframes horizontally, make sure that the dataframes have an equal number of rows. You can use the

concat() method to concatenate dataframes horizontally, as well. However, you will need to pass 1 as the value for the **axis** attribute. Furthermore, to reset dataset indexes, you need to pass True as the value for the **ignore_index** attribute.

Script 12:

```
df1 = final_data[:200]
print(df1.shape)
df2 = final_data[200:]
print(df2.shape)

final_data2 = pd.concat([df1, df2], axis = 1, ignore_index =
True)
print(final_data2.shape)
```

Output:

(200, 12)

(200, 12)

(400, 24)

Further Readings – Pandas concat [3]

To study more about the Pandas concat() method, please check Pandas' official documentation for the concat method. Try to execute the concat method with a different set of attributes, as mentioned in the official documentation.

6.6. Sorting Dataframes

To sort the Pandas dataframe, you can use the **sort_values()** function of the Pandas dataframe. The list of columns used for sorting needs to be passed to the **by** attribute of the **sort_values()** method. The following script sorts the Titanic dataset in by ascending order of the passenger's age.

Script 13:

```
age_sorted_data = titanic_data.sort_values(by=['Age'])
age_sorted_data.head()
```

Output:

	PassengerId	Survived	Pclass	Name	Sex	Age	SibSp	Parch	Ticket	Fare	Cabin	Embarked
803	804	1	3	Thomas, Master. Assad Alexander	male	0.42	0	1	2625	8.5167	NaN	C
755	756	1	2	Hamalainen, Master. Viljo	male	0.67	1	1	250649	14.5000	NaN	S
644	645	1	3	Baclini, Miss. Eugenie	male	0.75	2	1	2666	19.2583	NaN	C
469	470	1	3	Baclini, Miss. Helene Barbara	male	0.75	2	1	2666	19.2583	NaN	C
78	79	1	2	Caldwell, Master. Alden Gates	male	0.83	0	2	248738	29.0000	NaN	S

To sort by descending order, you need to pass False as the value for the **ascending** attribute of the **sort_values()** function. The following script sorts the dataset by descending order of age.

Script 14:

```
age_sorted_data = titanic_data.sort_values(by=['Age'],
ascending = False)
age_sorted_data.head()
```

Output:

	PassengerId	Survived	Pclass	Name	Sex	Age	SibSp	Parch	Ticket	Fare	Cabin	Embarked
630	631	1	1	Barkworth, Mr. Algernon Henry Wilson	male	80.0	0	0	27042	30.0000	A23	S
851	852	0	3	Svensson, Mr. Johan	male	74.0	0	0	347060	7.7750	NaN	S
493	494	0	1	Artagaveytia, Mr. Ramon	male	71.0	0	0	PC 17609	49.5042	NaN	C
96	97	0	1	Goldschmidt, Mr. George B	male	71.0	0	0	PC 17754	34.6542	A5	C
116	117	0	3	Connors, Mr. Patrick	male	70.5	0	0	370369	7.7500	NaN	Q

You can also pass multiple columns to the **by** attribute of the **sort_values()**function. In such a case, the dataset will be sorted by the first column, and in case of equal values for two or more records, the dataset will be sorted by the second column and so on. The following script first sorts the data by Age and then by Fare, both by descending orders.

Script 15:

```
age_sorted_data = titanic_data.sort_
values(by=['Age','Fare'], ascending = False)
age_sorted_data.head()
```

Output:

	PassengerId	Survived	Pclass	Name	Sex	Age	SibSp	Parch	Ticket	Fare	Cabin	Embarked
630	631	1	1	Barkworth, Mr. Algernon Henry Wilson	male	80.0	0	0	27042	30.0000	A23	S
851	852	0	3	Svensson, Mr. Johan	male	74.0	0	0	347060	7.7750	NaN	S
493	494	0	1	Artagaveytia, Mr. Ramon	male	71.0	0	0	PC 17609	49.5042	NaN	C
96	97	0	1	Goldschmidt, Mr. George B	male	71.0	0	0	PC 17754	34.6542	A5	C
116	117	0	3	Connors, Mr. Patrick	male	70.5	0	0	370369	7.7500	NaN	Q

Further Readings – Pandas sort_values [4]

To study more about the Pandas sort_values() method, please check Pandas' official documentation forsort_values() method. Try to execute the sort_values() method with a different set of attributes, as mentioned in the official documentation.

6.7. Apply Function

The **apply()** function is used to apply a function on multiple rows or on rows of a particular column. A lambda expression is passed to the **apply()** function. The lambda expression basically specifies the operation performed by the **apply()** function. For instance, in the following **apply()** function adds 2 to all the values in the **Pclass** column of the Titanic dataset.

Script 16:

```
updated_class = titanic_data.Pclass.apply(lambda x : x + 2)
updated_class.head()
```

The output shows that all the values in the Pclass column have been incremented by 2.

Output:

0 5

1 3

2 5

3 3

4 5

Name: Pclass, dtype: int64

In addition to a lambda expression, you can also pass a concrete function to the **apply()** method. In the following script, we define a **mult()** function, which multiplies the parameter passed to it by 2 and returns the resultant value. In the apply function, we simply pass the name of the **mult()** method. All the values in the **Pclass** column will be multiplied by 2 as shown in the output of the script 17.

Script 17:

```
def mult(x):
    return x * 2

updated_class = titanic_data.Pclass.apply(mult)
updated_class.head()
```

Output:

0 6

1 2

2 6

3 2

4 6

Name: Pclass, dtype: int64

Further Readings – Pandas apply [5]

To study more about the Pandas apply method, please check Pandas' official documentation for the apply method. Try to execute the apply method with a different set of attributes, as mentioned in the official documentation.

6.8. Pivot & Crosstab

You have already seen a Pivot operator in action in the last chapter when we studied heat maps in Seaborn. Here, we will briefly revise the pivot operation via the flights dataset. The following script downloads the flights dataset.

Script 18:

```
import matplotlib.pyplot as plt
import seaborn as sns


flights_data = sns.load_dataset('flights')

flights_data.head()
```

Output:

	year	month	passengers
0	1949	January	112
1	1949	February	118
2	1949	March	132
3	1949	April	129
4	1949	May	121

Script 19:

```
flights_data_pivot =flights_data.pivot_table(index='month',
columns='year', values='passengers')
flights_data_pivot.head()
```

Output:

year month	1949	1950	1951	1952	1953	1954	1955	1956	1957	1958	1959	1960
January	112	115	145	171	196	204	242	284	315	340	360	417
February	118	126	150	180	196	188	233	277	301	318	342	391
March	132	141	178	193	236	235	267	317	356	362	406	419
April	129	135	163	181	235	227	269	313	348	348	396	461
May	121	125	172	183	229	234	270	318	355	363	420	472

The **crosstab()** function is used to plot the cross-tabulation between two columns. Let's plot a cross tab matrix between passenger class and age columns for the Titanic dataset.

Script 20:

```
import pandas as pd
titanic_data = pd.read_csv(r»E:\Data Visualization with
Python\Datasets\titanic_data.csv»)
titanic_data.head()

pd.crosstab(titanic_data.Pclass, titanic_data.Age,
margins=True)
```

Output:

Age Pclass	0.42	0.67	0.75	0.83	0.92	1.0	2.0	3.0	4.0	5.0	...	63.0	64.0	65.0	66.0	70.0	70.5	71.0	74.0	80.0	All
1	0	0	0	0	1	0	1	0	1	0	...	1	2	2	0	1	0	2	0	1	186
2	0	1	0	2	0	2	2	3	2	1	...	0	0	0	1	1	0	0	0	0	173
3	1	0	2	0	0	5	7	3	7	3	...	1	0	1	0	0	1	0	1	0	355
All	1	1	2	2	1	7	10	6	10	4	...	2	2	3	1	2	1	2	1	1	714

4 rows × 89 columns

6.9. Arithmetic Operations with Where

The **where** clause from the N**umpy** library can be used to perform arithmetic operations on the Pandas dataframe. For instance, in the following script, the **where** clause is used to add 5 to the rows in the Fare column, **where** passengers' ages are greater than 20.

Script 21:

```
import numpy as np
titanic_data.Fare = np.where( titanic_data.Age > 20,
titanic_data.Fare +5 , titanic_data.Fare)

titanic_data.head()
```

Output:

	PassengerId	Survived	Pclass	Name	Sex	Age	SibSp	Parch	Ticket	Fare	Cabin	Embarked
0	1	0	3	Braund, Mr. Owen Harris	male	22.0	1	0	A/5 21171	17.2500	NaN	S
1	2	1	1	Cumings, Mrs. John Bradley (Florence Briggs Th...	female	38.0	1	0	PC 17599	81.2833	C85	C
2	3	1	3	Heikkinen, Miss. Laina	female	26.0	0	0	STON/O2. 3101282	17.9250	NaN	S
3	4	1	1	Futrelle, Mrs. Jacques Heath (Lily May Peel)	female	35.0	1	0	113803	63.1000	C123	S
4	5	0	3	Allen, Mr. William Henry	male	35.0	0	0	373450	18.0500	NaN	S

Hands-on Time – Exercise

Now, it is your turn. Follow the instructions in **the exercises below** to check your understanding of the data analysis with the Pandas library. The answers to these questions are given at the end of the book.

Exercise 6.1

Question 1

In order to horizontally concatenate two Pandas dataframe, the value for the axis attribute should be set to:

A- 0
B- 1
C- 2
D- None of the above

Question 2

Which function is used to sort a Pandas dataframe by column value?

A- sort_dataframe()
B- sort_rows()
C- sort_values()
D- sort_records()

Question 3

To filter columns from a Pandas dataframe, you have to pass a list of column names to one of the following method:

A- filter()
B- filter_columns()
C- apply_filter()
D- None of the above()

Exercise 6.2

Use the apply function to subtract 10 from the Fare column of the Titanic dataset, without using lambda expression.

References

1 https://pandas.pydata.org/pandas-docs/stable/reference/api/pandas.DataFrame.filter.html

2 https://pandas.pydata.org/pandas-docs/stable/reference/api/pandas.DataFrame.append.html

3 https://pandas.pydata.org/pandas-docs/stable/reference/api/pandas.concat.html

4 https://pandas.pydata.org/pandas-docs/stable/reference/api/pandas.DataFrame.sort_values.html

5 https://pandas.pydata.org/pandas-docs/stable/reference/api/pandas.DataFrame.apply.html

7

Pandas for Data Visualization

7.1. Introduction

In the previous chapter, you saw how to work with the Pandas library for data analysis. You saw how to read CSV files into the Pandas dataframe, and how to analyze data by performing a variety of functions on the Pandas dataframe. In this chapter, you will see how the Pandas library can be used to plot different types of visualizations. As a matter of fact, the Pandas library is probably the easiest library for data plotting, as you will see in this chapter.

Requirements – Anaconda, Jupyter, Matplotlib, and Pandas

- All the scripts in this book have been executed via the Jupyter notebook. Therefore, you should have the Jupyter notebook installed.
- It goes without saying that we will be using the Matplotlib library.
- The Numpy and Pandas libraries should also be installed before this chapter.

Hands-on Time - Source Codes

All IPython notebooks for the source code of all the scripts in this chapter can be found in Resources/Chapter 7.ipynb. I would suggest that you write all the code in this chapter yourself and see if you can get the same output as mentioned in this chapter.

7.2. Loading Datasets with Pandas

Before you can plot any visualization with the Pandas library, you need to read data into a Pandas dataframe. The best way to do so is via the **read_csv()** method. The following script shows how to read the Titanic dataset into a dataframe named **titanic_data.** You can give any name to the dataframe.

Script 1:

```
import pandas as pd
titanic_data = pd.read_csv(r»E:\Data Visualization with
Python\Datasets\titanic_data.csv»)
titanic_data.head()
```

Output:

	PassengerId	Survived	Pclass	Name	Sex	Age	SibSp	Parch	Ticket	Fare	Cabin	Embarked
0	1	0	3	Braund, Mr. Owen Harris	male	22.0	1	0	A/5 21171	7.2500	NaN	S
1	2	1	1	Cumings, Mrs. John Bradley (Florence Briggs Th...	female	38.0	1	0	PC 17599	71.2833	C85	C
2	3	1	3	Heikkinen, Miss. Laina	female	26.0	0	0	STON/O2. 3101282	7.9250	NaN	S
3	4	1	1	Futrelle, Mrs. Jacques Heath (Lily May Peel)	female	35.0	1	0	113803	53.1000	C123	S
4	5	0	3	Allen, Mr. William Henry	male	35.0	0	0	373450	8.0500	NaN	S

7.3. Plotting Histograms with Pandas

Let's now see how to plot different types of plots with the Pandas dataframe. The first plot we are going to plot is a Histogram. There are multiple ways to plot a graph in Pandas. The first way is to select the dataframe column by specifying the name of the column in square brackets that follows the dataframe name and then append the plot name via dot operator. The following script plots a histogram for the Age column of the Titanic dataset using the **hist()** function. It is important to mention that behind the scenes, the Pandas library makes use of the Matplotlib plotting functions. Therefore, you need to import the **Matplotlib's pyplot** module before you can plot Pandas visualizations.

Script 2:

```
import matplotlib.pyplot as plt
titanic_data['Age'].hist()
```

Output:

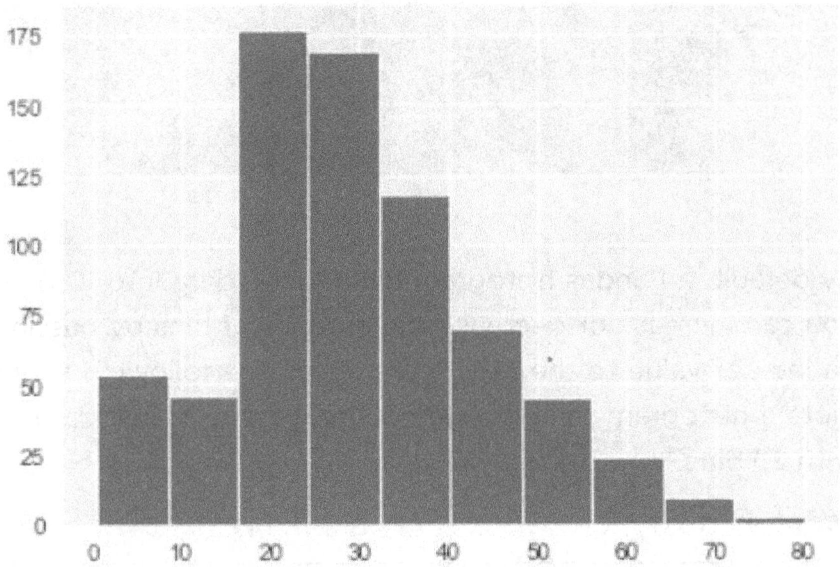

The other way to plot a graph via Pandas is by using the **plot()** function. The type of plot you want to plot is passed to the kind attribute of the **plot()** function. The following script uses the **plot()** function to plot a histogram for the Age column of the Titanic dataset.

Script 3:

```
import matplotlib.pyplot as plt
titanic_data['Age'].plot(kind='hist')
```

Output:

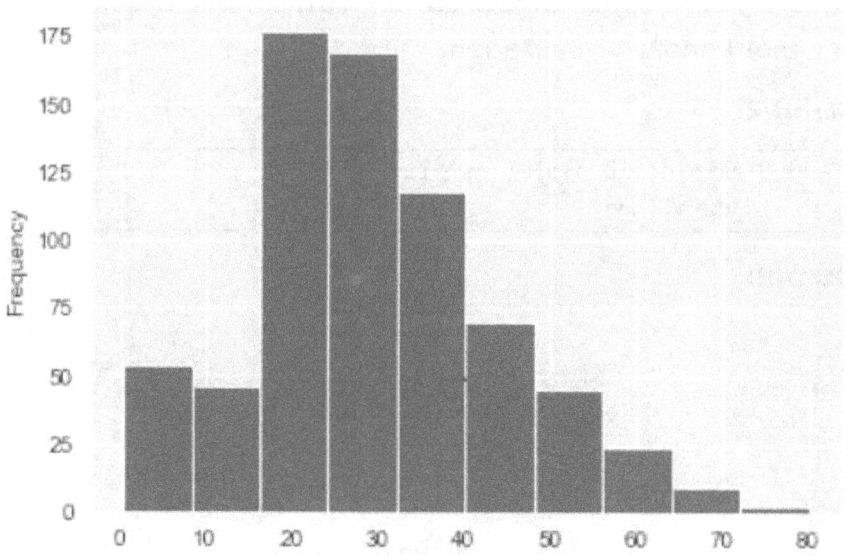

By default, a Pandas histogram divides the data into 10 bins. You can increase or decrease the number of bins by passing an integer value to the **bins** parameter. The following script plots a histogram for the Age column of the Titanic dataset with 20 bins.

Script 4:

```
import matplotlib.pyplot as plt
import seaborn as sns
sns.set_style('darkgrid')
titanic_data['Age'].hist(bins = 20)
```

Output:

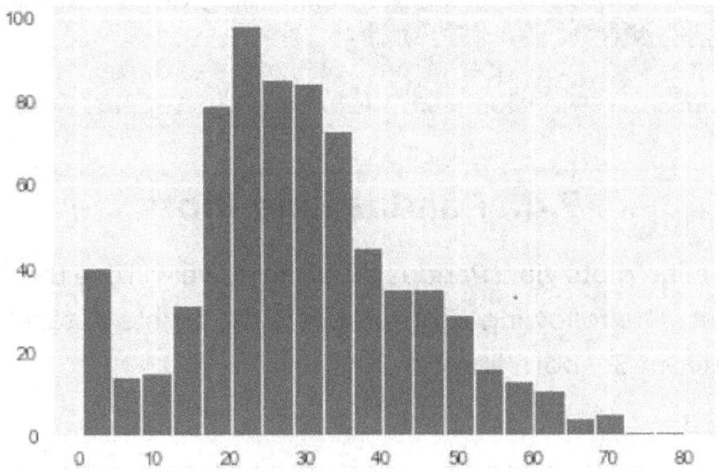

Finally, you can change the color of your histogram by specifying the color name to the color attribute, as shown below.

Script 5:

```
titanic_data['Age'].hist(bins = 20, color = 'orange')
```

Output:

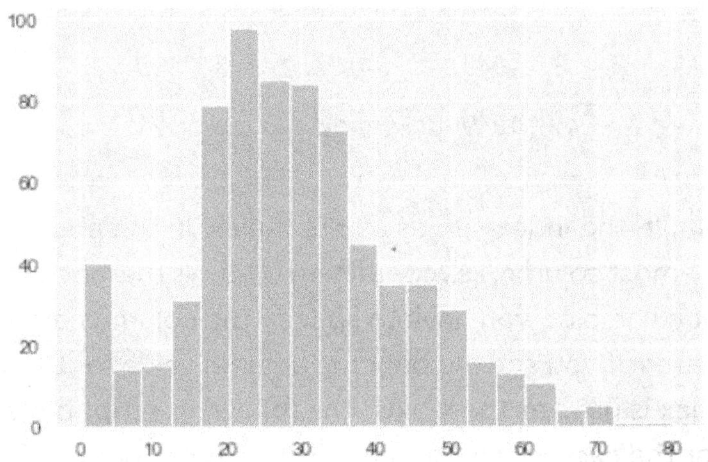

Further Readings – Pandas Histogram [1]

To study more about the Pandas histogram, please check Pandas' official documentation for a histogram. Try to execute the histogram method with a different set of attributes, as mentioned in the official documentation.

7.4. Pandas Line Plots

To plot line plots via a Pandas dataframe, we will use the flights dataset. The following script imports the flights dataset from the built-in Seaborn library.

Script 6:

```
flights_data = sns.load_dataset('flights')

flights_data.head()
```

Output:

	year	month	passengers
0	1949	January	112
1	1949	February	118
2	1949	March	132
3	1949	April	129
4	1949	May	121

By default, the index serves as the x-axis. In the above script, the left-most column, i.e., containing 0,1,2 ... is the index column. To plot a line plot, you have to specify the column names for x and y axes. If you specify only the column value for the y-axis, the index is used as the x-axis. The following script plots a line plot for the `passengers` column of the `flights` data.

Script 7:

```
flights_data.plot.line( y='passengers', figsize=(8,6))
```

Output:

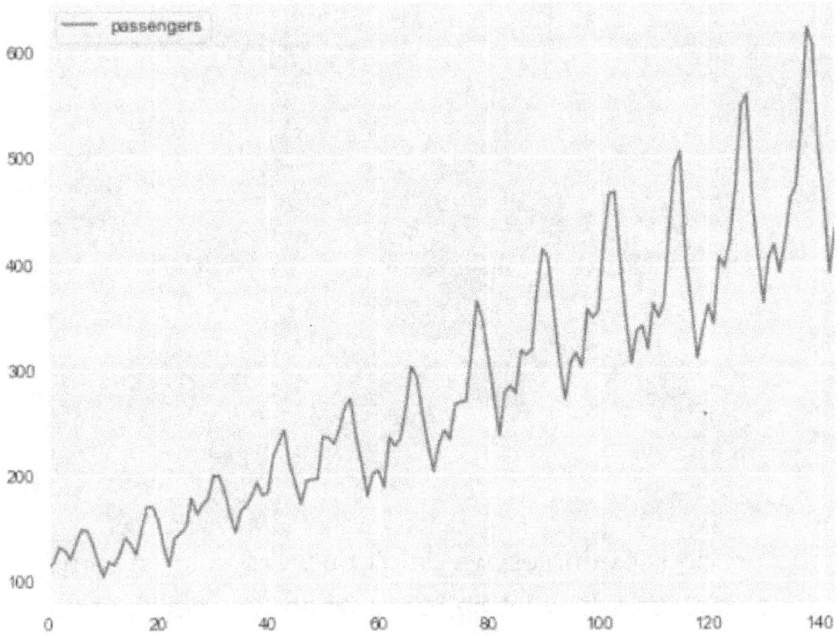

Similarly, you can change the color of the line plot via the color attribute, as shown below.

Script 8:

```
flights_data.plot.line( y='passengers', figsize=(8,6), color
= 'orange')
```

Output:

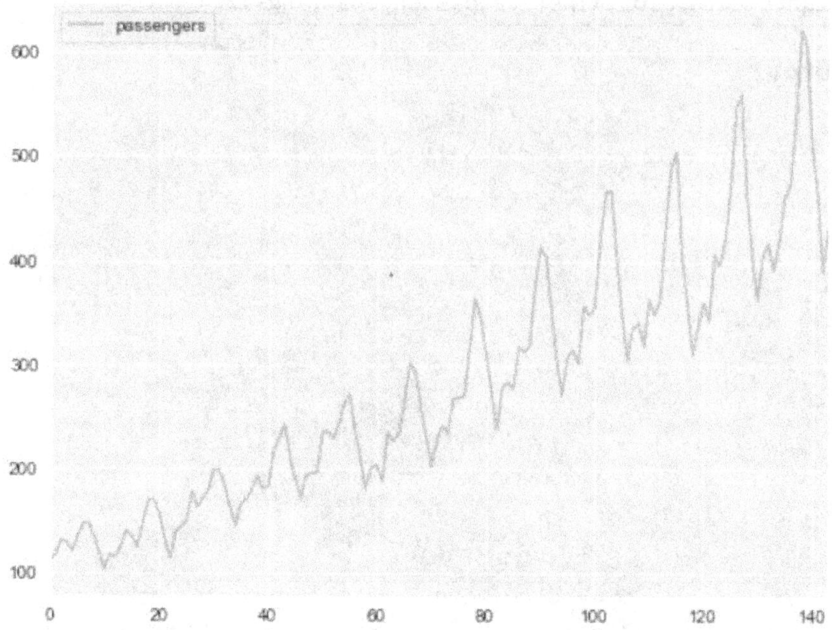

In the previous examples, we didn't pass the column name for the x-axis. Let's see what happens when we specify the year as the column name for the x-axis.

Script 9:

```
flights_data.plot.line(x ='year', y='passengers',
figsize=(8,6), color = 'orange')
```

Output:

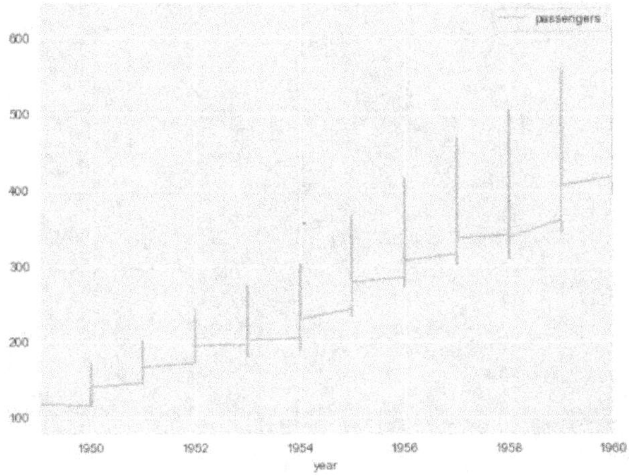

The output shows that for each year, we have multiple values. This is because each year has 12 months. However, the overall trend remains the same and the number of passengers traveling by air increases as the years pass.

Further Readings – Pandas Line Plots [2]

To study more about Pandas line plots, please check Pandas' official documentation for line plots. Try to execute the line() method with a different set of attributes, as mentioned in the official documentation.

7.5. Pandas Scatter Plots

To plot scatter plots with Pandas, the **scatter()** function is used. The following script plots a scatter plot containing the year on the x-axis, and the number of passengers on the y-axis.

Script 10:

```
flights_data.plot.scatter(x='year', y='passengers',
figsize=(8,6))
```

Output:

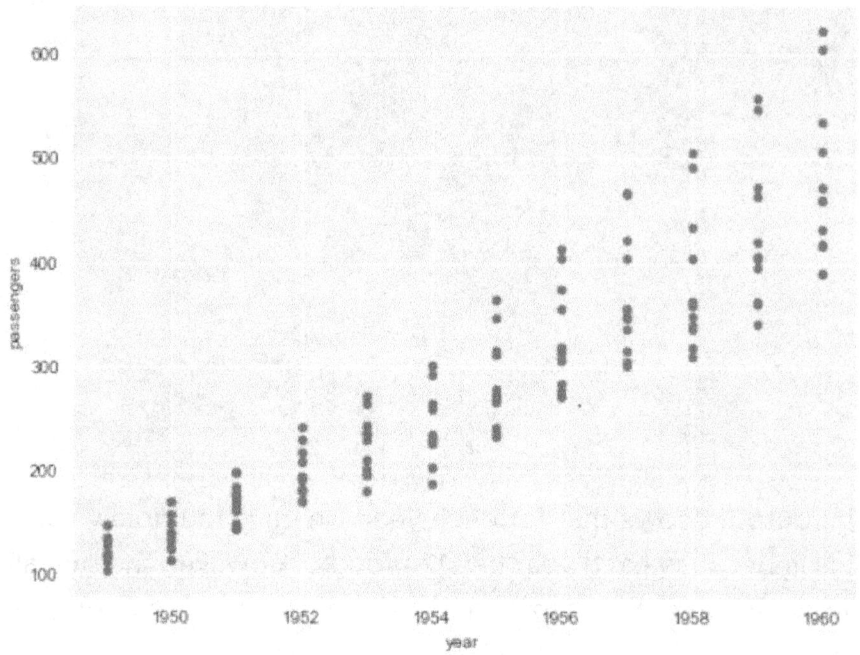

Like a line plot and histogram, you can also change the color of a scatter plot by passing the color name as the value for the color attribute. Look at the following script.

Script 11:

```
flights_data.plot.scatter(x='year', y='passengers',
color='red', figsize=(8,6))
```

Output:

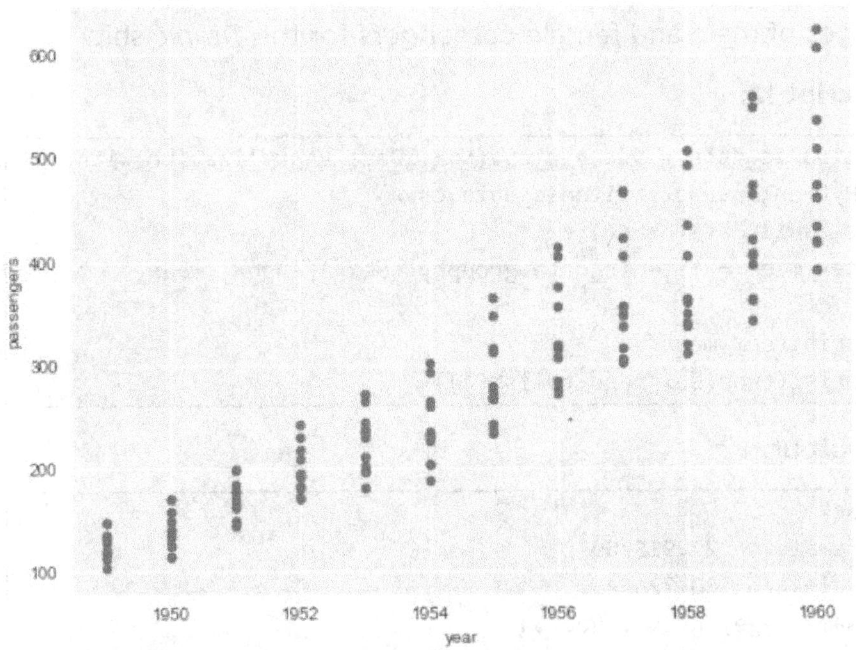

Further Readings – Pandas Scatter Plots [3]

To study more about Pandas scatter plots, please check Pandas' official documentation for scatter plots. Try to execute the scatter() method with a different set of attributes, as mentioned in the official documentation.

7.6. Pandas Bar Plots

To plot bar plots with Pandas, you need a list of categories and a list of values. This list of categories and the list of values must have the same length. Let's plot a bar plot that shows the average age of male and female passengers.

To do so, first, we need to calculate the mean age of both male and female passengers traveling in the unfortunate Titanic ship. The **groupby()** method of the Pandas dataframe can be used to apply aggregate function with respect to categorical columns. The following script returns the mean values for the ages of male and female passengers for the *Titanic* ship.

Script 12:

```
titanic_data = pd.read_csv(r»E:\Data Visualization with
Python\Datasets\titanic_data.csv»)
titanic_data.head()
sex_mean = titanic_data.groupby(«Sex»)[«Age»].mean()

print(sex_mean)
print(type(sex_mean.tolist()))
```

Output:

```
Sex
female    27.915709
male      30.726645
Name: Age, dtype: float64
<class 'list'>
```

Next, we need to create a new Pandas dataframe with two columns: Gender and Age. Then, we can simply use the **bar()** method to plot a bar plot that displays the average ages of male and female passengers for the *Titanic* ship.

Script 13:

```
df = pd.DataFrame({'Gender':['Female', 'Male'], 'Age':sex_
mean.tolist()})
ax = df.plot.bar(x='Gender', y='Age', figsize=(8,6))
```

Output:

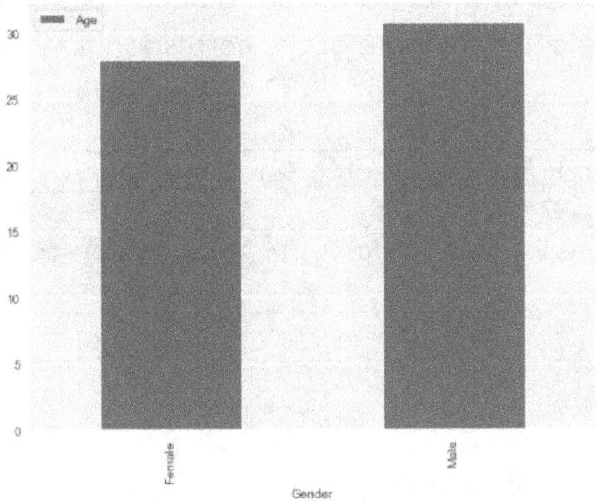

You can also plot horizontal bar plots via the Pandas library. To do so, you need to call the **barh()** function, as shown in the following example.

Script 14:

```
df = pd.DataFrame({'Gender':['Female', 'Male'], 'Age':sex_
mean.tolist()})
ax = df.plot.barh(x='Gender', y='Age', figsize=(8,6))
```

Output:

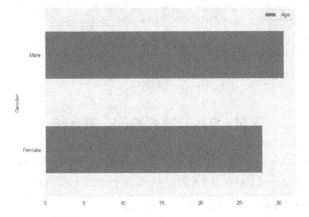

Finally, like all the other Pandas plots, you can change the color of both vertical and horizontal bar plots by passing the color name to the color attribute of the corresponding function.

Script 15:

```
df = pd.DataFrame({'Gender':['Female', 'Male'], 'Age':sex_
mean.tolist()})
ax = df.plot.barh(x='Gender', y='Age', figsize=(8,6), color
= 'orange')
```

Output:

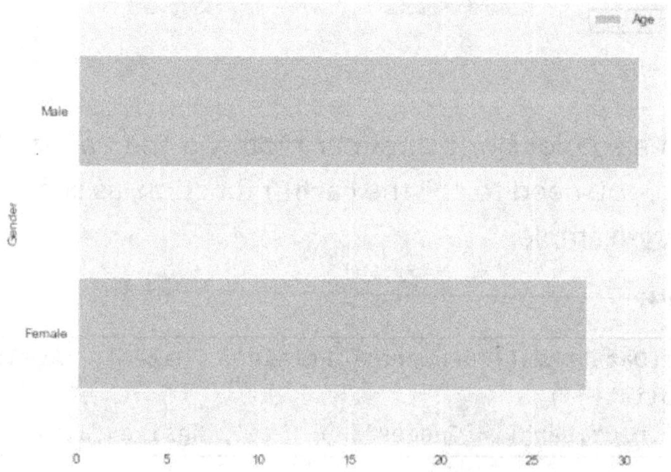

Further Readings – Pandas Bar Plots [4]

To study more about Pandas bar plots, please check Pandas' official documentation for bar plots. Try to execute the bar plot methods with a different set of attributes, as mentioned in the official documentation.

7.7. Pandas Box Plots

To plot box plots via the Pandas library, you need to call the **box()** function. The following script plots box plots for all the numeric columns in the Titanic dataset.

Script 16:

```
titanic_data = pd.read_csv(r»E:\Data Visualization with
Python\Datasets\titanic_data.csv»)
titanic_data.plot.box(figsize=(10,8))
```

Output:

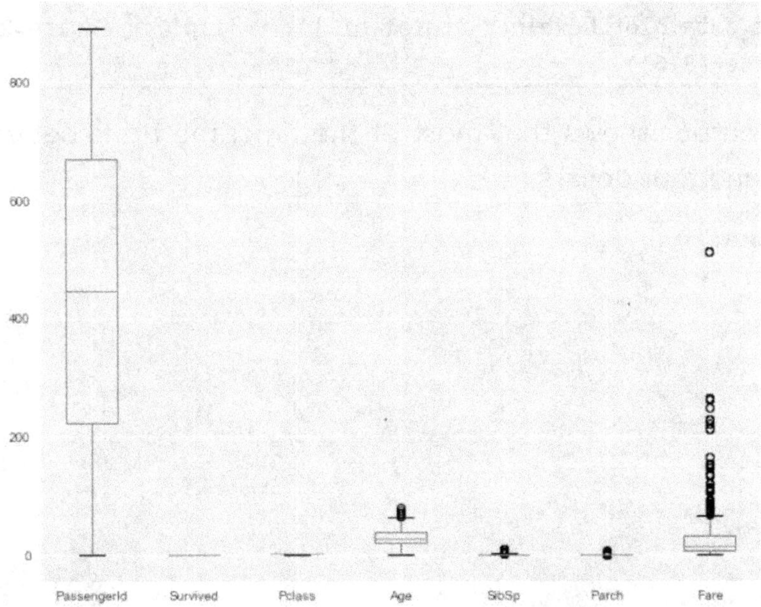

Further Readings – Pandas Box Plots [5]

To study more about Pandas box plots, please check Pandas' official documentation for box plots. Try to execute the box plot methods with a different set of attributes, as mentioned in the official documentation.

7.8. Pandas Hexagonal Plots

Hexagonal plots are used to plot the density of occurrence of values for a specific column. The hexagonal plots will be explained with the help of the **tips** dataset. The following script loads the **tips** dataset from the Seaborn library and then plots a hexagonal plot that shows values from the **total_bill** column on the x-axis and values from the **tip** column on the y-axis.

Script 17:

```
tips_data = sns.load_dataset('tips')

tips_data.plot.hexbin(x='total_bill', y='tip', gridsize=20, figsize=(8,6))
```

The output shows that most of the time, the tip is between two and four dollars.

Output:

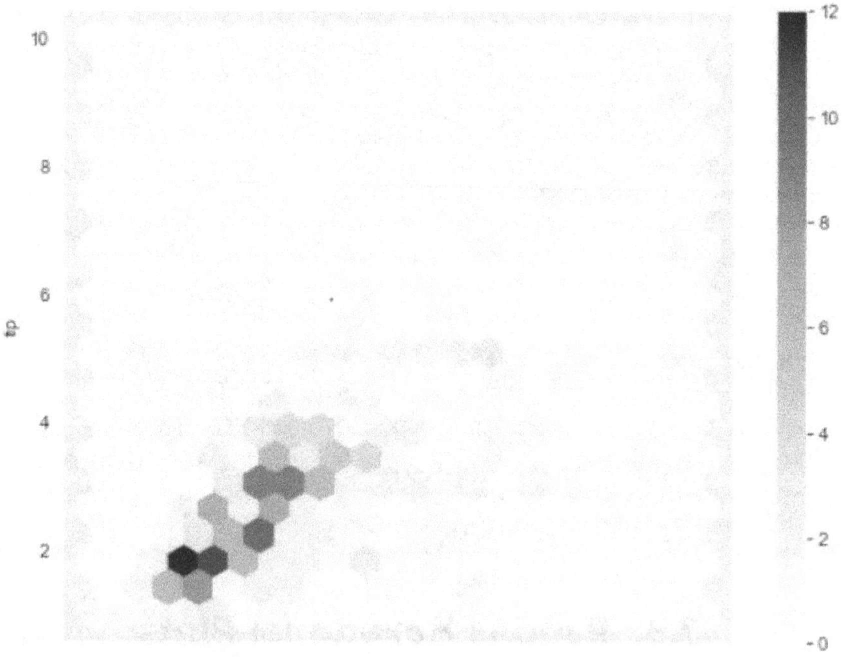

As always, you can change the color of the hexagonal plot by specifying the color name for the color attribute, as shown below.

Script 18:

```
tips_data.plot.hexbin(x='total_bill', y='tip', gridsize=20,
figsize=(8,6), color = 'blue')
```

Output:

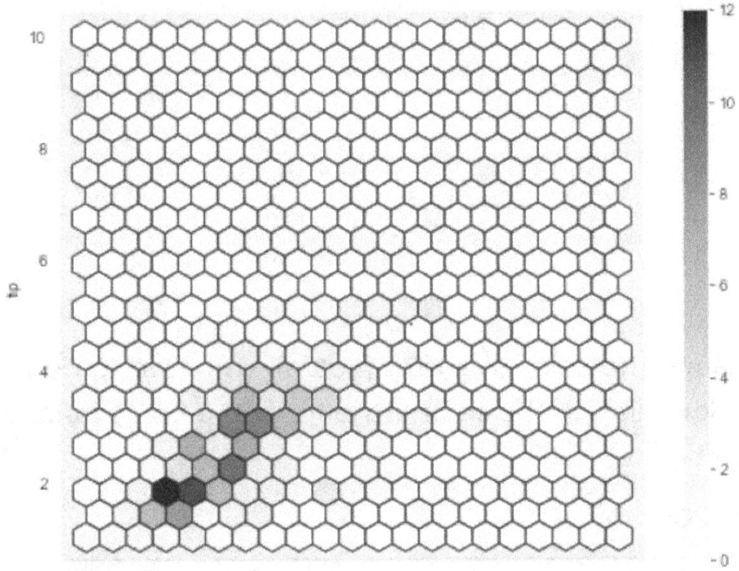

Further Readings - Pandas Hexagonal Plots [6]

To study more about the Pandas hexagonal plots, please check Pandas' official documentation for hexagonal plots. Try to execute the hexagonal plot methods with a different set of attributes, as mentioned in the official documentation.

7.9. Pandas Kernel Density Plots

You can also plot Kernel Density Estimation plots with the help of the Pandas **kde()** function. The following script plots a KDE for the tip column of the **tips** dataset.

Script 19:

```
tips_data.plot.kde( y='tip',  figsize=(8,6), color = 'blue')
```

Output:

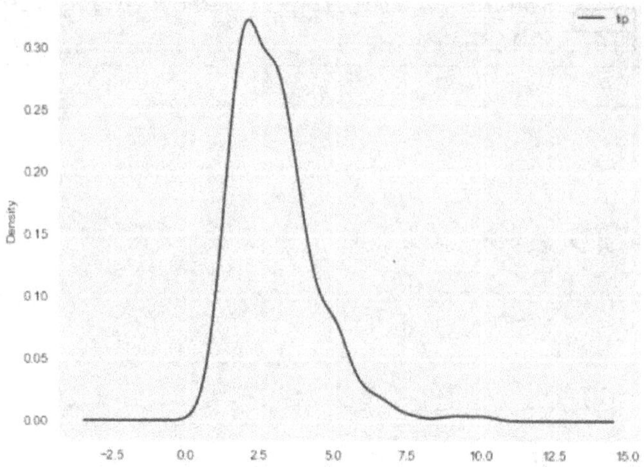

To change the color of a KDE plot, all you have to do is pass the color name to the color attribute of the **kde()** function, as shown below.

Script 20:

```
tips_data.plot.kde( y='total_bill',  figsize=(8,6), color =
'red')
```

Output:

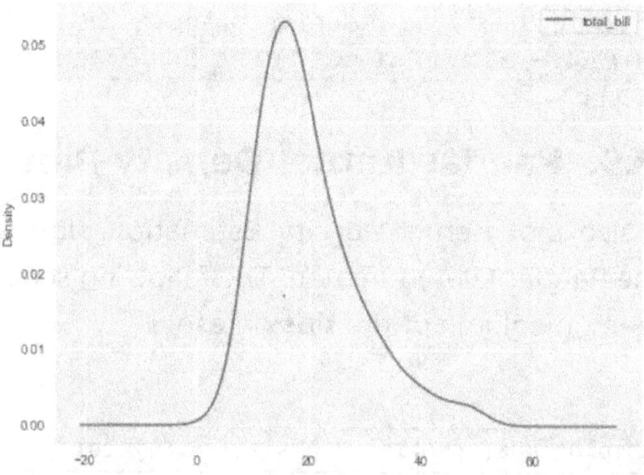

Further Readings – Pandas KDE Plots [7]

To study more about Pandas KDE plots, please check Pandas' official documentation for KDE plots. Try to execute the kde plot methods with a different set of attributes, as mentioned in the official documentation.

7.10. Pandas for Time Series Data Visualization

Pandas library also contains some useful methods that can be used to visualize time series data. Time series data is a type of data that is dependent on time and changes with time. For instance, hourly temperature for a specific place changes after every hour and is dependent upon time.

In this section, you will see how to plot time series data with Pandas. You will work with Google Stock Price data from 7thJanuary 2015 to 7th January 2020. The dataset is available in the *resources* folder by the name **google_data.csv**. The following script reads the data into a Pandas dataframe.

Script 21:

```
google_stock = pd.read_csv(r»E:\Data Visualization with
Python\Datasets\google_data.csv»)
google_stock.head()
```

Output:

	Date	Open	High	Low	Close	Adj Close	Volume
0	2015-01-06	513.589966	514.761719	499.678131	500.585632	500.585632	2899900
1	2015-01-07	505.611847	505.855164	498.281952	499.727997	499.727997	2065000
2	2015-01-08	496.626526	502.101471	489.655640	501.303680	501.303680	3353500
3	2015-01-09	503.377991	503.537537	493.435272	494.811493	494.811493	2071300
4	2015-01-12	493.584869	494.618011	486.225067	491.201416	491.201416	2326700

If you look at the dataset header, the index column by default is the left-most column. If we plot a line plot, the x-axis will use the index column to plot a line plot. However, we want to plot stock prices with respect to date. To do so, we first need to set the date as the index column. The date column currently contains dates in a string format.

We first need to convert values in the date column to date format. We can use **pd.to_datetime()** function for that purpose. Next, to set the Date column as the index column, we can use the **set_index()** function, as shown below. Next, we can simply use the **line()** function and pass the column name to visualize the y parameter. The following script prints the opening stock prices of Google stock over a period of five years.

Script 22:

```
google_stock['Date'] = google_stock['Date'].apply(pd.to_
datetime)
google_stock.set_index('Date', inplace=True)
google_stock.plot.line( y='Open', figsize=(12,8))
```

Output:

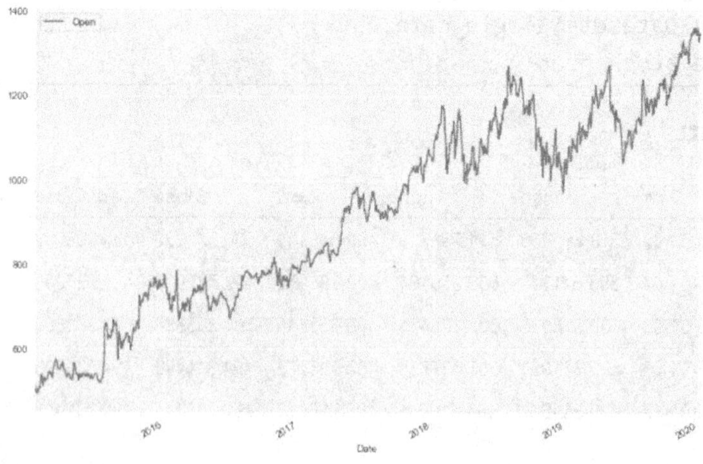

In the next two sections, we will see how to perform time sampling and time shifting with time series data.

7.10.1. Time Sampling with Pandas

Time sampling refers to grouping data over a certain period of time using an aggregate function such as min, max, count, mean, etc. To do resampling, you have to use the **resample()** function. The time frame is passed to the **rule** attribute of the **resample()** function. Finally, you have to append the aggregate function at the end of the **resample()** function. The following script shows the average values for all the columns of Google stock data, grouped by year. In the output, you can see five rows since our data set contains five years of Google stock prices. Here, we pass A as the value for the **rule** attribute, which refers to yearly data.

Script 23:

```
google_stock.resample(rule='A').mean()
```

Output:

	Open	High	Low	Close	Adj Close	Volume
Date						
2015-12-31	602.676217	608.091468	596.722047	602.678382	602.678382	2.071960e+06
2016-12-31	743.732459	749.421629	737.597905	743.486707	743.486707	1.832266e+06
2017-12-31	921.121193	926.898963	915.331412	921.780837	921.780837	1.476514e+06
2018-12-31	1113.554101	1125.777606	1101.001658	1113.225134	1113.225134	1.741965e+06
2019-12-31	1187.009821	1196.787599	1178.523734	1188.393057	1188.393057	1.414085e+06
2020-12-31	1346.470011	1379.046672	1345.697998	1374.079997	1374.079997	1.441767e+06

Similarly, to plot the monthly mean values for all the columns in the Google stock dataset, you will need to pass **M** as a value for the **rule** attribute, as shown below.

Script 24:

```
google_stock.resample(rule='M').mean()
```

Output:

Date	Open	High	Low	Close	Adj Close	Volume
2015-01-31	510.388728	515.352041	503.988300	510.248006	510.248006	2.595550e+06
2015-02-28	534.448454	540.111910	530.943141	536.519088	536.519088	1.715495e+06
2015-03-31	558.825290	562.627577	554.057018	558.183871	558.183871	1.756709e+06
2015-04-30	539.966811	543.839108	535.114912	539.304467	539.304467	2.017938e+06
2015-05-31	535.470502	539.167248	530.856650	535.238998	535.238998	1.593295e+06
...	...	...	...	...	...	...
2019-09-30	1217.599005	1228.892249	1209.628491	1220.839520	1220.839520	1.344970e+06
2019-10-31	1230.809995	1242.260774	1223.923043	1232.711744	1232.711744	1.250361e+06
2019-11-30	1302.348492	1311.498956	1296.424707	1304.278992	1304.278992	1.246170e+06
2019-12-31	1340.861415	1348.178531	1334.039190	1340.867635	1340.867635	1.302719e+06
2020-01-31	1346.470011	1379.046672	1345.697998	1374.079997	1374.079997	1.441767e+06

61 rows × 6 columns

In addition to aggregate values for all the columns, you can resample data with respect to a single column. For instance, the following script prints the yearly mean values for the opening stock prices of Google stock over a period of five years.

Script 25:

```
google_stock['Open'].resample('A').mean()
```

Output:

```
Date
2015-12-31     602.676217
2016-12-31     743.732459
2017-12-31     921.121193
2018-12-31    1113.554101
2019-12-31    1187.009821
2020-12-31    1346.470011
Freq: A-DEC, Name: Open, dtype: float64
```

The list of possible values for the rule attribute is given below:

B	business day frequency
C	custom business day frequency (experimental)
D	calendar day frequency
W	weekly frequency
M	month end frequency
SM	semi-month end frequency (15th and end of the month)
BM	business month end frequency
CBM	custom business month end frequency
MS	month start frequency
SMS	semi-month start frequency (1st and 15th)
BMS	business month start frequency
CBMS	custom business month start frequency
Q	quarter end frequency
BQ	business quarter end frequency
QS	quarter start frequency
BQS	business quarter start frequency
A	year end frequency
BA	business year end frequency
AS	year start frequency
BAS	business year start frequency

BH	business hour frequency
H	hourly frequency
T	minutely frequency
S	secondly frequency
L	milliseonds
U	microseconds
N	nanoseconds

You can also append plot functions with the **resample()** function in order to plot the different types of plot based on aggregate values. For instance, the following script plots a bar plot for the opening stock price of Google over a period of five years.

Script 26:

```
google_stock['Open'].resample('A').mean().plot(kind='bar',
figsize=(8,6))
```

Output:

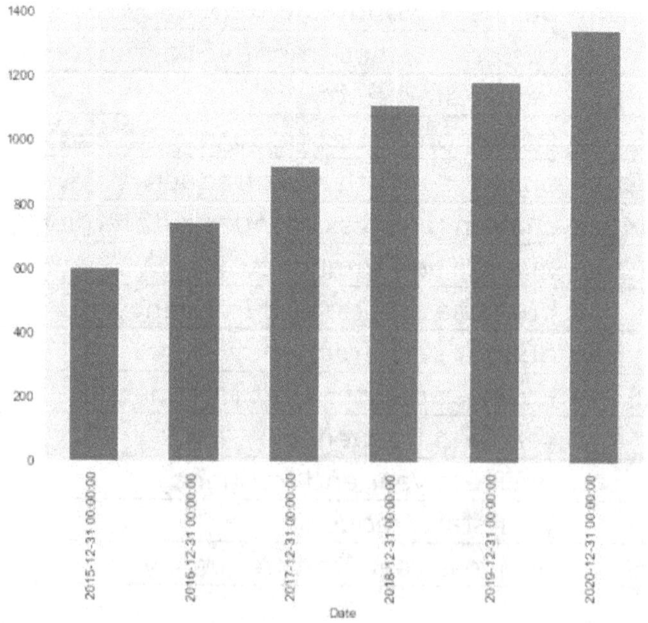

Similarly, here is the line plot for the yearly mean opening stock prices for Google stock over a period of five years.

Script 27:

```
google_stock['Open'].resample('A').mean().plot(kind='line',
figsize=(8,6))
```

Output:

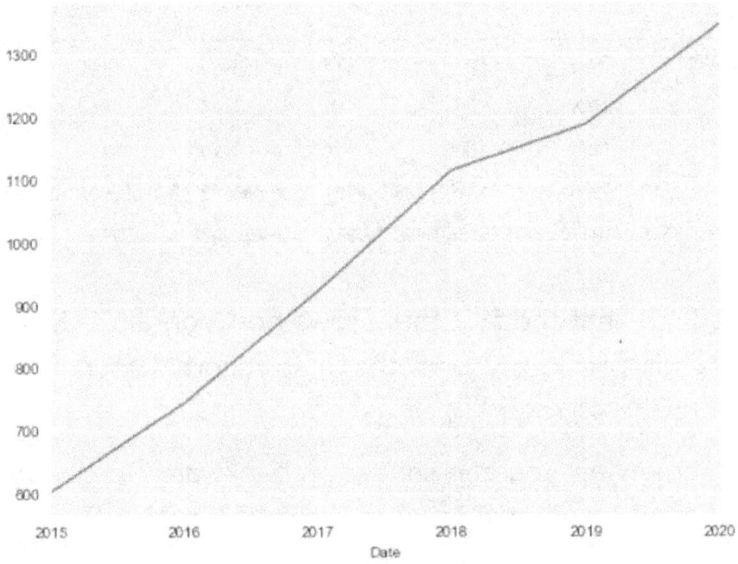

Further Readings - Pandas Resample Method [8]

To study more about the Pandas time sampling functions for time series data analysis, please check Pandas' official documentation for the resample function. Try to execute the time resample() method with a different set of attributes, as mentioned in the official documentation.

7.10.2. Time Shifting with Pandas

Time shifting refers to shifting rows forward or backward. To shift rows forward, you can use the **shift()** function and pass it a positive value. For instance, the following script shifts records three rows ahead and prints the header of the dataset.

Script 28:

```
google_stock.shift(3).head()
```

Output:

Date	Open	High	Low	Close	Adj Close	Volume
2015-01-06	NaN	NaN	NaN	NaN	NaN	NaN
2015-01-07	NaN	NaN	NaN	NaN	NaN	NaN
2015-01-08	NaN	NaN	NaN	NaN	NaN	NaN
2015-01-09	513.589966	514.761719	499.678131	500.585632	500.585632	2899900.0
2015-01-12	505.611847	505.855164	498.281952	499.727997	499.727997	2065000.0

You can see that the first three rows now contain null values, while what previously was the first record has now been shifted to the 4th row.

In the same way, you can shift rows backward. To do so, you have to pass a negative value to the shift function.

Script 29:

```
google_stock.shift(-3).tail()
```

Output:

Date	Open	High	Low	Close	Adj Close	Volume
2019-12-30	1347.859985	1372.5	1345.543945	1360.660034	1360.660034	1186400.0
2019-12-31	1350.000000	1396.5	1350.000000	1394.209961	1394.209961	1732300.0
2020-01-02	NaN	NaN	NaN	NaN	NaN	NaN
2020-01-03	NaN	NaN	NaN	NaN	NaN	NaN
2020-01-06	NaN	NaN	NaN	NaN	NaN	NaN

Further Readings - Pandas Shift Method [9]

To study more about the Pandas time shifting functions for time series data analysis, please check Pandas' official documentation for the shift() function. Try to execute the time shift() method with a different set of attributes, as mentioned in the official documentation.

Hands-on Time - Exercice

Now, it is your turn. Follow the instructions in **the exercises below** to check your understanding of the data visualization with the Pandas library. The answers to these questions are given at the end of the book.

Exercise 7.1

Question 1

Which attribute is used to change the color of the Pandas graph?

A- set_color()

B- define_color()

C- color()

D- None of the above

Question 2

Which Pandas function is used to plot a horizontal bar plot?

A- horz_bar()

B- barh()

C- bar_horizontal()

D- horizontal_bar()

Question 3

How to time shift Pandas dataframe five rows backward?

A - shift_back(5)
B - shift(5)
C - shift_behind(-5)
D - shift(-5)

Exercise 7.2

Display a bar plot using the Titanic dataset that displays the average age of the passengers who survived vs. those who did not survive.

References

1. https://pandas.pydata.org/pandas-docs/stable/reference/api/pandas.DataFrame.hist.html
2. https://pandas.pydata.org/pandas-docs/version/0.23/generated/pandas.DataFrame.plot.line.html
3. https://pandas.pydata.org/pandas-docs/stable/reference/api/pandas.DataFrame.plot.scatter.html
4. https://pandas.pydata.org/pandas-docs/stable/reference/api/pandas.DataFrame.plot.bar.html
5. https://pandas.pydata.org/pandas-docs/stable/reference/api/pandas.DataFrame.boxplot.html
6. https://pandas.pydata.org/pandas-docs/stable/reference/api/pandas.DataFrame.plot.hexbin.html
7. https://pandas.pydata.org/pandas-docs/stable/reference/api/pandas.DataFrame.plot.kde.html
8. https://pandas.pydata.org/pandas-docs/stable/reference/api/pandas.Series.resample.html
9. https://pandas.pydata.org/pandas-docs/stable/reference/api/pandas.DataFrame.shift.html

8

3D Plotting with Matplotlib

In the second and third chapters of this book, you saw how the Matplotlib library can be used to plot two-dimensional (2D) plots. In fact, in all the previous chapters, you saw how to plot 2D plots with different Python libraries. In this chapter, you will briefly see how the Matplotlib library can be used to plot 3D plots.

Requirements – Anaconda, Jupyter, Matplotlib, and Pandas

- All the scripts in this book have been executed via the Jupyter notebook. Therefore, you should have the Jupyter notebook installed.
- It goes without saying that we will be using the Matplotlib library.
- The Numpy and Pandas libraries should also be installed before this chapter.

Hands-on Time – Source Codes

All IPython notebooks for the source code of all the scripts in this chapter can be found in Resources/Chapter 8.ipynb. I would suggest that you write all the code in this chapter yourself and see if you can get the same output as mentioned in this chapter.

8.1. 3D Line Plot

The first 3D plot that we are going to plot is the line plot. To plot a 3D plot, you do not need to install any external library as the Matplotlib library provides support for plotting 3D plots. All you have to do is import **axes3d** class from the **mpl_toolkits.mplot3d library**. Next, you simply have to import the **pyplot** module from Matplotlib. Also, make sure that you execute the **%matplotlib notebook** command because that will plot your 3D plot inside the Jupyter notebook.

To actually plot a graph, you have to create a **figure** object. Next, you add an axis to the figure object by calling the **add_subplot()** method. Finally, to plot 3D plots, you pass the three list of items to the **plot()** function of the axis object. The following script plots a line plot for the x, y, z lists that contain random integers from 1 to 10.

Script 1:

```
from mpl_toolkits.mplot3d import axes3d
import matplotlib.pyplot as plt
%matplotlib notebook


figure1 = plt.figure()
axis1 = figure1.add_subplot( projection='3d')

x = [1,7,6,3,2,4,9,8,1,9]
y = [4,6,1,8,3,7,9,1,2,4]
z = [6,4,9,2,7,8,1,3,4,9]
```

```
axis1.plot(x,y,z)

axis1.set_xlabel('X-axis')
axis1.set_ylabel('Y-axis')
axis1.set_zlabel('Z-axis')

plt.show()
```

Output:

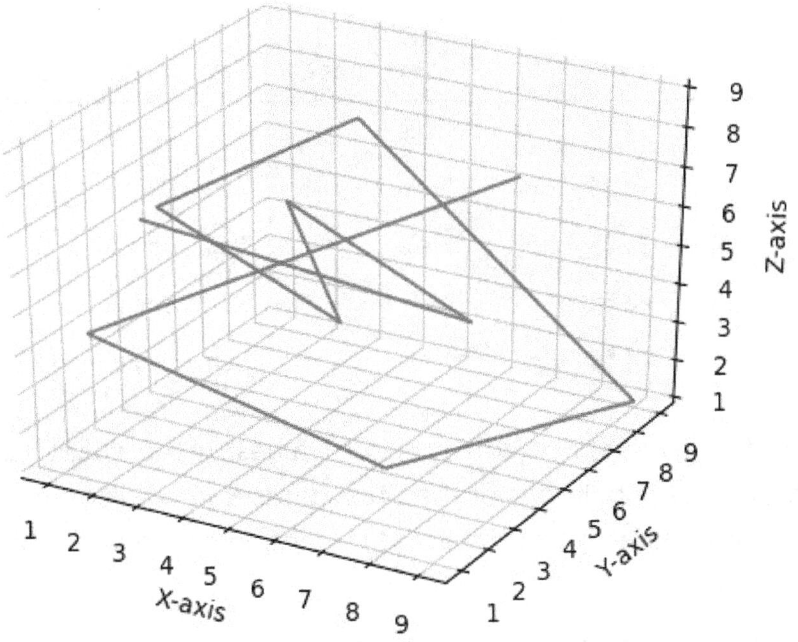

In the previous section, we plotted a 3D plot with random integers. Let's now plot a 3D line plot that shows the relationship between the values in the **total_bill, tip**, and **size** columns of the **tips** dataset.

Script 2:

```
import seaborn as sns

plt.rcParams[«figure.figsize»] = [10,8]

tips_data = sns.load_dataset('tips')

tips_data.head()
```

Output:

	total_bill	tip	sex	smoker	day	time	size
0	16.99	1.01	Female	No	Sun	Dinner	2
1	10.34	1.66	Male	No	Sun	Dinner	3
2	21.01	3.50	Male	No	Sun	Dinner	3
3	23.68	3.31	Male	No	Sun	Dinner	2
4	24.59	3.61	Female	No	Sun	Dinner	4

The following script converts the values in the `total_bill`, `tip`, and `size` columns of the **tips** dataset into a list of values that will be passed to the **`plot()`** function of the **axis** object.

Script 3:

```
bill = tips_data['total_bill'].tolist()
tip = tips_data['tip'].tolist()
size = tips_data['size'].tolist()
```

Finally, the following script plots a 3D line plot that shows the relationship between the total_bill, tip, and size columns of the **tips** dataset.

Script 4:

```
from mpl_toolkits.mplot3d import axes3d
import matplotlib.pyplot as plt
%matplotlib notebook


figure2 = plt.figure()
axis2 = figure2.add_subplot( projection='3d')


axis2.plot(bill,tip,size)

axis2.set_xlabel('bill')
axis2.set_ylabel('tip')
axis2.set_zlabel('size')

plt.show()
```

Output:

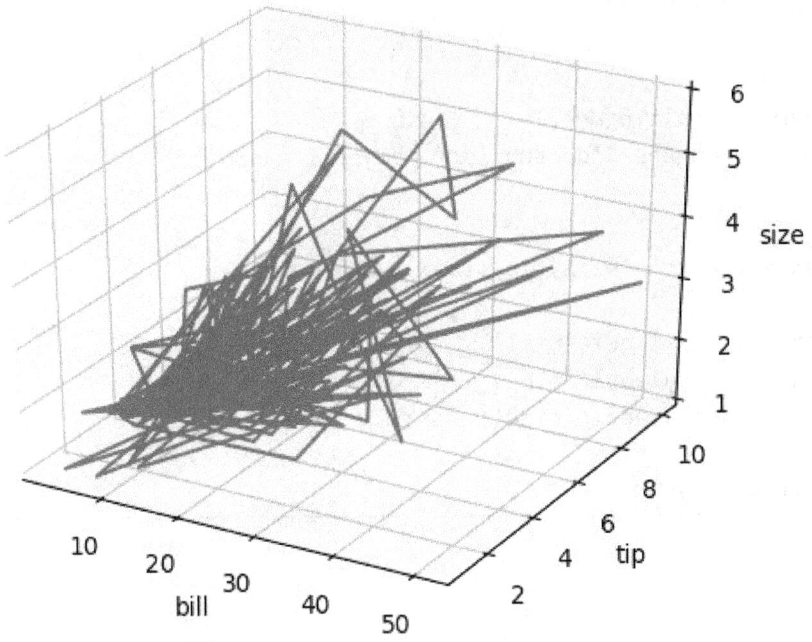

Further Readings - Matplotlib 3D Line Plot (1)

To study more about Matplotlib 3D line plot functions, please check Matplotlib's official documentation. Try to execute the plot() method with a different set of attributes, as mentioned in the official documentation.

8.2. 3D Scatter Plot

In the previous section, you saw how to plot a 3D line plot via the plot() function of the axis object. To plot a scatter plot, everything remains the same, except you use the scatter() function. The following script plots a scatter plot that shows the relationship between the `total_bill`, `tip`, and `size` columns of the **`tips`** dataset.

Script 5:

```
from mpl_toolkits.mplot3d import axes3d
import matplotlib.pyplot as plt
%matplotlib notebook


figure2 = plt.figure()
axis2 = figure2.add_subplot( projection='3d')


axis2.scatter(bill,tip,size)

axis2.set_xlabel('bill')
axis2.set_ylabel('tip')
axis2.set_zlabel('size')

plt.show()
```

Output:

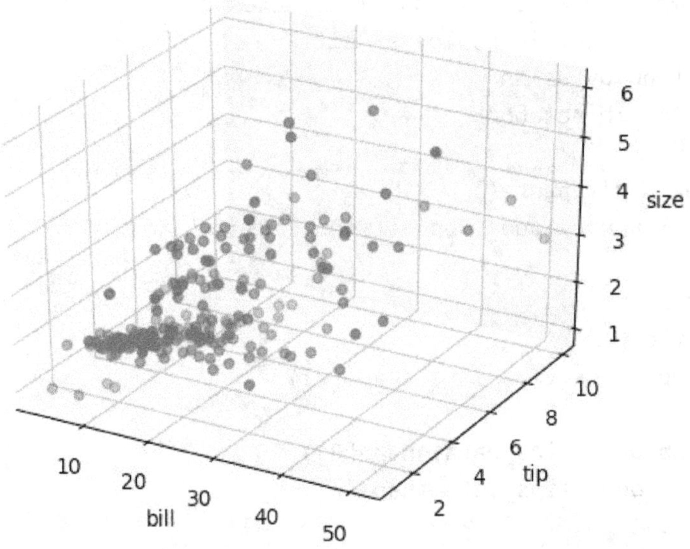

Further Readings - Matplotlib 3D Scatter Plot (2)

To study more about Matplotlib 3D scatter plot functions, please check Matplotlib's official documentation. Try to execute the scatter () method with a different set of attributes, as mentioned in the official documentation.

8.3. 3D Bar Plot

Finally, to plot a 3D bar plot, you have to use the bar3d function of the axis object, as shown below. The following script plots a bar plot displaying the relationship between the `total_bill` and `tip` columns of the **`tips`** dataset.

Script 6:

```
from mpl_toolkits.mplot3d import axes3d
import matplotlib.pyplot as plt
import numpy as np
%matplotlib notebook

figure2 = plt.figure()
axis3 = figure2.add_subplot( projection='3d')

x3 =bill
y3 = tip
z3 = np.zeros(tips_data.shape[0])

dx = np.ones(tips_data.shape[0])
dy = np.ones(tips_data.shape[0])
dz = bill

axis3.bar3d(x3, y3, z3, dx, dy, dz)

axis3.set_xlabel('bill')
axis3.set_ylabel('tip')
axis3.set_zlabel('size')

plt.show()
```

Output:

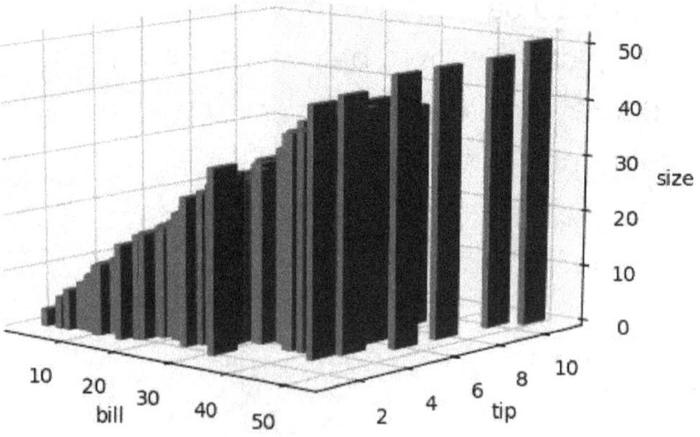

Further Readings - Matplotlib 3D Bar Plot (2)

To study more about Matplotlib 3D bar plot functions, please check Matplotlib's official documentation.

Further Readings - Matplotlib Remaining 3D Plots

To study more about Matplotlib 3D plot functions, please check Matplotlib's official documentation.

Hands-on Time - Exercice

Now, it is your turn. Follow the instructions in **the exercises below** to check your understanding of 3D data plotting with Matplotlib. The answers to these questions are given at the end of the book.

Exercise 8.1

Plot a scatter plot that shows the distribution of `pclass, age,` and `fare` columns from the Titanic dataset.

References

1. https://matplotlib.org/mpl_toolkits/mplot3d/tutorial.html#line-plots
2. https://matplotlib.org/mpl_toolkits/mplot3d/tutorial.html#scatter-plots
3. https://matplotlib.org/mpl_toolkits/mplot3d/tutorial.html#bar-plots

9

Interactive Data Visualization with Bokeh

In all the chapters till now, you have been plotting static graphs. In this chapter and the next one, you will see how to plot interactive graphs. Interactive graphs are the type of graphs that show different information based on the actions performed by the users. In this chapter, you will see how to plot interactive plots with Python's Bokeh library. In the next chapter, you will see how to plot interactive plots with Plotly.

9.1. Installation

Use the pip installer to install the Bokeh library. To do so, execute the following command on your command line.

```
$ pip install bokeh
```

Requirements – Anaconda, Jupyter, Matplotlib, Pandas

- All the scripts in this book have been executed via the Jupyter notebook. Therefore, you should have the Jupyter notebook installed.
- Needless to say, we will be using the Matplotlib library.
- The Numpy and Pandas libraries should also be installed before this chapter.

Hands-on Time – Source Codes

All IPython notebooks for the source code of all the scripts in this chapter can be found in Resources/Chapter 9.ipynb. I would suggest that you write all the code in this chapter yourself and see if you can get the same output as mentioned in this chapter.

9.2. Line Plots

The first plot that we are going to plot using the Bokeh library is the line plot that displays the number of passengers traveling between 1949 and 1960. The following script imports the dataset.

Script 1:

```
import pandas as pd
import numpy as np
%matplotlib inline
import seaborn as sns

flights_data = sns.load_dataset('flights')

flights_data.head()
```

Output:

	year	month	passengers
0	1949	January	112
1	1949	February	118
2	1949	March	132
3	1949	April	129
4	1949	May	121

Next, to plot a line plot, we have to first create an object of the **figure** class. The following script imports the classes required to plot the Bokeh plots.

Script 2:

```
from bokeh.plotting import figure, output_file, show
```

A bokeh plot is stored locally on your hard drive. To specify the path where the plot will be stored, you need to call the **output_file()** method and pass it the file location.

Script 3:

```
output_file('E:/bokeh.html')
```

Finally, to create a plot, you have to first create an object of the **figure()** class. The **figure()** class is used to set the title, the x and y labels, and the width and height of the plot. Execute the following script to create a figure class object.

Script 4:

```
plot = figure(
  title = 'Years vs Passengers',
  x_axis_label ='Year',
  y_axis_label ='Passengers',
  plot_width=600,
  plot_height=400
)
```

Next, you need data sources that you will use to plot a graph. We will be plotting the year against the number of passengers.

Script 5:

```
year = flights_data['year']
passengers = flights_data['passengers']
```

Finally, to create a line plot, you have to pass the list of values for the x- and y-axis to the **line()** function of the **figure** class object. The **line_width** attribute here is used to set the width of the line.

Script 6:

```
plot.line(year,passengers, legend='Years vs Passengers',
line_width=2)
```

At this point in time, the plot has been created and saved. However, to display the plot, you have to call the **show()** method, as shown below.

Script 7:

```
show(plot)
```

Once the above method is executed, you will see that an interactive line plot will be populated inside your default browser.

Output:

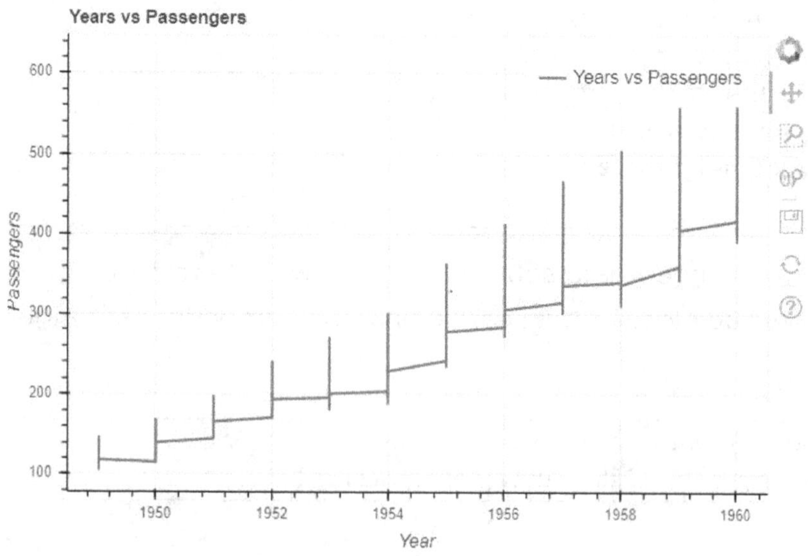

Further Readings - Bokeh Line Plot (1)

To study more about Bokeh's line plot functions, please check Bokeh's official documentation for line()function. Try to execute the line() method with a different set of attributes, as mentioned in the official documentation.

9.3. Bar Plots

To plot bar plots with Bokeh, you need a list of categorical values for each bar plot and the corresponding numerical values that will represent the height of the bar plot. The following script returns all the month names in the flights data along with the number of passengers traveling each month.

Script 8:

```
month_passengers = flights_data.groupby(«month»)
[«passengers»].mean()
print(month_passengers.index.tolist())
print(month_passengers.tolist())
```

Output:

```
['January', 'February', 'March', 'April', 'May', 'June',
'July', 'August', 'September', 'October', 'November',
'December']
[241.75, 235.0, 270.1666666666667, 267.0833333333333,
271.8333333333333, 311.6666666666667, 351.3333333333333,
351.0833333333333, 302.4166666666667, 266.5833333333333,
232.83333333333334, 261.8333333333333]
```

The **month_passengers** variable is a series where the index names correspond to the month names, and the corresponding values represent the number of total passengers traveling that month. Next, you need to create a **figure()** object and pass the index names, i.e., the names of the month to the **x_range** attribute.

Script 9:

```
plot2 = figure(
  x_range = month_passengers.index.tolist(),
  title = 'Month vs Passengers',
  x_axis_label ='Month',
  y_axis_label ='Passengers',
  plot_height=400
)
```

Finally, you need to call the **vbar()** method to actually plot a vertical bar plot. The first parameter should be the month names, and the second parameter should be the numeric values representing the number of passengers traveling during that month.

Script 10:

```
plot2.vbar(x = month_passengers.index.tolist() , top =
month_passengers.tolist(), legend='Months vs Passengers',
width = 0.7)
show(plot2)
```

The output clearly shows that the highest number of passengers traveled during the months of July and August. The holiday season might be the reason behind the surge in the number of passengers traveling during these months.

Output:

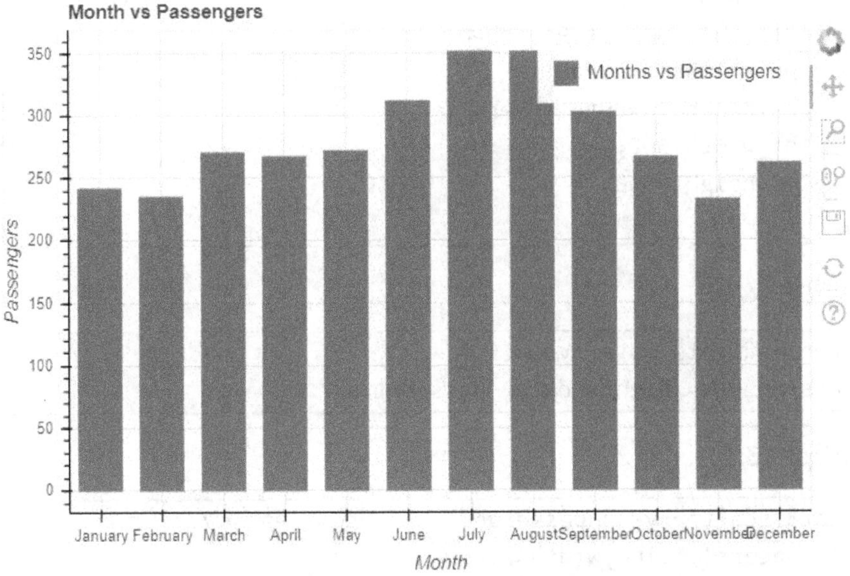

Further Readings – Bokeh Vertical Bar Plot (2)

To study more about Bokeh's vertical bar plot function, please check Bokeh's official documentation for the vbar() plot. Try to execute the vbar() method with a different set of attributes, as mentioned in the official documentation. For a horizontal bar, you can execute the hbar() function.

9.4. Scatter Plots

To plot a scatter via Bokeh, you need to call the **scatter()** function of the **figure** object. The following script plots a scatter plot that shows years on the x-axis and the number of passengers traveling in that year on the y-axis.

Script 11:

```
plot3 = figure(
  title = 'Years vs Passengers',
  x_axis_label ='Year',
  y_axis_label ='Passengers',
  plot_width=600,
  plot_height=400
)
```

Script 12:

```
year = flights_data['year']
passengers = flights_data['passengers']
```

Script 13:

```
plot3.scatter(year,passengers, legend='Years vs
Passengers', line_width=2)
show(plot3)
```

Output:

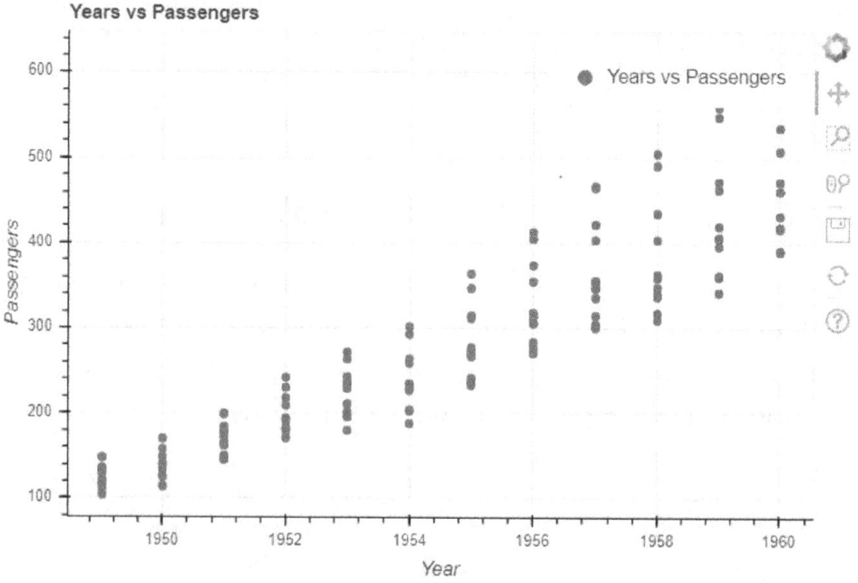

Let's plot another scatter plot using the **tips** dataset. The scatter plot shows the values from the **total_bill** column on the x-axis and the **tips** on the y-axis. The following script loads the **tips** dataset.

Script 14:

```
import seaborn as sns

tips_data = sns.load_dataset('tips')

tips_data.head()
```

Output:

	total_bill	tip	sex	smoker	day	time	size
0	16.99	1.01	Female	No	Sun	Dinner	2
1	10.34	1.66	Male	No	Sun	Dinner	3
2	21.01	3.50	Male	No	Sun	Dinner	3
3	23.68	3.31	Male	No	Sun	Dinner	2
4	24.59	3.61	Female	No	Sun	Dinner	4

And the following script plots a scatter plot showing the distribution of **total_bill** vs. **tips**.

Script 14:

```
plot4 = figure(
  title = 'Total Bill vs Tips',
  x_axis_label ='Totall Bill',
  y_axis_label ='Tips',
  plot_width=600,
  plot_height=400
)
```

Script 15:

```
total_bill = tips_data['total_bill']
tips = tips_data['tip']
```

Script 16:

```
plot4.scatter(total_bill, tips, legend='Total Bill vs Tip', 
line_width=2)
show(plot4)
```

Output:

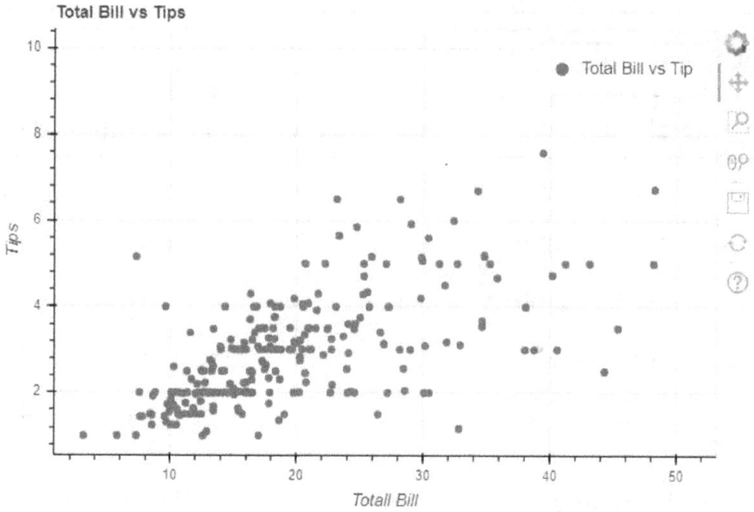

Another way to plot a scatter plot is via the circle() function of the figure object, as shown.

Script 17:

```
plot5 = figure(
  title = 'Total Bill vs Tips',
  x_axis_label ='Totall Bill',
  y_axis_label ='Tips',
  plot_width=600,
  plot_height=400
)
```

The sizes of the circle points on a scatter plot can be controlled by the radius attribute.

Script 18:

```
plot5.circle(total_bill, tips, radius = 0.5)
show(plot5)
```

Output:

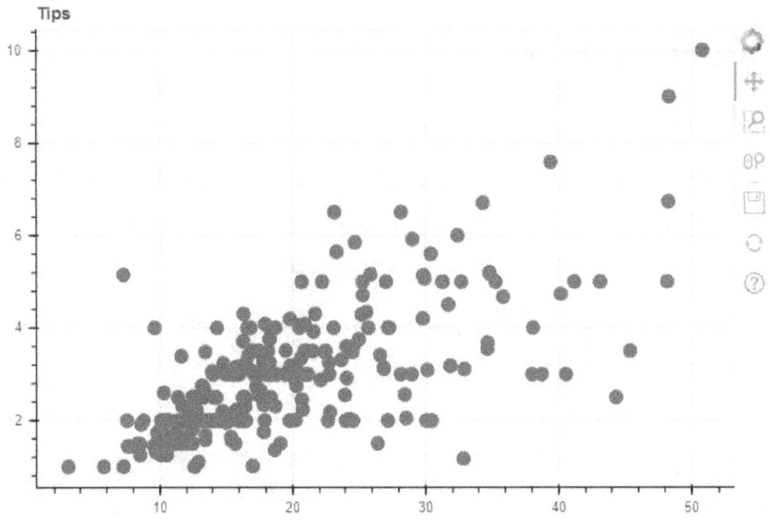

In this chapter, you saw how to plot interactive plots via the Bokeh library. In the next chapter, you will see how to plot interactive plots via the Plotly library, which is yet another useful library for interactive data plotting.

Further Readings - Bokeh Scatter Plot (3)

To study more about Bokeh's scatter plot function, please check Bokeh's official documentation for the circle()plot. Try to execute the circle () method with a different set of attributes, as mentioned in the official documentation.

Exercise 9.1

Question 1

Which object is used to set the width and height of a plot in Bokeh?

A- figure()

B- width()

C- height()

D- None of the above

Question 2

Which attribute is used to set the width of the line in a line plot in Bokeh?

A- line

B- width

C- line_width

D- length

Question 3

In the Bokeh library, the list of values used to plot bar plots is passed to the following attribute of the bar plot:

A- values

B- legends

C- y

D- top

Exercise 9.2

Plot a bar plot using the Titanic dataset that displays the average age of both male and female passengers.

References

1. https://docs.bokeh.org/en/latest/docs/reference/plotting.html#bokeh.plotting.figure.Figure.line
2. https://docs.bokeh.org/en/latest/docs/reference/plotting.html#bokeh.plotting.figure.Figure.vbar
3. https://docs.bokeh.org/en/latest/docs/reference/plotting.html#bokeh.plotting.figure.Figure.circle

10

Interactive Data Visualization with Plotly

In the previous chapter, you saw how to plot interactive plots with the Bokeh library. In this chapter, you will see how to plot interactive plots with Python's Plotly library. Plotly is an interactive Python platform where the user can interact with plots. An interactive plot is a plot that changes according to the actions performed by a user such as a mouse hover, mouse click, keyboard button presses, etc. Though Plotly is an online platform, you can also plot Plotly graphs within the Jupyter notebook.

Requirements – Anaconda, Jupyter, Matplotlib, and Pandas

- All the scripts in this book have been executed via the Jupyter notebook. Therefore, you should have the Jupyter notebook installed.
- Needless to say, we will be using the Matplotlib library.
- The Numpy and Pandas libraries should also be installed before this chapter.

Hands-on Time – Source Codes

All IPython notebooks for the source code of all the scripts in this chapter can be found in Resources/Chapter 10.ipynb. I would suggest that you write all the code in this chapter yourself and see if you can get the same output as mentioned in this chapter.

10.1 Installation

To plot interactive plots with Plotly, you have to first download the Plotly library using the following script.

```
$ pip install plotly
```

As I said earlier, Plotly is a web platform which plots different types of interactive plots using Javascript inside your browser. To plot Plotly graphs inside the Jupyter Notebook, you can make use of Pandas plots. To do so, you will need to download the Cufflinks library. The Cufflinks library basically connects the Pandas library with Plotly, which helps you plot interactive visualizations within the Jupyter notebook. Execute the following script on your command terminal to download Cufflinks:

```
$ pip install cufflinks
```

Before we plot with Plotly library, let's first import the required libraries:

```
import pandas as pd
import numpy as np
%matplotlib inline
```

Since we will be plotting Plotly graphs offline, we need to import **plotly.offline** module, along with the other modules required to plot Plotly graphs.

```
from plotly.offline import download_plotlyjs, init_notebook_
mode, plot, iplot
```

Finally, the following statement will make Plotly plots appear in the Jupyter notebook.

```
init_notebook_mode(connected=True)
import cufflinks as cf cf.go_offline()
```

10.2. Line Plot

Let's now plot a simple line plot using Plotly. We will be using the flights dataset to plot our first line plot. The following script downloads the flights dataset.

Script 1:

```
flights_data = sns.load_dataset('flights')

flights_data.head()
```

Output:

	year	month	passengers
0	1949	January	112
1	1949	February	118
2	1949	March	132
3	1949	April	129
4	1949	May	121

Let's first plot a very simple line plot using Pandas only. To do so, you need to select the column for which you want to plot a static line plot and then call the "plot()" method. The following script plots plot for the passengers columns of the flights dataset.

Script 2:

```
dataset_filter = flights_data[[«passengers»]]
dataset_filter.plot()
```

Output:

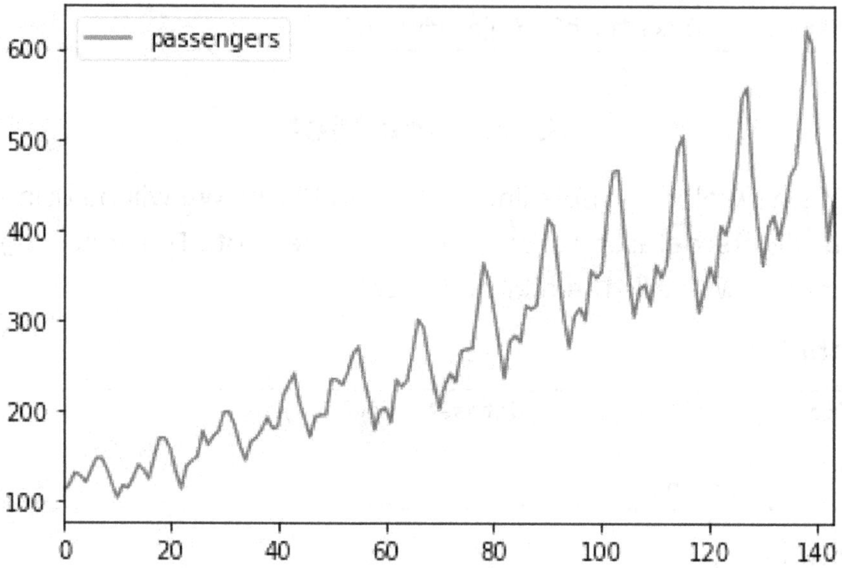

Now to plot an interactive line plot, you have to call the **iplot()** method on the Pandas dataframe as shown below.

Script 3:

```
dataset_filter.iplot()
```

Now, if you hover over the chart below in Jupyter notebook, you can see the interactive features of the plots. The runtime values of the **passengers** column.

Output:

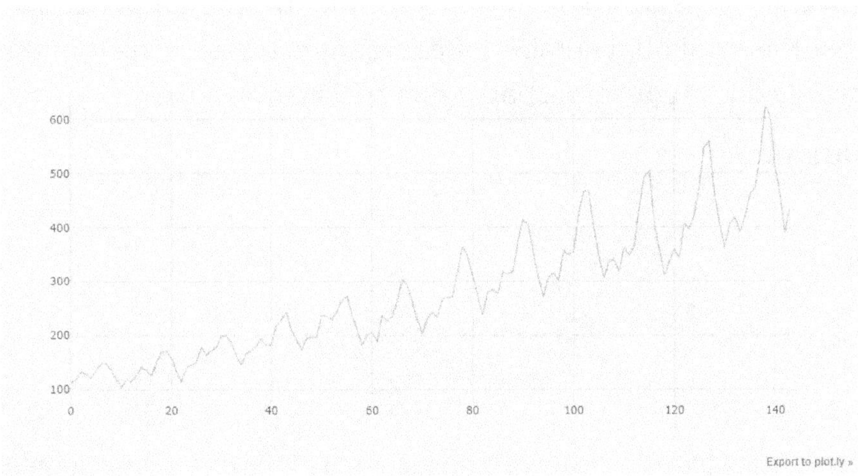

Further Readings - Plotly Cufflink Line Plots[1]

To study more about the Plotly cufflinks line functions, please check Cufflinks' official documentation for the cufflinks line plot functions. Try to execute the cufflinks iplot() method with a different set of attributes, as mentioned in the official documentation.

It is important to mention here that the output only contains a screenshot. To actually interact with the plots, you can run the plots from the Python Jupyter notebook for chapter 10 in the resources.

10.3. Bar Plot

You can also plot interactive bar plots via Plotly. To do so, you need to specify **bar** as the value for the **kind** attribute of the **iplot()** function.

Script 4:

```
flights_data.iplot(kind='bar', x=['month'],y= 'passengers')
```

If you hover the mouse below, you will see the actual number of passengers traveling in a specific month. The output shows that the maximum number of passengers travel in the months of July and August, probably due to vacation.

Output:

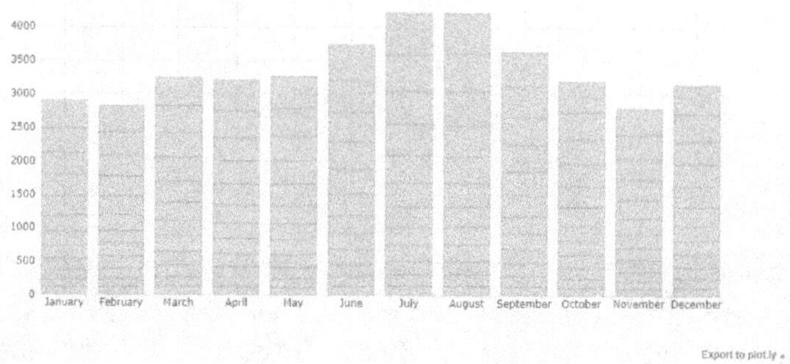

To plot horizontal bar plots, you have to pass **barh** as the value for the **kind** attribute of the **iplot()** function. Look at the following example.

Script 5:

```
flights_data.iplot(kind='barh', x=['month'],y= 'passengers')
```

Output:

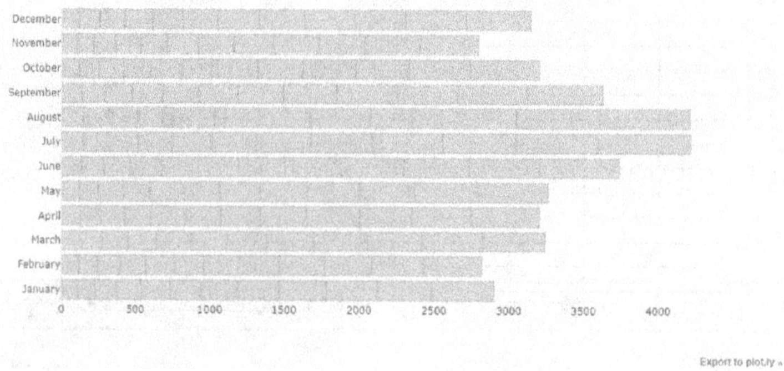

Further Readings - Plotly Cufflinks Bar Plots[2]

To study more about Plotly Cufflinks bar plot functions, please check Cufflinks' official documentation for the Cufflinks bar plot function. Try to execute the cufflinks bar plot method with a different set of attributes, as mentioned in the official documentation.

10.4. Scatter Plot

To plot a scatter plot via the **iplot()** function, you have to pass scatter as the value to the **kind** attribute of the **iplot()** function. In addition, you have to set the value of the **mode** attribute to **markers**. The following script plots a scatter plot of the number of passengers traveling each month using the flights dataset.

Script 6:

```
flights_data.iplot(kind='scatter', x= 'month', y=
'passengers', mode= 'markers')
```

Output:

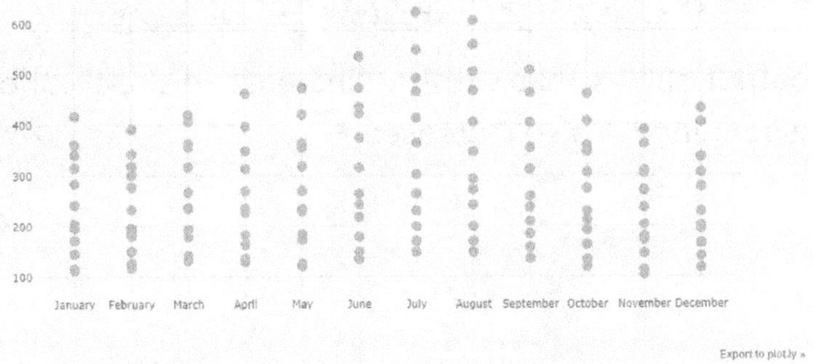

Let's plot a scatter plot using the **tips** dataset. The following script imports the **tips** dataset from the Seaborn library.

Script 7:

```
import seaborn as sns

tips_data = sns.load_dataset('tips')

tips_data.head()
```

Output:

	total_bill	tip	sex	smoker	day	time	size
0	16.99	1.01	Female	No	Sun	Dinner	2
1	10.34	1.66	Male	No	Sun	Dinner	3
2	21.01	3.50	Male	No	Sun	Dinner	3
3	23.68	3.31	Male	No	Sun	Dinner	2
4	24.59	3.61	Female	No	Sun	Dinner	4

The following script plots Plotly scatter plot, which shows values in the **total_bill** column on the x-axis and values for the **tip** column on the y-axis.

Script 8:

```
tips_data.iplot(kind='scatter', x='total_bill', y='tip',
mode='markers', color = 'blue')
```

The output shows that with the increase in the total bill, the corresponding tip also increases.

Output:

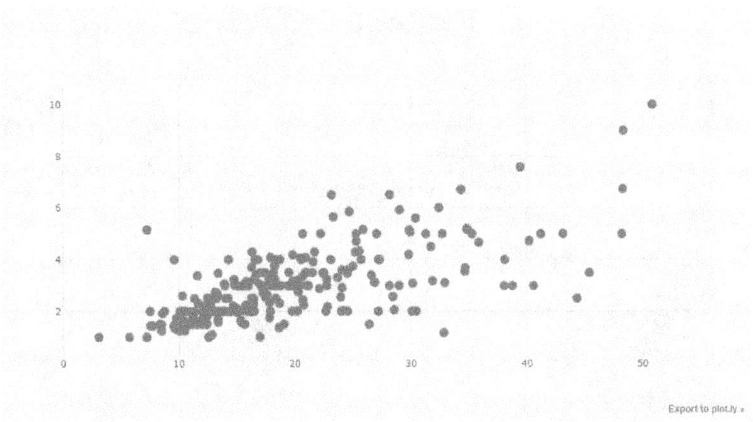

Further Readings – Plotly Cufflinks Scatter Plots [3]

To study more about Plotly Cufflinks scatter plot functions, please check Cufflinks' official documentation for the Cufflinks scatter plot functions. Try to execute the cufflinks scatter plot method with a different set of attributes, as mentioned in the official documentation.

10.5. Box Plot

In the previous chapters, you saw how to plot box plots with the Pandas and Seaborn libraries. You can also plot box plots via the Plotly and Cufflinks libraries. The following script plots the box plot for the numeric columns of the **tips** dataset.

Script 9:

```
tips_data.iplot(kind='box')
```

Output:

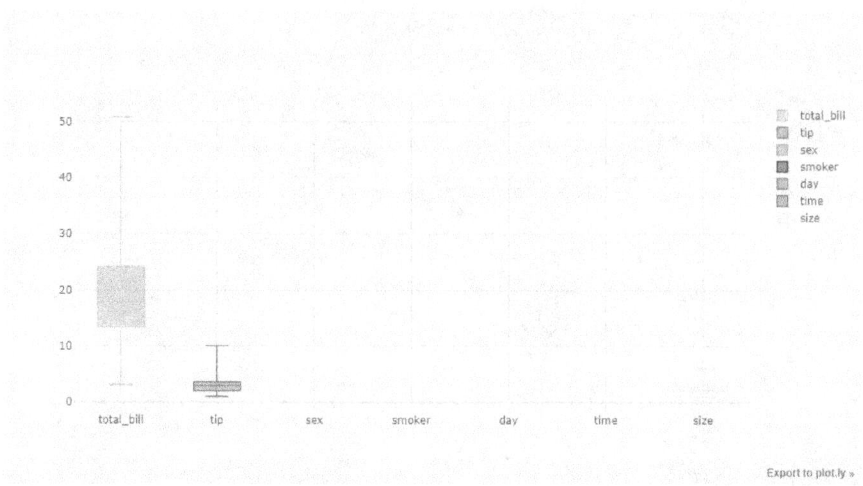

Further Readings – Plotly Cufflinks Box Plots [4]

To study more about Plotly Cufflinks box plot functions, please check Cufflinks' official documentation for the cufflinks box plot functions. Try to execute the cufflinks box plot method with a different set of attributes, as mentioned in the official documentation.

10.6. Histogram

Histograms show the distribution of values in a numeric column. Let's plot the histogram for the age column of the Titanic dataset. To do so, you first need to import the Titanic dataset using the following script.

Script 10:

```
titanic_data = pd.read_csv(r»E:\Data Visualization with
Python\Datasets\titanic_data.csv»)
titanic_data.head()
```

Output:

	PassengerId	Survived	Pclass	Name	Sex	Age	SibSp	Parch	Ticket	Fare	Cabin	Embarked
0	1	0	3	Braund, Mr. Owen Harris	male	22.0	1	0	A/5 21171	7.2500	NaN	S
1	2	1	1	Cumings, Mrs. John Bradley (Florence Briggs Th...	female	38.0	1	0	PC 17599	71.2833	C85	C
2	3	1	3	Heikkinen, Miss. Laina	female	26.0	0	0	STON/O2. 3101282	7.9250	NaN	S
3	4	1	1	Futrelle, Mrs. Jacques Heath (Lily May Peel)	female	35.0	1	0	113803	53.1000	C123	S
4	5	0	3	Allen, Mr. William Henry	male	35.0	0	0	373450	8.0500	NaN	S

Now to plot an interactive histogram via Plotly and Cufflinks, pass **hist** as a value to the **kind** attribute of the **iplot()** function.

Script 11:

```
titanic_data['Age'].iplot(kind='hist',bins=25)
```

Output:

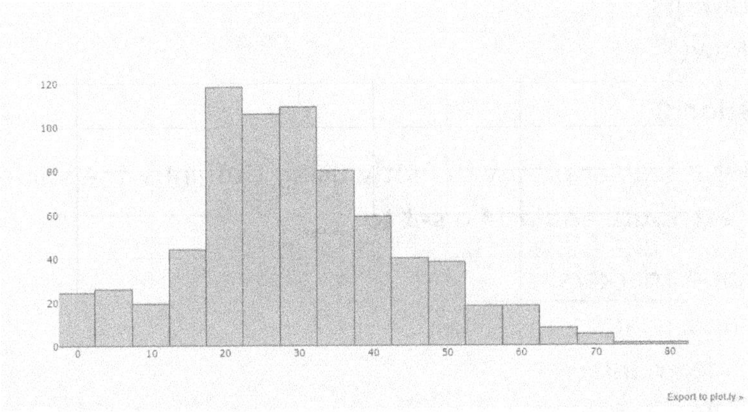

Further Readings – Plotly Cufflinks Histograms [5]

To study more about Plotly Cufflinks histogram functions, please check Cufflinks' official documentation for the cufflinks histogram functions. Try to execute the cufflinks histogram method with a different set of attributes, as mentioned in the official documentation.

Hands-on Time – Exercice

Now, it is your turn. Follow the instructions in **the exercises below** to check your understanding of the data visualization with the Pandas library. The answers to these questions are given at the end of the book.

Exercise 10.1

Question 1

Which top-level function is used to plot interactive plots with Plotly using Cufflinks?

A- plot()

B- iplot()

C- draw()()

D- idraw()

Question 2

To plot a scatter plot with Plotly using Cufflinks, the value of __ **attribute should be set to** ___:

A- shape, markers

B- shape, scatter

C- mode, marker

D- mode, scatter

Question 3

To plot a histogram with Plotly and Cufflinks, the kind attribute of the iplot() function should be set to:

A- histogram()
B- histo()
C- hist()
D- none of the above

Answer: C

Exercise 10.2

Plot an interactive histogram for the PClass column of the Titanic dataset.

References

1. https://plot.ly/python/v3/ipython-notebooks/cufflinks/#line-charts
2. https://plot.ly/python/v3/ipython-notebooks/cufflinks/#bar-charts
3. https://plot.ly/python/v3/ipython notebooks/cufflinks/#scatter-plot
4. https://plot.ly/python/v3/ipython-notebooks/cufflinks/#box-plots
5. https://plot.ly/python/v3/ipython-notebooks/cufflinks/#histograms

Hands-on Project

In this section, you will see how to visualize a dataset from scratch. The dataset that we are going to Analyze is available in a CSV file named customer_churn.csv in the *resources* folder.

It is important to mention that a dataset can be visualized in different ways, and it mainly depends upon the task that you want to perform after visualizing the data. The following section explains the dataset we have and the task that we want to perform after the visualization.

The dataset can be explained by best looking at it. The following script reads the CSV file and stores the dataset in a Pandas dataframe.

Script 1:

```
titanic_data = pd.read_csv(r»E:\Data Visualization with
Python\Datasets\titanic_data.csv»)
titanic_data.head()
```

Output:

CustomerId	Surname	CreditScore	Geography	Gender	Age	Tenure	Balance	NumOfProducts	HasCrCard	IsActiveMember	EstimatedSalary	Exited
15634602	Hargrave	619	France	Female	42	2	0.00	1	1	1	101348.88	1
15647311	Hill	608	Spain	Female	41	1	83807.86	1	0	1	112542.58	0
15619304	Onio	502	France	Female	42	8	159660.80	3	1	0	113931.57	1
15701354	Boni	699	France	Female	39	1	0.00	2	0	0	93826.63	0
15737888	Mitchell	850	Spain	Female	43	2	125510.82	1	1	1	79084.10	0

Another way to view all the columns in the dataset is by using the columns attribute of the Pandas dataframe, as shown below.

Script 2:

```
data_columns = customer_churn.columns.values.tolist()
print(data_columns)
```

Output:

```
['RowNumber', 'CustomerId', 'Surname', 'CreditScore',
'Geography', 'Gender', 'Age', 'Tenure', 'Balance',
'NumOfProducts', 'HasCrCard', 'IsActiveMember',
'EstimatedSalary', 'Exited']
```

The dataset has 14 columns. The dataset basically refers to bank customers' information. The first 13 columns contain customers' personal information while the data in the 14th column, i.e., Exited, was recorded six months after the data for the first 13 columns was recorded. The dataset tells that based on the information in the first 13 columns, whether a customer left the bank after six months or not. If a customer left the bank, a 1 was added in the Exited column, else a 0 was added.

We assume that the task here is to predict whether or not a new customer will leave the bank after 6 months, based on the information available in the first 13 columns.

The very first step in data visualization is to identify which data is actually important. In the case of our data, the columns RowNumber, CustomerId, and Surname are random and not important since they have no role in deciding whether a bank customer will leave the bank or not.

As a first data visualization step, try to plot a pair plot.

Script 3:

```
sns.pairplot(data=customer_churn)
```

Output:

```
<seaborn.axisgrid.PairGrid at 0x1b4500f9488>
```

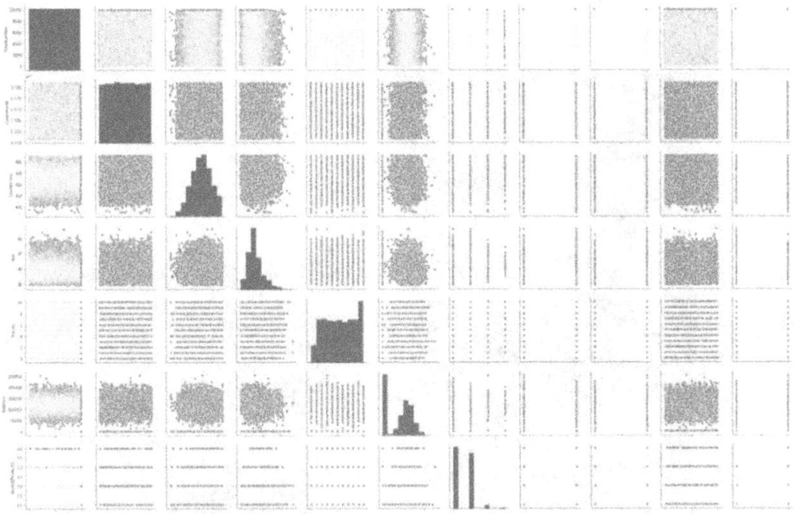

A pair plot can give you high-level information about the relation between different columns. It is important to mention that you should have knowledge of all the important data visualization libraries and should be able to decide which library to use in order to plot your desired plot.

Also, depending upon your screen, you should increase or decrease your default plot size.

Script 4:

```
plt.rcParams[«figure.figsize»] = [10,8]
```

After pair plot, you are free to choose whichever plot you want to plot depending upon the task. Let's see if gender plays any role in customer churn. You can plot the bar chart for that, as shown below.

Script 5:

```
sns.barplot(x='Gender', y='Exited', data=customer_churn)
```

Output:

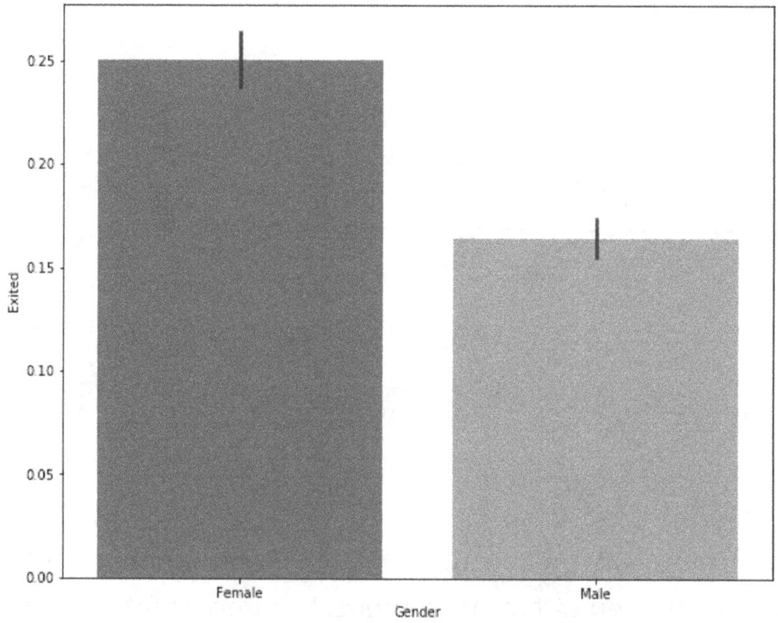

The output shows that 25 percent of the women left the bank compared to 15 percent of the men, which means that women are more likely to leave the bank than men.

I would suggest that you plot a bar plot to see if Geography has any impact on customer churn.

Let's now plot a histogram for the Age column of our dataset.

Script 6:

```
plt.title('Age Histogram')
plt.hist(customer_churn[«Age»])
```

Output:

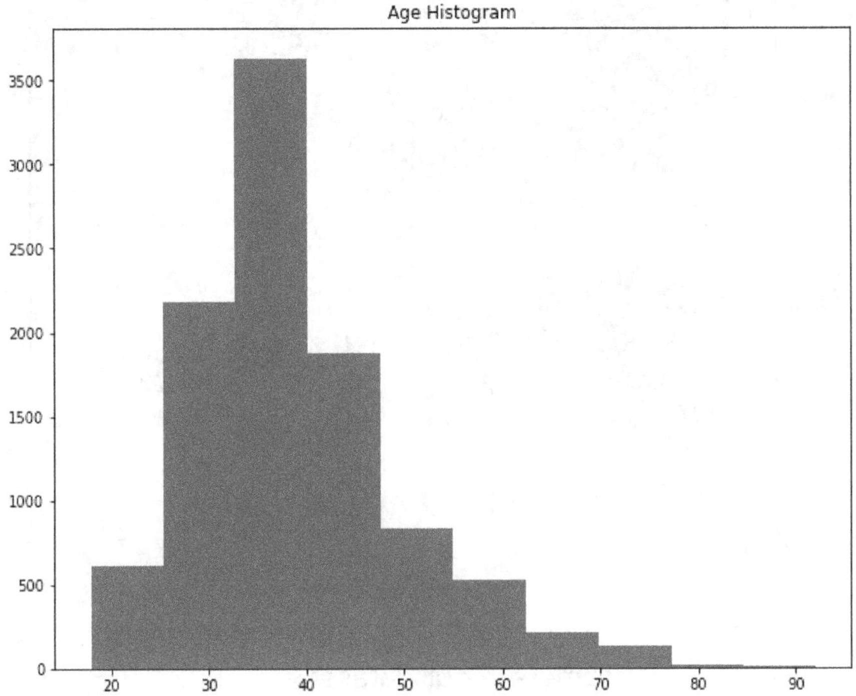

The output shows that most of our customers are aged between 25 to 50 years.

Let's plot a scatter plot to see if a customer's Age and Salary has any correlation.

Script 7:

```
plt.scatter(customer_churn[«Age»], customer_
churn[«EstimatedSalary»], c = 'g')
```

The output indicates that there is no significant correlation between a customer's age and estimated salary. Even a person as young as 20 earns 200k a month.

Output:

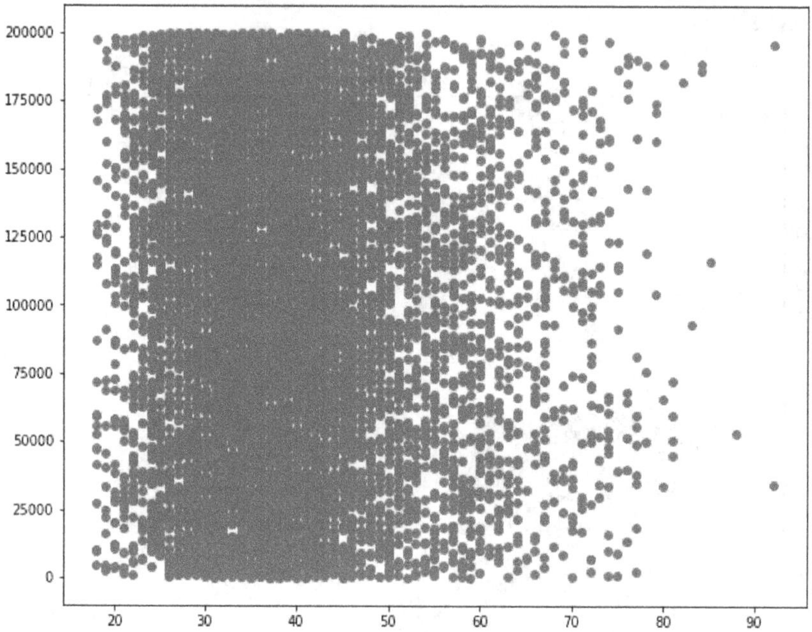

Let's now plot a pie chart that shows the geographical distribution of customers in our dataset.

Script 8:

```
countries = customer_churn[«Geography»].value_counts()

labels = countries.index.values.tolist()
values = countries.values.tolist()
explode = (0.05, 0.05, 0.05)

plt.pie(values, explode=explode, labels=labels,
autopct='%1.1f%%', shadow=True, startangle=140)
plt.show()
```

Output:

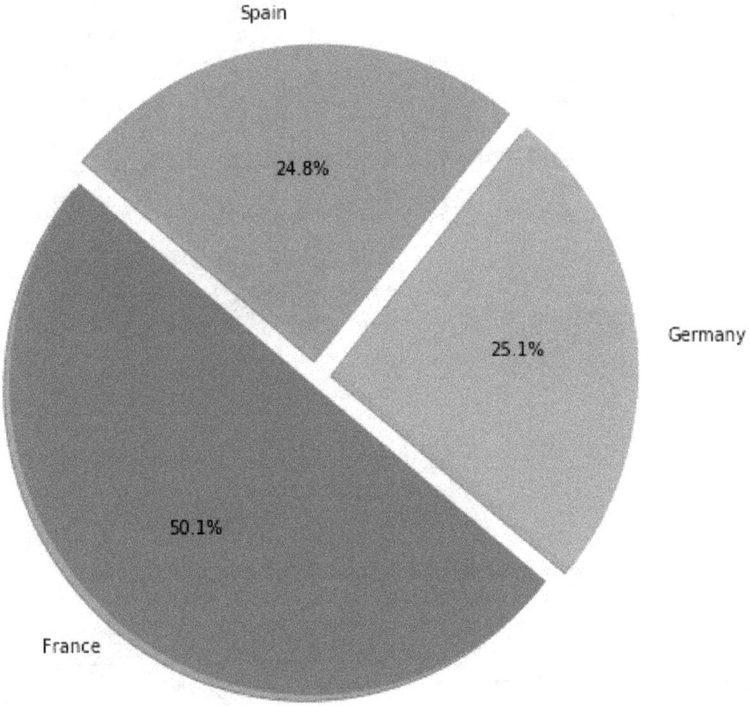

The output shows that 50 percent of the customers are from France, while around 25 percent belong to Germany and Spain each.

Let's plot a box plot showing the percentile of age for the passengers who left the bank and for those who didn't leave the bank with respect to gender.

Script 9:

```
sns.boxplot(x='Exited', y='Age', hue =
'Gender',data=customer_churn)
```

The output shows that the average age of the customers who left the bank is slightly higher than those who didn't leave the bank.

Output:

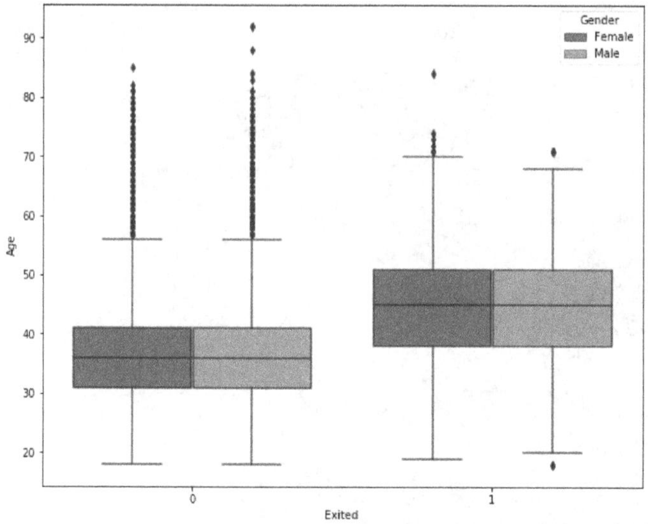

You can plot the same information via a violin plot.

Script 10:

```
sns.violinplot(x='Exited', y='Age', hue =
'Gender',data=customer_churn)
```

Output:

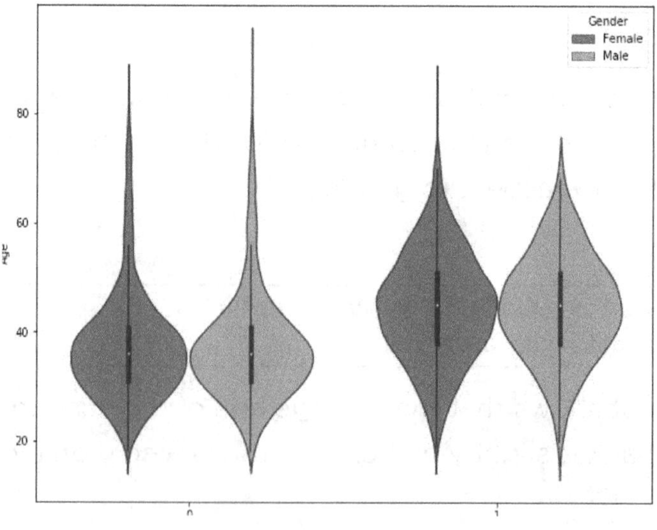

Furthermore, you can find correlation between numeric columns by plotting a heat map as shown below:

Script 11:

```
corr_values = customer_churn.corr()
sns.heatmap(corr_values, annot= True)
```

Output:

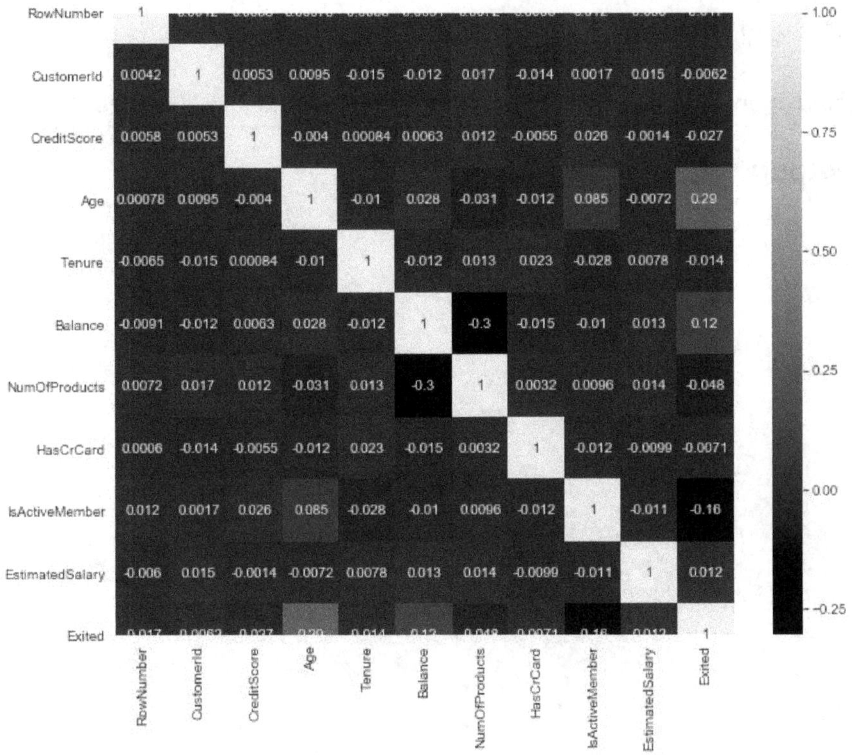

Interactive plots reveal a lot of runtime information. If you are interested in runtime information, I would suggest that you plot an interactive plot. The following script plots an interactive bar plot for gender and age columns of our dataset using the Plotly library.

Script 12:

```
import pandas as pd
import numpy as np
%matplotlib inline

from plotly.offline import download_plotlyjs, init_notebook_
mode, plot, iplot
init_notebook_mode(connected=True)
import cufflinks as cf
cf.go_offline()

customer_churn.iplot(kind='bar', x=['Gender'],y= 'Age')
```

Output:

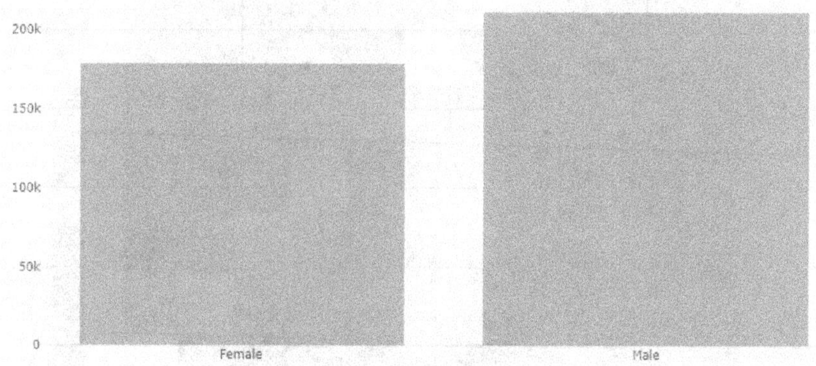

Exercise Solutions

§ Exercise 1.1

Question 1

Which iteration should be used when you want to repeatedly execute a code a specific number of times?

A- For Loop

B- While Loop

C- Both A and B

D- None of the above

Answer: A

Question 2

What is the maximum number of values that a function can return in Python?

A- Single Value

B- Double Value

C- More than two values

D- None

Answer: C

Question 3

Which of the following membership operators are supported by Python?

A- In
B- Out
C- Not In
D- Both A and C

Answer: D

§ Exercise 1.2

Print the table of integer for 9 using a while loop.

Solution

```
j=1
while j< 11:
    print(«9 x «+str(j)+ « = «+ str(9*j))
    j=j+1
```

Output:

```
9 x 1 = 9
9 x 2 = 18
9 x 3 = 27
9 x 4 = 36
9 x 5 = 45
9 x 6 = 54
9 x 7 = 63
9 x 8 = 72
9 x 9 = 81
9 x 10 = 90
```

§ Exercise 2.1

Question 1

Which is the one parameter that you must specify in order to make a scatter plot in Matplotlib?

A- color

B- c

C- r

D- None of the above

Answer: C

Question 2

To create a legend, the value for which of the following parameter needs to be specified?

A- title

B- label

C- axis

D- All of the above

Answer: B

Question 3

How are percentage values shown on a matplotlib pie chart?

A - autopct = '%1.1f%%'

B - percentage = '%1.1f%%'

C - perc = '%1.1f%%'

D - None of the Above

Answer: A

§ Exercise 2.2

Create a pie chart that shows the distribution of passengers with respect to their gender, in the unfortunate *Titanic* ship. You can use the T*itanic* dataset for that purpose.

Solution:

```
import pandas as pd
data = pd.read_csv(r"E:\Data Visualization with Python\
Datasets\titanic_data.csv")
data.head()

sex= data["Sex"].value_counts()
print(sex)

labels = sex.index.values.tolist()
values = sex.values.tolist()
explode = (0.05, 0.05)

plt.pie(values, explode=explode, labels=labels,
autopct='%1.1f%%', shadow=True, startangle=140)
plt.show()
```

Output:

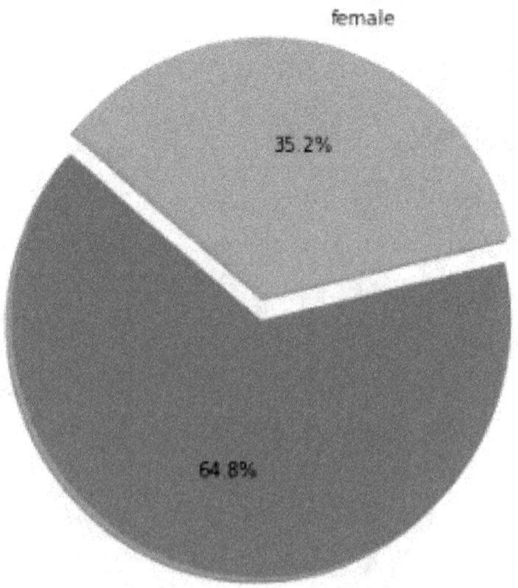

§ Exercise 3.1

Question 1

Which plot function will you use to plot a graph in the 5th cell of a plot multiple plot figure with four rows and two columns?

A- plt.subplot(5,4,2)

B- plt.subplot(2,4,5)

C- plt.subplot(4,2,5)

D- None of the Above

Answer: C

Question 2

How will you create a subplot with five rows and three columns using the subplots() function?

A- plt.subplots(nrows=5, ncols=3)

B- plt.subplots(5,3)

C- plt.subplots(rows=5, cols=3)

D- All of the Above

Answer: A

Question 3

Which function is used to save a graph?

A- figure.saveimage()

B- figure.savegraph()

C- figure.saveplot()

D- figure.savefig()

Answer: D

§ Exercise 3.2

Draw multiple plots with three rows and one column. Show the sine of any 30 integers in the first plot, the cosine of the same 30 integers in the second plot, and the tangent of the same 30 integers in the third plot.

Solution:

```
import matplotlib.pyplot as plt
import numpy as np
import math

plt.rcParams["figure.figsize"] = [12,8]

x_vals = np.linspace(0, 30, 30)
y1_vals = [math.sin(i) for i in x_vals]
y2_vals = [math.cos(i) for i in x_vals]
y3_vals = [math.tan(i) for i in x_vals]

plt.subplot(3,1,1)
plt.plot(x_vals, y1_vals, 'bo-')

plt.subplot(3,1,2)
plt.plot(x_vals, y2_vals, 'rx-')

plt.subplot(3,1,3)
plt.plot(x_vals, y3_vals, 'g*-')
```

Output:

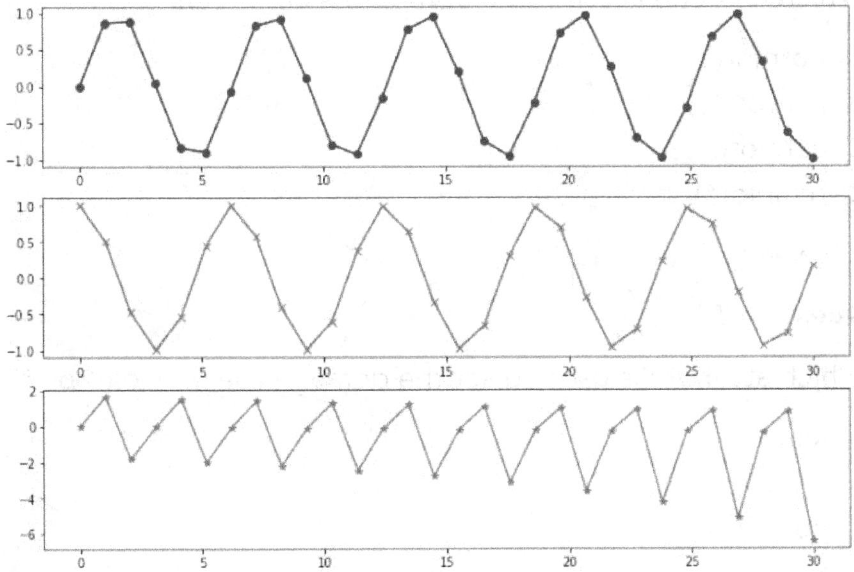

§ Exercise 4.1

Question 1

Which plot is used to plot multiple joint plots for all the combinations of numeric and Boolean columns in a dataset?

A- Joint Plot

B- Pair Plot

C- Dist Plot

D- Scatter Plot

Answer: B

Question 2

Which function is used to plot multiple bar plots?

A- barplot()

B- jointplot()

C- catplot()

D- mulplot()

Answer: C

Question 3

Which attribute is used to set the default type of a joint plot?

A- kind

B- type

C- hue

D- col

Answer: A

§ Exercise 4.2

Plot a swarm violin plot using the Titanic data that displays the fare paid by male and female passengers. Further, categorize the plot by passengers who survived and by those who didn't.

Solution:

```
sns.swarmplot(x='sex', y='fare',
hue='survived',data=titanic_data, split = True)
```

Output:

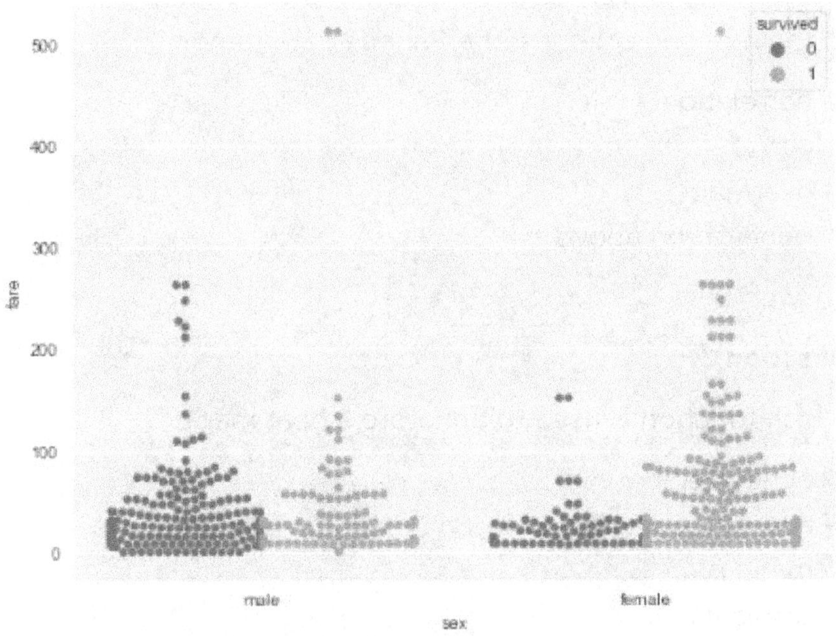

§ Exercise 5.1

Question 1

Which Seaborn function allows you to plot a graph that can be printed as a poster?

A- set_style ('darkgrid')
B- set_style ('whitegrid')
C- set_style ('poster')
D- set_context ('poster')

Answer: D

Question 2

Which function can be used to find the correlation between all the numeric columns of a Pandas dataframe?

A- correlation()

B- corr()

C- heatmap()

D- none of the above

Answer: B

Question 3

Which function is used to annotate a heat map?

A- annotate()

B- annot()

C- mark()

D- display()

Answer: B

§ Exercise 5.2

Plot two scatter plots on the same graph using the tips_dataset. In the first scatter plot, display values from the total_bill column on the x-axis and from the tip column on the y-axis. The color of the first scatter plot should be green. In the second scatter plot, display values from the total_bill column on the x-axis and from the size column on the y-axis. The color of the second scatter plot should be blue, and the markers should be x.

Solution:

```
sns.scatterplot(x=»total_bill», y=»tip», data=tips_data,
color = 'g')
sns.scatterplot(x=»total_bill», y=»size», data=tips_data,
color = 'b', marker = 'x')
```

Output:

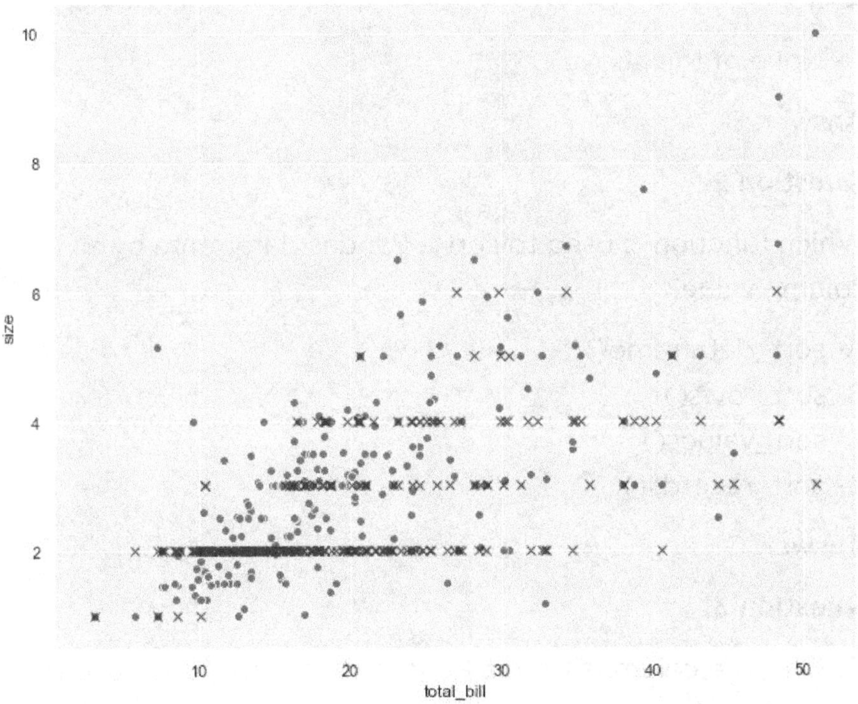

§ Exercise 6.1

Question 1

In order to horizontally concatenate two Pandas dataframes, the value for the axis attribute should be set to:

A- 0
B- 1
C- 2
D- None of the above

Answer: B

Question 2

Which function is used to sort a Pandas dataframe by a column value?

A- sort_dataframe()
B- sort_rows()
C- sort_values()
D- sort_records()

Answer: C

Question 3

To filter the columns from a Pandas dataframe, you have to pass a list of column names to one of the following method:

A- filter()
B- filter_columns()
C- apply_filter ()
D- None of the above()

Answer: A

§ Exercise 6.2

Use the apply function to subtract 10 from the Fare column of the Titanic dataset, without using lambda expression.

Solution:

```
def subt(x):
    return x - 10

updated_class = titanic_data.Fare.apply(subt)
updated_class.head()
```

Output:

```
0     2.2500
1    66.2833
2     2.9250
3    48.1000
4     3.0500
Name: Fare, dtype: float64
```

§ Exercise 7.1

Question 1

Which attribute is used to change the color of a Pandas graph?

A- set_color()
B- define_color()
C- color()
D- None of the above

Answer: C

Question 2

Which Pandas function is used to plot a horizontal bar plot?

A- horz_bar()

B- barh()

C- bar_horizontal()

D- horizontal_bar()

Answer: B

Question 3

How to time shift a Pandas dataframe five rows back?

A - shift_back(5)

B - shift(5)

c - shift_behind(-5)

D - shift(-5)

Answer: D

§ Exercise 7.2

Display a bar plot using the Titanic dataset that displays the average age of the passengers who survived vs. those who did not survive.

Solution:

```
titanic_data = pd.read_csv(r»E:\Data Visualization with
Python\Datasets\titanic_data.csv»)
titanic_data.head()
surv_mean = titanic_data.groupby(«Survived»)[«Age»].mean()

df = pd.DataFrame({'Survived':['No', 'Yes'], 'Age':surv_
mean.tolist()})
ax = df.plot.bar(x='Survived', y='Age', figsize=(8,6))
```

Output:

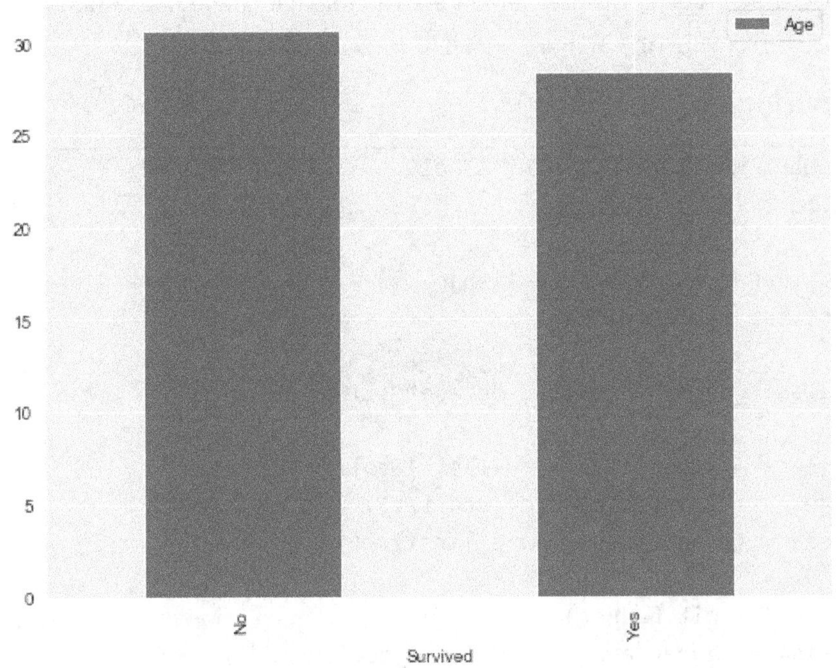

§ Exercise 8.1

Plot a scatter plot that shows the distribution of pclass, age, and fare columns from the Titanic dataset.

Solution:

```
import matplotlib.pyplot as plt
import seaborn as sns

plt.rcParams[«figure.figsize»] = [8,6]
sns.set_style(«darkgrid»)

titanic_data = sns.load_dataset('titanic')

pclass = titanic_data['pclass'].tolist()
age = titanic_data['age'].tolist()
fare = titanic_data['fare'].tolist()

figure4 = plt.figure()
axis4 = figure4.add_subplot( projection='3d')


axis4.scatter(bill,tip,size)

axis4.set_xlabel('pclass')
axis4.set_ylabel('age')
axis4.set_zlabel('fare')

plt.show()
```

Output:

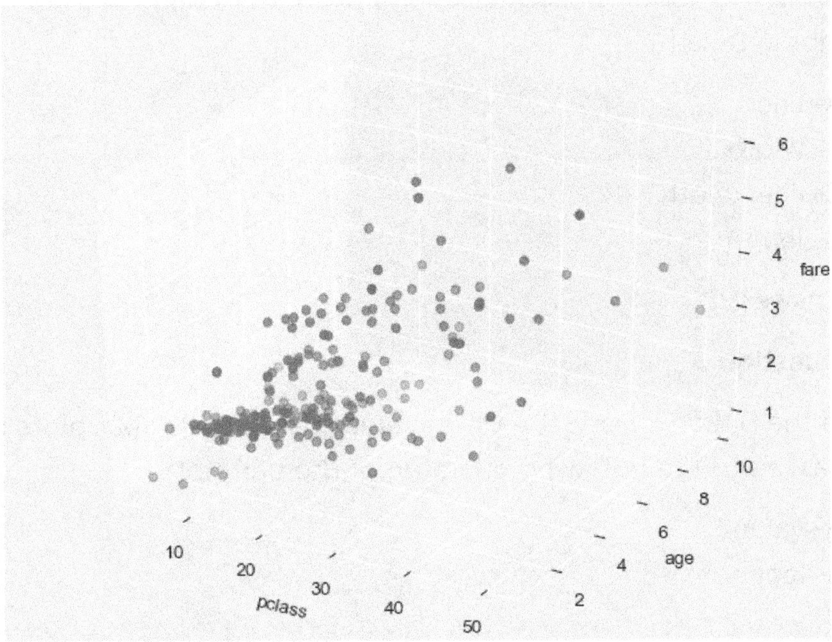

§ Exercise 9.1

Question 1

Which object is used to set the width and height of a plot in Bokeh?

A- figure()
B- width()
C- height()
D- None of the above

Answer: A

Question 2

Which attribute is used to set the width of the line in a line plot in Bokeh?

A- line

B- width

C- line_width

D- length

Answer: C

Question 3

In the Bokeh library, the list of values used to plot bar plots is passed to the following attribute of the bar plot:

A- values

B- legends

C- y

D- top

Answer: D

§ Exercise 9.2

Plot a bar plot using the Titanic dataset that displays the average age of both male and female passengers.

Solution:

```
titanic_data = pd.read_csv(r"E:\Data Visualization with
Python\Datasets\titanic_data.csv")

titanic_data = pd.read_csv(r"E:\Data Visualization with
Python\Datasets\titanic_data.csv")

sex_mean = titanic_data.groupby("Sex")["Age"].mean()

plotx = figure(
  x_range = sex_mean.index.tolist(),
  title = 'Sex vs Age',
  x_axis_label ='Sex',
  y_axis_label ='Age',
  plot_height=400
)

plotx.vbar(x = sex_mean.index.tolist() , top = sex_mean.
tolist(), legend='Sex vs Age', width = 0.7)
show(plotx)
```

Output:

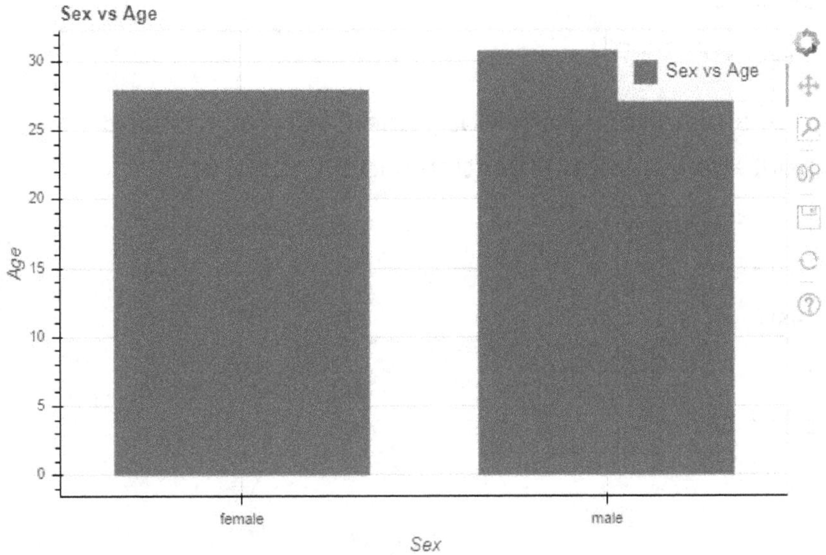

§ Exercise 10.1

Question 1

Which top-level function is used to plot interactive plots with Plotly using Cufflinks?

A- plot()

B- iplot()

C- draw()()

D- idraw()

Answer: B

Question 2

To plot a scatter plot with Plotly using Cufflinks, the value of __ attribute should be set to ___.

A- shape, markers

B- shape, scatter

C- mode, marker

D- mode, scatter

Answer: C

Question 3

To plot a histogram with Plotly and Cufflinks, the kind attribute of the iplot() function should be set to:

A- histogram()

B- histo()

C- hist()

D- none of the above

Answer: C

§ Exercise 10.2

Plot an interactive histogram for the PClass column of the Titanic dataset.

Solution:

```
titanic_data = pd.read_csv(r»E:\Data Visualization with
Python\Datasets\titanic_data.csv»)

titanic_data['Pclass'].iplot(kind='hist')
```

Output:

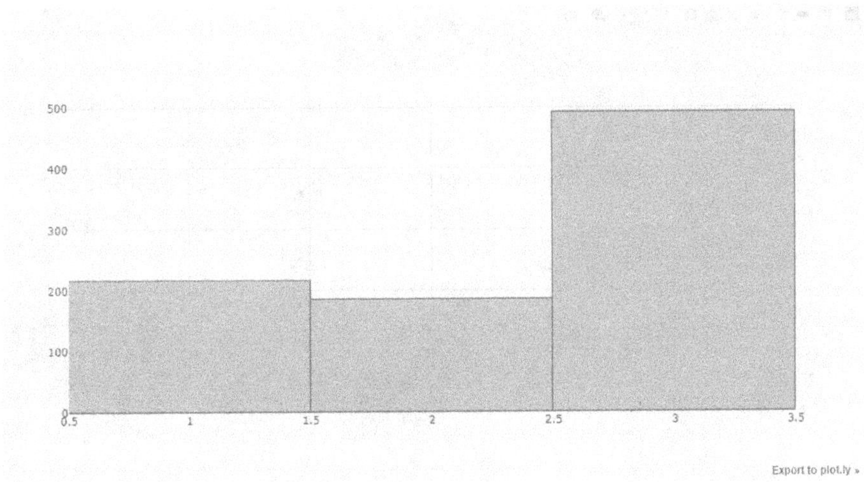